Ten Years
of
Madness

TEN YEARS
OF
MADNESS

Oral Histories
of China's
Cultural Revolution

FENG JICAI

CHINA BOOKS
& PERIODICALS, INC.
San Francisco

Cover design by Wendy K. Lee
Text design by Linda Revel
Chinese calligraphy by Yiping You

First Edition, October 1996

Library of Congress Catalog Card Number: 96-085844
ISBN 0-8351-2584-X

Printed in Canada

 **CHINA BOOKS**
& Periodicals, Inc.

TABLE OF CONTENTS

PREFACE

WHEN THE HISTORY OF THE TWENTIETH CENTURY IS WRITTEN, the most heavily laden language imaginable will be used to record its two greatest human tragedies: the atrocities of the Fascist reign, and the calamities of the Cultural Revolution. Anyone who has personally experienced either of those horrors tries hard to forget them, but cannot. Writers and historians record events in different ways: it is historical fact that matters most to historians, while a writer is more concerned with the heart and soul of those who suffer. In this book I have sought to record faithfully the pain inflicted upon the hearts and souls of a hundred ordinary Chinese during the Cultural Revolution, so as to reveal the truth about this unprecedented calamity.

A decade is but the mere blink of an eye in the long history of the world. But for a generation of Chinese, one particular decade seemed to last a hundred years. Hardly anyone born before the 1960s can claim that his fate was unchanged by its evil content. Over the course of those ten years, a civilization whose abundant roots reach back into antiquity miraculously all but vanished: people turned on each other in a barbarous performance of blood-letting; goodness and beauty went underground, ugliness and evil were given wanton release; tens of thousands of households were ravaged, hundreds of thousands of lives were devoured. We became a nation of sacrificial victims, those who fell under the crashing waves and those who unleashed them alike. Even the most seasoned personalities were subjected to intense remolding. Strengths were turned into weaknesses, honesty became deceit, tranquillity gave way to frenzy, brightness turned to gloom. Everything that contributes to the nobility of man— character, humanity, human rights, dignity, and self worth— was exposed to public abuse. While this was not war fought with conventional weapons of destruction, we witnessed acts of savagery—the brutal destruction of the soul—unmatched by the most bitterly fought battle. If one can say that Fascist atrocities left in their wake an incalculable number of bloody corpses, then the calamitous Cultural Revolution will go down as having bequeathed an incalculable number of invisible yet deeply scarred human souls.

Now that the catastrophic events are behind us, who must answer to all those innocent victims? The best restitution we can offer them, the living and the dead, is to dedicate ourselves to unearthing the causes of the calamity and eradicating the soil in which it took root. A generation that paid such a grievous price deserves an ironclad guarantee that history will not repeat itself. The foundation of this guarantee must be a thorough understanding of what happened. Regardless of how absurd or chaotic things once were, awakening is the first step on the road ahead. Each generation lives, and dies, for the generations that follow. If we succeed in helping future generations remain vigilant against a reenactment of the tragedies that befell us, our misfortunes may make us the worthiest generation of all.

I am frequently dismayed by the sad awareness that our people forget too easily. The Cultural Revolution has been over a mere ten years, and already one seldom hears it mentioned. Where are the dark shadows that once shrouded the face of everyone you knew? Maybe thousands of years of oppressive feudal government has taught us to deal with adversity by simply wiping clear our memory. Such optimism can hardly be viewed as the sign of a people's greatness. It could at best be deemed an endearing ignorance. Hard-earned wealth accrues from the mistakes of history, and discarding this wealth can only lead to a new recklessness.

From writing this book I gain many new insights.

The people who recounted their experiences during the Cultural Revolution were all strangers to me. When they heard of my desire to record their Cultural Revolution experiences, they eagerly sought me out, any way they could. Struck by their sense of urgency, I placed only a single demand upon them, that they willingly open their hearts to me. I knew it would not be easy. Life has taught me that deep down everyone has secrets shared with no one, and that the greater the pain the more deeply it is buried. But as these people revealed their most intimate secrets through their tears, I finally understood that the most heavily laden thing on this earth is the human heart. Unable to hold back their anguish, they yearned to break down the barriers of their hearts, for they knew they could not remain silent forever, knew that they would not remain silent. There was a quest for deliverance, for consolation, for release, for revenge, and most importantly for true understanding. In the wake of an era when people turned on each other and relinquished their faith in their fellow man, I was immensely gratified to have gained their trust, free and unconditional.

To protect the privacy of these people, and ensure that their comments do not come back to haunt them, I have found it necessary to conceal their identities. But I can assure my readers that I have not altered or enhanced the stories they told me. My goal has been to show how certain people in our midst made it through the Cultural Revolution one way or another; I also want future generations to be aware of the incredible experiences of a group of people who once inhabited this earth. They are not characters from the pen of a novelist, but living, breathing human beings whose lives were molded by the Cultural Revolution.

I often ask myself: Where have the perpetrators of all that evil gone, now that the calamity has passed? After the Fascist rule of terror, many of the evildoers, whether German or Japanese, took their own lives, unable to cope with the guilt hidden deep in their hearts. Is it really possible that the evildoers of the Cultural Revolution have simply picked up where they left off, as if nothing had happened, without so much as a twinge of conscience? As a people we seem to have nerves of steel, a notion that has always made me shudder. But this time I was blessed to hear the sounds of guilty consciences, to hear heavily laden admissions of remorse. My ears rang with the dulcet tones of a spring brook, the benevolent run-off of frozen evil as it thaws. I came to understand that the tragedy of the Cultural Revolution was not set in motion solely by distant historical inevitability or by more immediate social politics. The frailty of human nature, manifested in jealousy, timidity, selfishness, and vanity, as well as such human strengths as courage, loyalty, and devotion, all combined to form a frightful driving force. I could now affirm that when politics strays from the spirit of humanity, tragic social dramas are virtually assured.

The Cultural Revolution erupted out of a mix of politics, culture, and the chronic ills of our people, and a full reckoning will not be achieved overnight; besides, no age is ever concluded and made separate because of any one event. The ties that bind the inter personal relations and personal interests of yesterday and today are closely intermeshed, and courage is required to sort things out, that and time; perhaps only those who come after us will complete the task. That is why this book lays no claim to providing its readers with pat answers, and why I want to let these honest-to-goodness facts speak for themselves; by focusing once again on the spiritual tableaux of people who lived through the Cultural Revolution, we can ponder life more deeply. If we allow ourselves to be satisfied with a mere smattering of information and are fearful of probing the depths, we stand no chance of finding answers that lay claim to truth. And history without answers is forever static.

While sincere in my desire to reflect the profound complexities of this ten-year national disaster by recounting the diverse experiences of a hundred individuals, I appreciate how difficult that is to achieve. Anyone attempting a sweeping overview of the experiences of hundreds of millions, will find the task beyond his abilities. What I have striven to do here is choose a few unique examples from those people with whom I came into contact, based upon how their hearts and souls were affected by their experiences. As for the uniqueness of the experience itself, there was no need for me to go searching. Confronted by the incomparable destructive power of the society, twists of fate that defy description surfaced, and scenarios devised by the boldest imagination pale in comparison. But I have no interest in collecting wondrous tales of horror; my sole intent has been to seek out the true state of the victims' hearts and souls. I purposely chose to record the experiences of common people, because truth that emanates from the lower classes is the essential truth of human life. One must cherish every blade of grass and every speck of verdant life, in order to embrace the entire prairie and to fully appreciate its spiritual qualities and astonishing endurance, its thirst for life and untiring pursuit of beauty, and its deep anxieties, as well as its eternal trust in the land itself, trust that borders on the absolute sincerity of a simpleton.

I believe that this book will resonate with victims of the Cultural Revolution and bring them tranquillity, and that it will awaken the consciences of those who launched the Cultural Revolution, making them squirm for the rest of their lives. I owe an eternal debt of gratitude to those strangers who became my friends in the reawakening of painful memories as they poured out their hearts for the sake of this book. Together we completed our sacred task: memorializing the past and offering inspiration for the future.

INTRODUCTION

ON A WINDY WINTER NIGHT OF 1967, there was a knock on my door. For a family like mine whose house had been frequently ransacked, a knock on the door was usually a bad omen. But this time, it was gentle and soft. It turned out to be a good friend of mine. He was a Chinese teacher at a suburban middle school. Ever since the Cultural Revolution started, we had completely lost touch with each other. I figured he must also have been a target of persecutions. And I was right. He had just been released from the "cow shed." During the time he was locked up there, several of his former students who knew he had the habit of sleep talking took turns waiting by his side at night in order to record anything he said. The next day he would be forced to confess the "reactionary meaning" of his slurring "black words." Therefore he was always afraid to sleep. In the end, he miraculously lost his ability to sleep. As a result, his health was damaged, and his spirit collapsed. Seeing him in front of me, I had the eerie feeling that he had been reduced to a dehydrated kernel.

At that time, both my family and my fiancee's family had been ransacked with very little left. At the mercy of the neighborhood security office, we were given a small room of several square meters so that we could get married and start a family. Because of our problematic class background, we lived nervously every day in the terror of the Cultural Revolution.

Both of us knew that the reality was even worse than we could imagine. Even though we hadn't seen each other for over half a year, we had nothing to say at this moment. All we did was smoke, one cigarette after another. They were low quality cigarettes, named "Fighting." The stinky smoke filled the small room, so dense that we could hardly see each other's faces. The only sound came from the twigs and leaves of an old tree outside the house that was gnawing in the wind, as if a beast was grinding its teeth. But suddenly he broke the silence and said in a loud voice, "Tell me, will people of future generations know what kind of life we are living now? Will they understand our situation and our miseries? If it goes on like this for a few decades, we will all have died. Then who will live to tell the real stories of our generation? Will we suffer for nothing? Do you think there are people who are writing down our sufferings today? Of course, that's impossible. Who would risk his life for that?"

In the dense smoke he struggled to open his eyes, the very eyes that had fought against sleep for six months and were now swamped with blood vessels. He looked desperately depressed.

From then on, I began to quietly write down the stories of people around me. Knowing that this could be a crime punishable by death, I changed the names and places to foreign names, and the time to the last century. Then I signed the stories with names of foreign authors, writers such as Thomas Mann, Gide, and Steinbeck. If they were ever discovered, I could claim that they were excerpts from foreign novels that I had copied many years before. I also chose to write on small pieces of papers that were easy to conceal. As soon as I finished a story, I'd hide it underneath a brick, inside a wall crack, in a flower pot, or in between quilts. Sometimes I glued a number of pieces together, covered them with Chairman Mao's quotations or Cultural Revolution posters, and hung them on the wall. I exhausted my brain trying to hide these "reactionary" writings. But for a person who has something to hide, the more skillful and secretive you think you are, the more you believe they might be discovered. So I dug them out and hid them again in other places. For a long time, it became my habit to write, hide, dig out, and hide again.

Once during the movement, we were assembled in a stadium for a public sentencing. The audience was assigned spaces according to their work units. We stood in rows, facing an ad hoc stage that was set up with wooden planks. On the stage were some loudspeakers and microphones. When the criminals—altogether twenty-two of them—were led onto the stage, the noises from the handcuffs and shackles were magnified by the loudspeakers and heard throughout the stadium, sending shivers of fear to everyone in the audience. Then the crimes of those criminals were read. One of them was charged with writing "counterrevolutionary" articles and journals. The most lenient sentence that day was twenty years imprisonment. Most of the accused were sentenced to death. The one who wrote "counterrevolutionary" articles was sentenced to life imprisonment.

When I went home and saw my wife, I was suddenly overwhelmed by a depressed feeling. What if I was also sentenced to life imprisonment, like the one who wrote "counterrevolutionary" articles? She would then have to live like a widow for the rest of her life. This was not just a psychotic fantasy. That disastrous era was full of disastrous possibilities. I hurried to dig out my writings and copied the most important ones onto some thinner paper. Then I disposed of the original pieces and rolled up the new ones. I wrapped them in oil paper and inserted them into my bicycle tube. But as soon as I felt a little safer, I began to worry that my bike might be stolen. At that time, people were mobilized to search for "clues of hidden enemies." I often fantasized that someone would spring at my bike and fish out my writings. Those were enough to sentence me to death. Eventually I could not stand the fears in my heart and quietly took out the papers in the bicycle tube. I tried to memorize the stories before I burnt some of the papers and flushed others in the toilet. I subsequently changed my way of writing. Whenever I had the urge to write, I would put my material on paper, memorize it, and then burn the paper. I couldn't afford to leave any trace of it. I carried on with this writing habit until the end of the Cultural Revolution.

The Great Tangshan Earthquake took place on July 28, 1976. And Tianjin was also affected. For me it was a double disaster. Our house collapsed. When I crawled out of the wreckage with my family, the first thing that came to my mind was to clean up the ruins. I knew that there were still pieces of my writings that I had left in cracks of the wall and underneath the bricks. The Cultural Revolution was not over yet, and I couldn't afford to let other people discover them. However, I couldn't just work on my own house. That would make others suspicious. So I offered to help my neighbors clean up their houses first. When it was finally time to clean up my own place, I turned down my neighbors' offer for help and carefully rummaged through the ruins to look for my writings. In the end, I collected a whole bagful of small pieces of paper.

In the 1980s, a Swedish TV station learned of my story and requested an interview with me. Talking about this peculiarity of my writing habits, which could only be imaginable for that era, they asked me, "What did you feel about those pieces of paper."

"Responsibility," I replied.

Today people no longer talk about the "responsibility" of literature. Perhaps the word is too heavily laden, or perhaps it is always associated with misery and suffering. Some have blamed responsibility for having slighted self-expression, and viewed it as a function that doesn't belong to literature. But for ten years, responsibility accompanied me on a lonely path laden with danger and hazards. In an era when literature virtually didn't exist, I was able to find the real value in literature. With my own life on the line, I attempted to build a museum of hearts and souls for a whole generation of people, without the slightest thought of profit. Historians record the events of history, and writers record the hearts and souls of people. The latter is the noblest literature imaginable. It is also the highest meaning of literature. All the rest is no match for the importance of this.

Since I started my literary career in 1979, I have authored many works of fiction, covering a variety of topics. Although I have not been bound to any particular subject, I have never given up the idea that possessed me at the start of the Cultural Revolution. That is to record the hearts and souls for a generation of ordinary Chinese. Since 1986, I have plunged into the writing of *Ten Years of One Hundred People*, a literary documentation of people's experiences during the Cultural Revolution. Ten years have passed. I have since received more than 4,000 letters from people who offered their stories, and I have interviewed several hundred of them. I have selected some of the most striking and unique stories for this book. This year marks the twentieth anniversary of the collapse of the Cultural Revolution. At this time of celebration, my ten-year endeavor has finally come to an end. As I write this introduction to reveal my heavily-laden experience of thirty years ago, I feel that a burden has finally been lifted from my heart.

Laying down my pen, I can't help but give out a long sigh.

JUNE 2, 1996, IN TIANJIN

Away
from Madness

MALE, *age 16 in*

1966

JUNIOR STUDENT
at a middle school
in E City

T he first thing I'd like to tell you is: I am a non-participant! I didn't join in any faction or organization during the Cultural Revolution. All I did was follow the crowd, raising my hand at mass meetings, humming songs about Chairman Mao's quotations, and playing poker. I didn't beat up anybody and I was not beaten up by others. Never did I gain any personal power, nor was I the target of attack. In one word, my body was in the movement but my mind was not. As a non-participant, I was as happy as I could be!

Now that you know my situation, I bet you've already lost interest in me. You may assume that a non-participant couldn't possibly have an unusual story to tell. Then you must be puzzled by my insistence on talking to you. Mind you, don't look down upon us non-participants!

Do you know why I became a non-participant? I had every opportunity to become a "rebel" because of my good class background[1] and my young age. I was only 16, pure and innocent. Then why should I stand aside with my ears covered and eyes closed? You might picture me as an eccentric, lacking enthusiasm for politics, or even being chicken-livered. Totally wrong! When I was a little boy, the thing that interested me most was to stir up a nest of wasps. On August 18, 1966, when Chairman Mao received the Red Guards[2] for the first time, I walked hundreds of li[3] to Beijing in order to be at Tiananmen Square at that time ... Well, have I caught your attention now? Good! I'll start from the very beginning.

I decided to be a non-participant soon after the Cultural Revolution began. With articles criticizing the Peking Opera *The Ghost Concubine Takes Revenge*[4] and the writing group named "Three-Family Village,"[5] the *People's Daily*[6] had kindled the flames of the Cultural Revolution, which swept my school like wild fire.

One day when I arrived at school, a huge poster caught my eye. It was hanging from the third floor of the main building all the way down to the ground. Four Chinese characters, each as large as one story, were written on the poster: Revolutionary Tempest. Students waving red flags were standing everywhere: outside and inside the main gate, and on top of the main building. All of a sudden, my heart was jumping so violently I could feel the Cultural Revolution was taking place right in front of my eyes.

Then all classes stopped to make way for revolution: putting up big-character posters[7] and struggling against the teachers. Those teachers who were considered "problematic" were dragged onto a stage to be criticized. Their heads were splashed with glue and donned with tall paper hats so that they would be humiliated. Many people were excited about what was happening. Some honestly felt justified in participating in this violent action of "one class overthrowing another." At first, I was also a little carried away. However, the attack on a fellow student, a boy named Zhao, completely changed my attitude.

Looking back, it is clear that people were totally out of their minds at the time, doing everything possible to search for class enemies. The students cast their eyes not only on their teachers, but also on their own schoolmates.

Zhao and I were in the same grade, but not the same class, so I don't even know his first name. He was nicknamed "Little Thumb" because of his small build. His shoulders were only half as broad as mine. He was a skinny and pale little boy with a pair of quite small feet. But it was said that he was a genius in mathematics. When he was still a second-year student at middle school, he was able to solve mathematical questions for high school seniors. Somehow the word came that he was the son of Xia Meng, a famous Hong Kong movie star. In those days, people with relatives overseas were all suspected of being "foreign spies." Someone suggested that he be hung over a tree branch with his ten fingers tightly fastened by flaxen threads. This they did, and I saw with my own eyes that his fingers lengthened, bit by bit, until they were doubly long. His screams were so horrible that I can remember them even today. Although I didn't take part in this cruel torture, being only a bystander, I felt guilty, as if it were I who had done such ghastly things to him.

But don't think I became a non-participant because of this incident alone. The Cultural Revolution was in many ways enchantingly attractive. On August 18, 1966, when I saw Chairman Mao at Tiananmen Square, I was once again attracted to the movement.

At noon the previous day, one of my classmates, Little Kong, came to me with a secret: Chairman Mao was going to review the Red Guards in Tiananmen Square! On hearing this, I felt as if the world was alight, as if I was on top of a mountain watching the sunrise. Little Kong warned me and another friend, Big-Eyed Chang, that we must keep this secret from others, including our parents. He didn't mention the source of the news, but we decided to set off for Beijing that very day at three o'clock in the afternoon. We started off on foot, and our hearts were filled with happiness. We had to cover the distance of several hundred *li* in order to arrive in Beijing early next morning. We thought that the review would most likely take place in the morning.

We walked and hitch-hiked until we finally made it to Tiananmen at 8:30 the next morning. Then we were told that the review would not take place until early in the afternoon. We stationed ourselves at a place near the ornamental column at the west side in front of Tiananmen Gate in order to have the best view of the reviewing stand where Chairman Mao would appear. We hadn't eaten or drunk anything since the previous afternoon, but we didn't feel thirsty or hungry at all. We were in high spirits, as if we had been bewitched.

In the early afternoon, groups of Red Guards and students began to swarm into the square carrying flags. I paid no attention to them and just fixed my eyes to the reviewing stand on top of the gate for fear I might miss some precious moment. As soon as Chairman Mao appeared, the shouting and greetings from the square were deafening. Because I was over excited, I could not distinguish the people on the reviewing stand. When I finally made out the figure of Chairman Mao, I jumped and shouted, throwing away my straw hat. Several times I almost lost my glasses. If I had, I would have never been able to find them again because I was sandwiched by a sea of people. I shouted at the top of my voice, but I couldn't hear myself.

When the ceremony ended and people dispersed, I could see that the ground was covered with hats, buttons and girls' shoe buckles. People were jubilant, their eyes shining and their faces burning. When I looked at my friends, Kong and Chang, their faces were as red as flames. We intended to tell each other how happy we were, but we had lost our voices. We held each other's hands and jumped around.

We were the first Red Guards reviewed by Chairman Mao! The next day, when we went back to our school, our schoolmates envied us more than people envy today's movie stars. We plunged ourselves into the movement right away as if injected with a new energy for the revolution.

After the "August 18th Review," the Red Guard movement was alive with added energy. The movement called "Destroying the Four Olds"[8] swept across the whole country. The Red Guards started to ransack people's homes and confiscate their property.

One day we heard that the Red Guards from No. 21 Middle School were attacking the old Xikai Church. We hurried to the spot, but were too late—everything in the church had already been smashed to pieces. Only the big cross on top of the church was still intact. Without fear, we climbed a ladder to reach the cross, 50 meters above the ground. We sawed it up, and when I tried to push it down to the ground, I almost fell. Luckily, Little Kong grabbed my belt to keep me from falling. Otherwise I wouldn't be sitting here today. However, I felt no fear at all. I stood high above the ground with my hands on my hips, looking at the people in the streets who were looking up at me. I felt like a real hero!

After destroying Xikai Church, I led my friends to another church, the one with a pinnacle not far from my own house. The iron fence was locked. I was the first one to climb over it. The main gate was locked, too. With an ax installed there in case of fire, I smashed the door open. There were no carved images in this church, only a few characters carved on the wall that said, "Lord, ye are ascending to Heaven!" We immediately chopped them away. There were metal monsters against the wall, appearing like some bazookas to us. Little Kong said, "They must be cannons hidden by the imperialists!" We threw ourselves onto the bazookas and smashed them on the ground. Only then did I realize it was just a pipe organ!

The greatest discovery in that church was its books. The two big rooms on both sides of the church were filled with books. Later we were told that church also served as the city library for reference materials about religion. At that time, however, we couldn't care less about "reference materials"— they were all reactionary propaganda to us. We piled the books in the courtyard and used two drums of gasoline to burn them. There were thousands of books to be burned, and their hard covers made the job difficult. We had to tear some of the covers off before we could set fire to them. There were more than twenty of us, and we spent the whole night and the next morning burning those books. When we finished, the trees across the street were scorched and our faces were smeared with dirt and ashes.

After that, we didn't go home but went on to ransack people's houses. If you had met me at that time, you would never have believed that I would become a "non-participant."

In fact, that was the only time I took part in a house raid, which was also the reason why I became a non-participant.

In one house we ransacked there lived a childless old couple. I heard that the man had once studied abroad and was one of the share-holders of a cement plant, which made him a capitalist who exploited the workers. The two-story building was tastefully furnished. This only made us more determined to tear it apart. Based on the logic at that time, the better a house was furnished, the more its owner had exploited the working class, and the more reactionary he must be.

When we searched the second floor, we found two boxes of Western glassware. As we were about to smash them, the man cried out, "Those are precious furnishings from the French Palace. I spent a fortune on them in France. Please don't smash them!" But his words only angered us more. We were the ones who would decide what to do. How dared he tell us not to smash the glassware. Little Kong jumped on the man and hit him with a club. He hit him in the mouth, but the sound was such that it was like hitting a piece of porcelain. When I looked at the man, I was appalled by the sight. With a mouthful of blood, the man spit out many teeth! It was as horrible as the sight of the lengthened fingers of Zhao, my schoolmate. I was completely stunned and just stood there until the other students reminded me that we were there to smash the glassware.

We threw the glassware, piece by piece, out of the window until every piece was broken. The man and his wife were on their knees behind us, crying their hearts out, as if we were throwing their children out of the window. When we finished and were ready to leave, I looked at the man. His toothless mouth was open, a gaping blood hole on his face. His stare was blank, yet he was concentrating as if he was trying to memorize every detail about me. I avoided his eyes. With a guilty feeling, I ran away from the house as quickly as I could.

When we had dinner that night, Grandmother suddenly asked me, "You didn't beat up people, did you?"

I was scared. Although I didn't beat up anyone, I felt as if I had. I learned that earlier that day Grandma had gone out to the vegetable market and saw a group of Red Guards parading some capitalists through the streets. One of the students thrashed the capitalists with the brass buckle on his belt. A man's eyeball popped out as a result of this treatment. Grandma was so frightened that she immediately came back home without buying anything.

Honestly speaking, I didn't think too much about the situation. But deep in my heart I knew I could not continue to do this kind of thing. Perhaps I was born with a soft heart. I couldn't stand seeing other people suffer, bleed, or weep. I found it hard to face those defenseless "targets of revolution." Without knowing it, I was drifting away from the "golden road of revolution" and becoming a "non-participant."

Towards the end of August 1966, the Red Guards began to travel around the country with free passage to "exchange revolutionary ideas"[9] and to "fan up revolutionary flames." I took advantage of the situation and traveled extensively from the summer of 1966 to the end of 1967. I went to Heilongjiang in the Northeast, Urumqi in Xinjiang in the Northwest, and to Xiamen, Guangzhou, Guilin, and Nanning in the South. I learned a great deal during these trips. At first I was welcomed everywhere I went as a Red Guard from a big city. Moreover, I had been among the Red Guards reviewed by Chairman Mao on August 18th, which made me feel as if I was sent down directly by the central authorities.

On my first visit to Urumqi, I found the city was as calm as a pond of stagnant water. As soon as we Red Guards alighted from the train, we were escorted to the guest house of the municipal government by the local army corps. We were treated well, but were not allowed to wander around. It seemed the local officials were afraid that we students from other cities might make trouble. Nevertheless, we did light the flames of revolution there. Not long after that, those flames swept across the whole country. Everywhere the Red Guards were smashing things, ransacking houses, and beating up innocent people. The seeds of doubt once again were planted deep in my heart.

Once I was caught in the middle of an armed fight in Baoding, Hebei Province, late at night. In the small hostel where I was staying, bullets were flying through the air and windows were broken. I found myself hidden under the bed without knowing how I got there. At dawn the city was death-

ly quiet. Peeping out of the window, I saw the whole street littered with trucks that couldn't move because of their flat tires.
There were dead bodies hanging in the trees. I thought this
must be what was called "exposing corpses," a form of punishment in ancient times. The image of the Cultural Revolution
was no longer gloriously radiant to me, but had become con-
fusingly blurred in my mind.

In order to show my respect for the "sacred place of
Chinese revolution," I walked all the way from Xi'an to
Yan'an.[10] However, when I chatted with the local people, I
found that they didn't know as much as I did about their
hometown. It was a blow to my sacred feeling towards the revolution. I was deeply hurt. My mind was full of question
marks. I now realize that people begin to change their attitude
with such question marks.

During these days of traveling around to "exchange
revolutionary ideas," I returned home several times to fetch
clothes and daily necessities. Once in November, when the
weather was getting cold, a friend of mine told me that
Chairman Mao was to review the Red Guards again, and he
dragged me along. Altogether Chairman Mao reviewed the Red
Guards eight times. Only the first time was there spontaneous
participation from the bottom up. The other times were strictly organized from the top down. Take this time for example.
Chairman Mao was in an open jeep, riding from west to east
in front of the Tiananmen Gate. The students had been waiting on the square for a long time, while soldiers forced them
to sit still. They were not allowed to stand. When the jeep
passed by, many students were on their knees in order to have
a better look of the Chairman. I had found a place in the front
row. Chairman Mao was only two meters away from me when
the jeep passed. We were separated only by a soldier who was
standing on guard in front of us.

Chairman Mao was stalwart, vigorously waving his
arm. When his jeep passed in front of me, he suddenly turned
towards my side, waving with his other arm. I saw his face
clearly, even his cigarette-stained teeth. The other students,
especially those from other cities, were shouting slogans and
showing extreme enthusiasm and excitement. When the ceremony ended and people dispersed, the square was littered

with even more hats, buttons, shoe-buckles, pens, and glasses than it was the first time I saw Chairman Mao. I picked up a small diary book left behind by some Red Guard from Shandong Province. He had taken detailed notes, by the hours and days, of how he came to Beijing on foot to be reviewed by Chairman Mao. The notes ended right before the appearance of Chairman Mao, when he wrote, "The magnificent tune of 'The East Is Red'[11] is now being broadcast in the Square..." Strangely such enthusiastic words no longer moved me. For several months I had gone through excitement, sacred feelings, zeal, fighting ... but everything had by now passed.

Those who joined Chairman Mao in reviewing us didn't seem to show any enthusiasm on their faces. They waved the Little Red Book[12] with no excitement. There was nothing solemn or sacred to it. Chen Boda[13] remained motionless, not even waving the Little Red Book in his hand. What, I wonder, was he thinking then?

Whenever people's enthusiasm reached its peak, the images of lengthened fingers, blood stained teeth, and dead bodies hanging in trees came back to me. They were like ghosts haunting me, cooling me down whenever I was about to get excited again.

After traveling around to "exchange revolutionary ideas," I came back home. By then, armed fighting had started between the two factions of the Red Guards, but I found myself completely removed from the movement. I would not even be a bystander. You remember my friend Little Kong? After becoming the leader of a faction, one of his legs was maimed and he could never ride a bike again.

As for me, I found a new joy in life: fishing. Even in the severest of winters, I would make a hole in the ice and go fishing. Today I have thirty years of experience in fishing and have won first prizes in many fishing contests. I found that if you want to be a non-participant, the best thing to do is go fishing. In other words, fishing is a career for non-participants. When you focus your eyes on a float that may sink at any moment, you won't bother thinking about the struggles in the world. I think I'll remain a non-participant for the rest of my life. If you take up fishing and sit by the water all day, you'd probably become a non-participant too.

Have I made it clear why I became a non-participant? To sum it up, it was all because I am soft-hearted, afraid to see people hurt and kill each other, afraid of the sight of blood and tears. It would be dishonest if I claimed that I thought more profoundly than others. Nobody could think independently in those days. Those were times full of attractions and temptations. Therefore I attribute my actions to my natural instinct. In other words, most of the non-participants in the Cultural Revolution were kind-hearted people. I believe they are the ones who have lived peacefully and free of guilt. What do you think?

Every Chinese who went through the self-inflicted disasters acted according to their own moral standard and basic instinct.

—AUTHOR

FOOTNOTES

1. During the Cultural Revolution, people were divided into different classes according to their family backgrounds. "Good class background" referred to the families of workers and poor peasants, and "bad class background" meant families of landlords, rich peasants, and capitalists.

2. The Red Guards were members of mass organizations formed by high school and college students "to defend the proletarian revolutionary line of Chairman Mao." Many of them were responsible for ransacking houses and beating people.

3. One *li* equals half a kilometer.

4. *Ghost Concubine Takes Revenge* is a traditional Peking Opera.

5. In 1966, Mao Zedong criticized Deng Tuo, Wu Han, and Liao Mosha for writing *Notes from Three-Family Village* and accused them of being anti-Party and anti-socialist.

6. The *People's Daily* is the official newspaper of the Communist Party of China.

7. Big-character posters refer to wall posters written in bold characters with ink and brush to denounce someone or voice complaints.

8. During the Cultural Revolution, the Red Guards were encouraged to destroy anything believed to belong to old ideas, old culture, old customs, or old habits.

9. In the early stages of the Cultural Revolution, the Red Guards were given a free ride to travel around the country to exchange revolutionary experiences.

10. Yan'an is an impoverished area in Northern Shaanxi Province. The Communist Party used it as its base area from 1935 to the late 1940s.

11. "The East Is Red" is a song that eulogizes Mao Zedong. It was the most popular revolutionary song during the Cultural Revolution.

12. The Little Red Book is also known as *Quotations from Chairman Mao*. The Chinese people were required to carry a copy of it and memorize it during the Cultural Revolution. Well over a million copies of its English edition have been sold in the United States since the 1960s.

13. Chen Boda served as Mao Zedong's secretary for many years. He was appointed director of the Central Cultural Revolution Group in 1966. During the Cultural Revolution, he sided with Lin Biao and Jiang Qing and persecuted a large number of Party cadres.

Trapped in the Great Northern Wilderness

MALE, age 17 in

1970

EDUCATED YOUTH at a farm in H Province

On May 17, 1970, we got on a train leaving M City for the far away Great Northern Wilderness.[1] Noises of wailing and crying filled the railway station. The educated youths[2] reached out from the windows to hold tightly onto the hands of their family members. Even when the train started moving, they wouldn't let go. The security officers had to hit their hands with clubs. It was like they were going to part forever!

Among the educated youths, I was probably the only one who had a different feeling. I was so excited that I beat the drums and gongs and shouted slogans at the top of my voice. I had just turned seventeen and was full of enthusiasm aroused by the Red Guard movement. I had only one thing in mind, a call by Chairman Mao: "The countryside is a vast world where much can be accomplished." Nothing concrete, just a feeling of warmth. As a youngster, I also had the silly wish to get away from home and explore the world. I was in high spirits all the way, shouting and singing. After two days and two nights of traveling, I lost my voice, even before the train reached its destination.

The train pulled into a station near the farm at midnight. When we opened the door, it was pitch dark outside. The rain was pouring down. When we left M City, the weather was hot, and we were all dressed in summer clothes. Now we all reached into our luggage to pull out our green-color padded coats. When we got off the train, all we could see in the dim light were the green coats everyone was wearing in the rain.

We were taken to the farm in large trucks. The farm was so big that it seemed to be boundless. We were assigned into different companies like in the army. Each company was assigned to a different place. Whenever the truck reached one of the company sites, some people got off the truck. I got off at Company X, along with sixty other educated youths. We were led to a huge room and ordered to sleep. It was so dark that we couldn't see anything around us. We could only feel that the room was muddy, yet we didn't pay much attention to that. We were too tired and were soon sound asleep, not even disturbed by dreams.

When we woke up the next morning, we were petrified by what we saw—it was hardly a room we had slept in. Instead, it was a huge, old-fashioned tent with lots of patches and holes. Wind whistled through it, and wild grass was growing from under the beds on the muddy ground. This was to be our shelter for a long time to come.

We had to walk 100 meters of muddy road to reach the kitchen and have our meals. Only then did I understand why the school authorities had told us again and again to bring rubber boots.

Facing this situation, some younger students began to cry and asked to be sent back home. But how was that possible? In the company I was assigned to, there were two tents some fifty meters apart, each housing thirty youths. That night, after we lay down in our beds, nobody said a word. Then there was the sound of sobbing, first from the girls, and then some of the boys joined in. Between the two tents, we could clearly hear each other wailing and crying. But we were in the Northern Wilderness, and no one paid any more attention to our crying than they would to the sound of the wind and water. We were only sixteen and seventeen years old!

Most of us were assigned to do farm work in the "Agricultural Company." The job was particularly tough because the field had no draining system. At harvest time, if we were caught in a storm, the field might be covered with sea of water, and it was impossible to put mechanical harvesters to use. Instead, we had to use sickles to cut the wheat, and we had to be fast. The wheat had to be cut at day break as soon as the dew went dry. We couldn't stop harvesting until it began to dew again at dusk. The dew made it more difficult to harvest. After a day's work, we were always completely exhausted.

Harvesting soybeans in September was even more difficult. By then the soybean fields were full of rain water, which froze at night. We had to put on our felt stockings, leather boots and sweat pants in order to tread the thin ice puddles. But when the sun rose, our backs were baked in the hot sunshine, and we had to take off our shirts because of the heat. It was miserable to feel hot in our bodies, yet to feel ice-cold in the feet. Because of these working conditions, many people suffered from arthritis, rheumatism, and nephritis for years afterwards. However, at that time, no one dared duck the hard work due to the pressure of public opinion. It was a shame to be lazy. One of our slogans was: "Long live our little sickles!" Sometimes we would rather use our sickles and put the harvesters aside, even if the conditions allowed us to use the machines, because only then could we be sure not to waste a single grain. It was real tough, and more so for the girls. They had to work in the same conditions even during their periods, because they were too shy to ask for sick leave. Most of the veteran workers on the farm were demobilized army men who had been transferred to work here. They knew nothing about taking care of young girls. Today, when I think of them, I still feel deeply sorry for them.

The hardship of life in the Northern Wilderness is difficult for outsiders to imagine.

Let me give you an example. When a person got sick, he/she was entitled to a "special patient's diet," which was nothing more than a bowl of noodles boiled with soybean oil, chopped unions and salt. One day two people got sick, but there was only one bowl of noodles left. In order to have all the noodles for himself, one man spit into the bowl. The other immediately did the same thing, saying, "If you don't mind, I don't. So let's share it."

We became accustomed to coarse meals: a steamed bun could weigh a quarter of a kilo and a stuffed bun 150 grams. Once every two months we had pork at a meal. On that day, the farm would be full of happy faces. Too bad I didn't have a camera then. Those were the prettiest faces I had ever seen! When we didn't have pork, we would try all kinds of other meat: cats, rabbits, birds, rats. Once our tractor ran over a snake. We cut it into small pieces with our pocket knives. I found an empty can and poured some water into it. We built a fire with tree branches and boiled the snake piece by piece. Oh boy, what a feast! When other youths heard of this, their mouths watered.

The scenery in the Northern Wilderness was not bad. There was a virgin forest on the mountains. Small lakes and green grass were everywhere. The vast grassland was free from pollution. If you went there as a tourist, it would seem nice. But if you had to live there for eight years, like me, I think you would have run away long ago!

Take the weather. In the cold winter, our ears and noses would be "hard frozen." Sometimes the veteran workers would try to play tricks on the youths. They might point to a pickax and say, "Do you know why the pick tastes sweet? Why don't you try it." If the kid was silly enough to really lick the pick, his tongue would stick to it because of the cold. If he tried to pull away, he would lose a piece of his tongue for sure. The only solution would be to quickly run back into the house with the pickax still stuck to the tongue and ask others to breathe warm air onto his tongue until it broke free from the pick.

The other thing to watch out for was the gusty winds after a heavy snow. If you were caught in a draught, you would soon see the snow pile up three meters high around you, and there was no way you could get out. If you lost your way in a snowy wind, you would most definitely freeze to death.

Yes, life was tough. But we didn't complain or whine. Once, on our way back from the mountains after we finished our works, our truck broke down half way. We had to walk for more than fifty kilometers to get back home. When we got thirsty, we chewed tree leaves to get a little juice. At one point, I saw some rainwater in a shallow ditch left by the wheels of carts. I lay down on my stomach, waving away the small insects on the surface and drank the rainwater from the rut. I was commended for this discovery. Everyone else followed my example and drank to their hearts' content. When we were no longer thirsty, we were again in high spirits, singing, shouting slogans, and reading Chairman Mao's quotations all the way home.

After the Cultural Revolution broke out, I never doubted its policies. At the start of the movement, I joined other students in denouncing one of the senior teachers in our school. She used to be the principal of the school. During the Anti-Rightist Movement,[3] she was labeled a "Rightist" and forced to become the janitor as a result. When we made her to "confess" her crime, some mischievous students stuffed garlic into her mouth until she couldn't bear it anymore. Then they mixed the garlic with shoe-polish and forced her to swallow that. They even stuffed her mouth with grape leaves wrapped around mud. At that time, it never occurred to me that we were being vicious. On the contrary, we felt justified and heroic because of our firm class stand. That was how we felt at the beginning of the Cultural Revolution.

Before I went to the Great Northern Wilderness, I joined a team of youngsters who were mobilizing other people to go to the countryside. Once we visited a family who wouldn't let their daughter go. We stayed in their home and talked to them day and night, not allowing them to sleep until they finally gave in. We hurriedly went through all the necessary procedures for the young girl to leave the city for the border areas. Looking back on it now, I realize we were really mean at the time. I remember that the girl's family had only the mother and her daughter. There were seven or eight of us who squeezed into their tiny room and never stopped talking. The mother and the daughter kept silent all the time. Finally I became so tired I fell asleep. When I woke up at dawn, I found everyone else was asleep. The room was filled with the noise of snoring. In the end, the mother and the daughter gave in.

I never asked myself: If Chairman Mao's call was so great, why should we resort to such compulsory means? Yet if you don't think, you don't feel the pain. Therefore I was always happy, daring, and energetic.

Our spare time was spent mainly at struggle sessions, which ironically was the only spiritual activity there was. After a day's work, we would be assembled for mass criticism meetings. For us, writing big-character posters was a means of practicing calligraphy; writing criticism articles was a way to practice composition; singing "The East Is Red" and "Sailing on the Sea Depends on the Helmsman"[4] was a way to practice singing techniques. Sometimes we wrote poems too, but they were poems to serve a political purpose, not expressions of personal feelings.

We were strictly forbidden to read any books other than the works of Marx, Engels, Lenin, Stalin, and Chairman Mao. If someone got hold of a novel, all of us would wait in line to read it. Of course we had to make sure that leaders of the Company didn't discover this. I remember someone got a copy of the Chinese edition of de Maupassant's *Bel Ami*. It was supper time when it was my turn to read it. I didn't stop reading until I finished it at two o'clock in the morning, when another fellow got up and started reading at 2:30. The utilization of this book couldn't have been better.

When a movie was shown, we felt as if it was a happy festival. The copy of a movie could only be borrowed from Division Headquarters and shown to one regiment at a time. Most of the time the movie was shown at a place where nearby companies could gather and see it together. When the educated youths from different companies got together, it was a grand party. We could meet old friends and make new ones. Once we were told that a Hong Kong film, *The Acrobatic Troupe*, was to be shown. We all gathered at the public square at dusk, but the film didn't arrive until three o'clock in the morning. All that time we just sat there and waited. When the film was finally delivered, we broke into deafening cheers, like the roar of thunder. Another time a Korean movie was shown. It was snowing hard both in the story depicted in the movie and on the square where we were standing. But no one left. Later, when the characters in the movie moved into a house, we were still outside in the snow, watching the movie. It was indeed a queer, yet wonderful feeling.

Since we had lots of spare time, love came to occupy our lonely hearts. The company commander was like a steward in feudal times. He often went to a small bridge or a cross-road to stop young couples who were taking a walk. Sometimes he even hid in a big truck to keep watch on our movements.

But we found a secret path behind the tents that led to the forest. This became the place for young lovers' rendezvous. We lovingly called it the "Ho Chi Minh Trail." It was covered by young birch trees, winding all the way through a piece of grass-land with blooming flowers. It was so beautiful, quiet, and secret that many young lovers, with trembling hearts, left their footsteps there.

There is another important detail I can't neglect. Looking afar from the courtyard of our company, there was a maple tree growing on a piece of flat grassland. It was the only tree there, perhaps the result of a struggle for existence. The tree was short, but large. Since it was far from the company, it presented a rather blurred image most of the time. But in the fall, the leaves would turn so red that it looked like a torch. When we felt lonely, we would take a look at the tree and feel much better. It was a symbol of hope. Sometimes when we felt really down, we would run towards the tree to be alone for a while, even to weep a little. Then we would feel much relieved. As a result, people started to say that the tree had a magic power that could dispel sufferings.

What about me? Well, I really don't want to talk about myself. But strangely I have started to think of that maple tree lately. I might go back there some day just to have another look at it! What? My eyes are turning red? Sorry, I stayed up too late last night.

The turning point in our life came with an unexpected incident: a veteran worker had an affair with a young girl. One night he couldn't control himself and sneaked into the girls' tent. He was caught on the spot. It was like a bomb exploding in the company. But things were not that simple—after being criticized and beaten up, the man confessed that he had had affairs with many other women, both local workers and female educated youths. My girlfriend was suspected of being one of them.

At that time, it was quite cold in the tent. There was only one empty petrol drum that was used as a stove with wood burning inside. But that couldn't keep the tent warm at all. My girlfriend had gone to stay in that man's house, keeping company with his daughter. Her real purpose, of course, was to keep herself warm. But Chinese are always interested in talking about other people's affairs, and have good imaginations. Thus there was a big question mark over my girlfriend: Could it be possible that this man wouldn't be moved by such a good-looking young girl living in his house?

But my girlfriend was a really nice girl. We had been schoolmates since primary school, and we had always liked each other. But people of our generation were educated in traditional values, and we couldn't express our love in any explicit way. Once, when I was poisoned by chlorine, she put her overcoat on me and gave me her gloves, an expression of true love that was more than a casual kiss between today's young people. The fact that she was suspected of having an affair with that man gave me a serious blow. The pressure of public opinion alone was too much for me to stand.

After this incident, there was another similar case. The company leaders then decided that this was quite a serious problem. They asked the educated youths and veteran workers to tell on each other. Dozens of people were involved, including many educated youths, especially young girls. All the men who were involved were locked up and beaten. It was called a "mass dictatorship"—these forced confessions and beatings. But forced or not, as people confessed, more and more became involved. We were all shocked. Wasn't this incest? Wasn't the company a gang of hooligans? We were especially unsympathetic to the young girls. They had disgraced the rest of us educated youths. At that time, we had a strong sense of collective respect and honor, and were quite enthusiastic about the movement of "settling in the country-side and mountain areas."

One day a girl from B City was unable to stand the cold, and went to the stable to buy milk. But her real purpose was to stay in the stable a little while to get warm. The milk seller was quite attentive. He not only warmed the milk for her, but also offered her comforting words and small favors. Like that, he was able to start an affair with the girl. And she got pregnant. Everybody blamed the girl. But no one ever thought why a beautiful girl like her, tall and with a nice body, had thrown herself into the arms of an old and ugly man, a man who was short and had a blind eye? Nobody showed her any sympathy. We felt that her shameless behavior had disgraced us all.

She went to the hospital at the Division Headquarters to have an abortion, but the hospital wouldn't allow her to stay afterwards. On her way back, she was not allowed to get on the bus because the nurses and the bus conductors were all educated youths. None of them showed any sympathy for this "cheap" girl.

Once she had an argument with another educated youth. A group of people jumped on her and tore off her clothes to humiliate her. After that, she became easy with men and soon had affairs with several other men. Because she was pretty, the Regiment Commander took her for himself. This good girl was destroyed like that! The incident made me quite depressed.

After that, similar scandals happened one after another. At one regiment, the head of the regiment guest house, the chief of staff, and the commander all ganged up and recruited many female educated youths to work as attendants at the guest house. The girls were promised good jobs, good food, and a waiver from toiling in the fields. But what really happened was that the three men gang-raped the girls, one after another, all together over one hundred of them. Among the girls was the daughter of a high-ranking official, who took the case all the way to the central authorities. Only then were the three men arrested and executed.

After this incident was exposed, we began to realize that the girls were innocent and showed them some sympathy. Leaving their families at a young age, they were lonely and desperate in this far away wilderness. They could, therefore, easily be cheated with small favors and bullied by people in power. Some girls stooped to compromise in order to have a chance to return to the city or go to college. How can we blame these helpless young girls?

Along with sympathy, questions arose in my mind.

Once I returned to the farm after visiting my family in M City. I gave the company commander a calendar as a gift. Such calendars were rarely seen in the wilderness. But I had no intention of bribing him. However, the commander transferred me to the farm primary school to be a teacher, a coveted position among the educated youths. The small calendar won me a big favor, but I was completely bewildered by the result. I no longer had any sense of loftiness. And it made me sick! How stupid I had been to believe in lofty ideals. I started to cool down in my enthusiasm for the cause after that.

However, there were more stupid things that I did. It was not until 1978 that I left the Northern Wilderness and returned to M City. I was among the last to leave. By then, the local people jokingly called me "a rare animal."

Starting in 1975, there was a new policy that allowed the educated youths to return to the city if they were chosen to go to college or if they could produce evidence of poor health. The movement of settling in the countryside was coming to an end. At that time there was a popular song among the educated youths, which we didn't dare to sing in public at the beginning. But later, even the company commander didn't bother to stop us. I don't remember all the lyrics. Part of them go like this:

> Farewell to Mother dear,
> Farewell to hometown,
> Farewell to student life, the golden years.
> So long as my name is carved in history,
> Nothing can be undone here.
>
> Farewell to Mother dear,
> Farewell to hometown,

We are sent to "repair the earth,"
That is our holy duty
Oh my poor destiny!

The lyrics were not well versed, but the song was quite popular. Its blue tune reflected our low spirits at the time. The government officials were smart, and they recognized something inauspicious in this song. Soon the central authorities began to send "comforting groups" from all over the country to see us. I remember the Harbin Group brought us antiphlogistic medicines; the Tianjin Group gave each of us a heavy sweater; the Shanghai Group ... well, I forget what they brought. But we purposely showed them our worst living quarters. We took them into our toilets, which were just pits in the ground without a flushing or sewerage system. Some wooden planks and straw mats were used as "walls." When the pits were full of excrement, little "icebergs" formed that made it impossible to squat as the "icebergs" would prick our butts. Therefore we had to take sticks with us when we used the toilet to break away the "icebergs" first.

The members of the "comforting groups" seemed to be surprised to see all this. But all they could do was say nice words. They were there to pacify us, not really comfort us. And we became more and more determined to find some way to go home.

One day I was in the tent alone with another man, R. We stripped ourselves bare to see if there were anything wrong on our bodies. I found that one of his arms was a little crooked. He immediately wrote a letter home and learned that his arm was broken when he was a baby. With this excuse, he was allowed to return home. On the day I saw him off, I was left all by myself on the vast wilderness. I felt deserted. Of course, the fact was that we had been deserted since as early as 1970. We were just too simple minded to realize that.

The last days at the farm would have definitely been impossible to stand for most people.

When we first arrived there, the clotheslines were full of clothes; now there were only a few. We used to wait in long lines at the canteen; now the lines were short. We were like a few buttons left on a worn-out jacket. In the huge tent, you wouldn't see a companion unless you looked hard.

When we first arrived, there was a small path between the highway and the Company. It was now a three-meter wide road. With most of the people gone, it seemed to turn narrow again. The "Ho Chi Minh Trail" was now covered with wild grass. When I felt lonely, I still went to the maple tree and sat there for a while. But even the tree was no longer efficacious. No matter how hard I wept, I could not dispel my loneliness and depression.

The youths with good family backgrounds or social connections had all returned to the cities. Thanks to some tips from local people, I bribed a laboratory assistant at the hospital with four rolls of fine noodles to alter my test reports to show that I was too sick to stay. My eight years in the Great Northern Wilderness were not worth as much as four rolls of noodles!

I returned to M City on December 30, 1978. When I reached my home, my sixty-year-old mother became so excited that she jumped to her feet like a child. No one since has ever asked me what we had left behind in the place where we spent eight years.

The educated youths in our company were the lucky ones. All sixty of us survived. In a nearby company, there was a girl who was working in a brick kiln when the kiln collapsed. She was buried alive. When they dug her body out, it was burned and disfigured. She was hastily buried in the wilderness, so that her family didn't have to see the disfigured body.

The worst incident was a forest fire. The regiment commander ordered all of the educated youths to fight the fire. During the day, the fire appeared to be only smoke; but at night, it was aflame. The temperature reached several hundred degrees. People who went into the fire were immediately burned. The only way to put it out was to build a fire prevention lane around the forest. However, the regiment commander didn't understand this, and acted recklessly. As a result, more than forty educated youths were burned to death. Most of them were girls who couldn't run as fast as boys. They died, but who has even bothered to pay a little respect for their young lives? If those girls had known that they might finally get a chance to go back to their parents, how much worse would they have felt? If they have souls in the nether world, they must be letting out miserable and indignant cries!

By the time I was about to leave the farm, the other educated youths in the various companies were boiling with rage. In one regiment, they burned the house of a personnel director. It was said that the man had collected piles of gifts from the educated youths. After the Gang of Four[5] was over-thrown, and the educated youths were allowed to return to the city without conditions, they all wanted to know why they had gone through all the miseries.

After the educated youths all left, another human tragedy appeared. Some of the youths had developed girl-friends in the countryside. When they went back to the city, these girlfriends were left behind to taste the bitterness of bro-ken relationships. Some committed suicide. One of them wrote in her last letter, "My advice is: Don't ever fall in love with boys from the city!" As a result, local people started to hate all the educated youths.

Misery is contagious. Who could tell all the harm that the Cultural Revolution did to Chinese society?

You want to know how I feel about my experience as an educated youth? To tell you the truth, I've had conflicting thoughts about it all along. I'm afraid it will remain so for the rest of my life. I believe this is also what other educated youths will tell you.

From a pessimistic point of view, the eight years of hardship and misery are not even our major concern. We were sent to the remote border areas when we were still teenagers. Now we are all over forty years old. The eight years of suffer-ings have left scars on us both physically and mentally. Many of us suffered from nephritis, stomach-aches, back-aches, rheumatism, etc. Perhaps we'll never recover from these health problems. Still, these are secondary problems to us. Our major loss was the loss of an opportunity for a better education. Many of the educated youths were originally quite talented. But without sufficient education and necessary cre-dentials, we are now in no position to compete with today's young college students and graduate students, although we are still in our prime. We are a wasted generation.

From an optimistic point of view, the eight years have tempered us. We have gone through everything: the coldest weather, the toughest life, and the most tiring work. There is nothing we fear anymore. We have the strongest adaptability, fear no difficulties, and are able to deal with all kinds of tough situations.

Not long after I returned to the city, the Power Supply Bureau was recruiting new employees. About a hundred people applied. Most of them were educated youths. When the Bureau announced that it was planning to build some more offices and was in need of carpenters, more than a dozen people immediately claimed to be qualified carpenters. Again, they were all educated youths who had just returned from the countryside. I must say that all educated youths are capable people. Like the Monkey King, who was steeled in the "Vesper's Stove," the educated youths had been steeled in the stove of the Cultural Revolution.

What made me most proud was the fact that all educated youths understood what they had done for our country. In 1970, the year after the Red Guard movement came to an end, China's national economy was close to bankruptcy. The state was unable to create enough jobs for the 20 million educated youths. It might result in trouble for so many young people to be in the city without jobs. Therefore we were exiled to all corners of the country under the high-sounding slogan: "The countryside is a vast world where much can be accomplished." Like a great army of "thousands of soldiers and horses," we were loyal to the country and were always ready to charge forward. In the end, we found ourselves in a trap that had been set long before. Although we were extremely sad and suffered all kinds of hardships, we were able to carry a heavy burden on our young shoulders, so heavy that even the state couldn't handle it. It was we, the educated youths, who supported the tilting pillar of our nation, so that it avoided total collapse. Can you say we are not a great generation? We are not heroes? We are not the pillars of the state? But, of course, we did not understand all these implications until many years later.

I often ask myself, however, who will recognize us self-crowned heroes? As I said earlier, who will ever pay a little respect for the forty young girls who were burned to death in the forest fire?

So much about my story. It's your turn now!

History has recorded all these things. It is up to the people who must decide whether to remember or forget them.

—*Author*

FOOTNOTES

1. The Great Northern Wilderness is in Heilongjiang Province in north-eastern China, bordering Russia. During the Cultural Revolution, it was a vast undeveloped area, and thousands of urban youths were sent there to cultivate the wasteland and swamps. The area has now become a prosperous farming area.

2. In 1968 Mao Zedong called on the educated urban youths to go to the countryside to settle and be re-educated by the peasants. Most of them had just graduated from high school or were still high school students. They were called "educated youths."

3. In 1957 some 550,000 intellectuals were labeled "Rightists" for criticizing or making suggestions to the policies of the Communist Party. They were wrongfully persecuted as anti-socialist reactionary elements.

4. "Sailing on the Sea Depends on the Helmsman" was a popular song during the Cultural Revolution, eulogizing Mao Zedong.

5. The Gang of Four refers to Jiang Qing, Zhang Chunqiao, Wang Hongwen and Yao Wenyuan, four Party leaders who are now blamed for the massive persecutions of Party cadres during the Cultural Revolution.

Stream of Miserable Consciousness

善雅意識流

MALE, *age 41 in*

1966

UNEMPLOYED *in*

J City

WHERE shall I begin? Last night when I was in bed, I was trying to get things into shape so that you could understand my story. But the more I tried, the muddier the picture became. Why? Because my life was torn to pieces long ago. Nothing that happened to me was logical. The episodes are totally unrelated to each other. Therefore you may find my story confusing. Call it a "stream of consciousness" if you like. Some parts may be flashbacks, some insertions, some just a tangle of events. Luckily you are a writer, so I'm sure you can follow my story. But don't blame me if you can't. As I told you, my whole life has been a total mess.

On the third page of the September 1, 1957 issue of XX *Daily*, there was an article: "Another Major Rightist Has Been Uncovered." That "Rightist" was none other than myself. Of course you know what happened as a result. I was criticized, struggled against, interrogated, and forced to confess. These are nothing new to you, and I won't go into details now.

Anyway I was struggled against for one month before I was sent to F Village in the western suburbs in October to be "reformed through labor." In the meantime, I was still waiting for a further verdict on my case. My job in the village was to feed pigs. Seeing the dirty pigsty, I somehow felt that I was one of the pigs waiting to be slaughtered.

You wonder why I should begin from 1957 rather than 1966. This is because it will be less confusing. If I had started from 1966, you wouldn't understand how I could be "unemployed." You see, my life has really been absurd.

I did physical labor in the village for four months when the Chinese New Year approached. In March 1958, to be exact, on the 28th day of December of the lunar calendar, we were told to go home for the Spring Festival. I was very happy about this. It's a Chinese tradition that family members reunite and have a New Year's dinner together. Every year, my wife and I visited my mother, who lived in another city, for the occasion. We bought the train tickets for New Year's Eve, and decided to put aside the "Rightist" affair for the time being and get ready to visit my mother.

On the day we were to leave, several people from the "Anti-Rightist Working Group" of the Cultural Bureau suddenly appeared. The group leader, Mr. B, was a well-known writer. You must have heard of his name too. As soon as he stepped in, he read out a decision by the Party committee and the Public Security Bureau that said I had been discharged from my job and should be sent to GG Farm to be re-educated through labor. I was very calm and asked when I should leave. Mr. B said with a stern face, "You must leave immediately." Hearing his answer, my wife collapsed and fell onto the ground.

I was going to beg them to let me go and see my mother first. I was, after all, only to be "re-educated." I was not a criminal, and couldn't possibly run away. Although they had decided to send me to a labor camp, I couldn't understand why they would force me to leave on New Year's Eve. But before I could say a word, I could see that Mr. B's face was as cold as ice. I said "OK" and put my luggage on my shoulder. It was the same luggage I had carried back three days before from F Village. I hadn't had time to unpack yet. Ironically, my bad luck just made things simpler for me, for once.

Did you ask how I was labeled a Rightist? How should I know. I was just about to ask you the same question. I thought everyone else seemed to know better why I was named a "Rightist."

From the time the Party encouraged people to "speak out freely and air views fully"[1] to the time the Anti-Rightist Campaign started, I was not even in my work unit, the Institute of Traditional Opera. I was, in fact, on "sabbatical leave" and was in Shanghai writing a script. One day the Institute sent me a telegraph, urging me to go back to take part in the movement. I remember I even smiled to my wife, saying that since I had not been involved in the movement at all, everything should be alright. I didn't even write a big-character poster or level any criticism against the leadership. How could I get into trouble?

On the second day after my return, I was told to attend a mass meeting. As soon as I entered the meeting room, I was stunned by a poster hanging across the stage that said, "Thoroughly Criticize the XYZ Anti-Party Clique." X was the president of the Institute, Y was the vice-president, and Z was myself, then in charge of the school's teaching program. When the meeting started, I found that there was nothing substantial against me. They were merely groundless accusations.

I was totally stunned. How could they accuse me without giving me any reasons? Never did I say a word against the Communist Party. Even if they had to make up things, I felt I was entitled to know why I was forced to don the hat of a Rightist!

Now let me skip ahead twenty-two years and tell you what happened in 1979. You see, this is a stream of consciousness indeed. Anyway, by 1979 the Cultural Revolution was over. A person from the Personnel Department of the Bureau was sent to straighten out my case. When he talked to me, he looked very surprised. "Honestly speaking," he said, "after I read all your dossier, I can't understand why you were labeled a Rightist in the first place." I still remember the surprise and bewilderment on his face.

He showed me a thick binder containing my files, which stunned me even more. How could these files be used as evidence of my "crime?" They were nothing but my suggestions and criticisms regarding certain operas and scripts.

All I could manage to say was, "Is there anything else?"

"That's all," he answered.

I wonder how you would react if the same thing had happened to you. I suffered a great deal for twenty-two years, but this was the heaviest blow of all. In all those years, I tried to find out why I was labeled a "Rightist." When I finally did, I was even more confused. I felt as if I had come into a completely new world, one about which I knew nothing.

Let me go back to March 1958. My wife went to visit my mother as planned. She made an excuse for my absence, telling my mother I was too busy to make the trip. Mom had already heard a little about my situation. When she found out that I couldn't come to visit her, she understood everything. She was stunned as she held my wife tightly in her arms and burst into tears. On that New Year's Eve, the two women just wept and wept.

I never saw my mother again. In the summer of 1960, when I was toiling on the GG farm, she was seriously ill. I asked for permission to visit her, but I wasn't allowed to go until two days after her death. By not allowing me to see my mother when she was alive, they punished me even more.

The only positive experience I've drawn from my life is that happiness will not bring you any enlightenment, while suffering can improve your character.

I was originally quite sentimental, sensitive, easily excited, even fragile. Since I was labeled a Rightist, I became rational, flexible, and strong-willed. I tried to look at the bright

side of things and to control myself. As I said, I was too fragile, for I could not stand the setbacks and humiliation. Several
times I almost took my own life.

The first time I thought about suicide was when I was
locked up in a storage room at the Institute after being labeled
a "Rightist." I had been one of the best teachers in my school,
which had won me a lot of friends and respect. But now I was
being treated like an animal in the zoo. Even little kids could
humiliate me by spitting on me or throwing stones through the
open window. It was too much, and I thought of death. But in
the empty room, I couldn't find anything hard enough to cut
my veins. The room was so dirty that a lot of flies came
through the window. I knew that flies carry bacteria, which
cause cholera or dysentery. I caught the flies and swallowed
them in the hope that I would die eventually. Once I swallowed
hundreds of flies in a single day, but without any "success"! I
have never even told my wife about this for fear that she
couldn't stand it. You are the only one who knows.

I thought of death again when Mr. B sent for me late
one night. He ordered me to hand in my "confession" the next
day. He told me that I had to write down all my "reactionary
thoughts." I felt it was too much to ask for. Not only had I
never said anything reactionary, I had never even had such
thoughts. As a script writer, all I thought about was how to
write good scripts. Mr. B and his gang couldn't find anything
wrong with what I had said, so they wanted to dig into my
mind. If I did confess to reactionary thoughts, that could be
used against me in the future. Mr. B threatened me by saying
that if I failed to hand in my "confession" the next day, he
would send me to the Public Security Bureau. I was scared
about that. How could I stand the humiliation of being arrested by the police? I made up my mind to die before that happened.

The next day I went out and bought myself a bottle of
strong liquor. I have always been a light drinker. A drop of
wine can make me drunk. I took the bottle with me and went
to a desolate place near the canal behind S Park. I was sure
that if I drank the whole bottle, I would be so drunk that I
could jump into the canal without fear. Thus I could end my
sufferings. As strange as it can be, I became even more sober-

minded after I finished the whole bottle of liquor. Perhaps the Devil was refusing to take me in. I shook my head vigorously, which made people nearby suspicious. I thought if I failed to die, I would be accused of the more serious charge of "attempting suicide to escape punishment," which would have doubled my "crime." Finally I gave up my plan of suicide and went home.

The ridiculous thing in those years was that people were not afraid to die, but were afraid to live.

After the aborted suicide, I changed into a different person.

When I went home that day, Mr. B and his gang were waiting for me. They accosted me, asking me where I had been, why I smelled of liquor, and where my confession was. Without thinking, I shouted back at them, "Do whatever you like to, but I have nothing to confess!" My yelling startled not only Mr. B, but also my wife and even myself. Afterwards my wife told me that my voice was very loud, even louder than Mr. B's. How did I become so bold? Perhaps it was because of the alcohol, or that I had just come back from death. I had changed.

At the GG Farm, there was a female student from the Chemistry Department of NK University. She was also labeled a Rightist and was in charge of laboratory tests for the farm. One day she drank some cyanide and died immediately. Nobody could understand why she suddenly killed herself, and she didn't leave a word of explanation. But one of her friends told me secretly that she had been saying lately, "I cannot stand the humiliation any longer." Nobody knew what kind of humiliation she was referring to, but I understood. She was too fragile and had too much self-respect. She didn't understand that the only way to survive humiliation is to get rid of all pride and dignity. In other words, she must reduce herself to nothing. Otherwise, she would only be more miserable and not be able to survive it.

Honestly speaking, one of the reasons I was able to put up with such a despicable life was my wife. She was six years older than I was, and we were childless. Having a good class background, she was headed for promotion before I became a Rightist. After that, many people tried to persuade her to divorce me. But she wouldn't do it. She supported my parents and me with her meager salary for all those years, and she never complained. She was allowed to visit me every other week. Every time she came, she would prepare my clothes and food and then get up at 3:00 a.m. in order to catch the bus that started out at dawn. She'd arrive at M village at 10:00 a.m. and walk another fifteen kilometers to GG Farm, not arriving until the afternoon. We were only allowed to meet for twenty minutes in a huge rectangle room with a long table that separated the visitors from the inmates. Every time she came, we could only exchange a few sentences before she had to leave, taking my dirty clothes with her. She had to walk back to the bus station and arrived home at night. On rainy or snowy days, when I watched the poor woman going away silently, I could think of nothing else. Deep in my heart, I promised her: "Don't you worry. I'll live on just for you!" I suppose when someone lives for another person, life becomes more meaningful.

Thirst for knowledge is the instinct of an intellectual. Ever since I was a child, I had cultivated the habit of asking myself before going to sleep if I had acquired any new knowledge that day. Sometimes when I realized that I had spent that day without learning anything new, I would panic and get up immediately to look for a book to read. Only then did I feel I could go to sleep with a clear conscience.

I could not do that on the farm. The inmates were not allowed to exchange ideas or complaints. They were not even allowed to borrow money or tell stories to each other. Others might live by such a lifestyle, but I couldn't. For me, the worst thing that could happen was to be deprived of a spiritual life.

I had to change my method of reflecting at night. Before going to sleep, I would close my eyes and think back over what had happened that day. I tried to learn from life instead of books. Of course, I sometimes still felt an emptiness in my mind.

Once something happened unexpectedly that changed my spiritual life considerably. Because I was a good script writer, the authorities at GG Farm asked me to organize a group of inmates into a theatrical troupe and put on some short plays for the purpose of political propaganda and ideological education. They gave me an old dog-eared copy of *Xinhua Chinese Dictionary* for my writing assignment. I asked a guard if I could keep it and read it everyday. Without thinking, he said, "This should be OK." At long last I had something to read!

From then on, whenever I had some free time, I would read the dictionary, word for word, item by item, page by page. In the six years, I read through the dictionary one and a half times, including the appendix at the end, which contained knowledge about history, geography, and science, almost an encyclopedia! I tried to learn it all by heart so I could recite these sections without difficulty. With a whole dictionary in my head, I felt like a great scholar. I attributed this unexpected achievement to the adversities in my life. How could I have done this if I had not been locked up and forbidden to read any other book?

Years later, after I was released, I told this to my friends. They all laughed at me. "How can you call that knowledge?" they asked. They were right. After a while, I found that none of this learning had any practical use. As time went by, I gradually forgot all I had memorized from that dictionary. Only then did I realize that my life had been completely wasted.

While at the GG Farm, a guard once said to me, "How can Mr. A, the director of the Cultural Bureau, be so hard on you? You have been here for more than a year, and have already been discharged from your work unit. Therefore you should not be under the authority of the Bureau anymore. But Mr. A has just signed another order to treat you as an 'ultra-Rightist'!"

That was extremely odd. Mr. A was a famous writer. When he was head of the Cultural Bureau, I was just an ordinary staff member at an institute under his jurisdiction. Although he did put on airs sometimes, whenever we met, he was quite polite to me. I actually thought that he liked my talent. It was indeed surprising that he should try to destroy me when I was already down on my luck.

In 1963, I was released from the GG Farm after serving my time there. But the Cultural Bureau refused to take me back. The farm sent my personal dossier[2] to the Bureau anyway and asked me to register for a residence at the local public security office. When I reported for duty at the Bureau, I was told that I should go back to the farm because I was an ultra-Rightist. Moreover, they said, they had not received my dossier. I started to panic. Without my dossier, I could not be assigned a job and would have to go without an income. I set out to look for my dossier everywhere, the Farm, the local public security office, the neighborhood committee, and the municipal Public Security Bureau. But they all claimed they had never seen it. Thus, from 1963 to 1979, for sixteen years, I was out of a job and had to be supported by my wife. Every day I lived like a baffling vagrant. As I told you earlier, it was not until 1979 that the Cultural Bureau suddenly showed me my personal dossier. Do you know why they did that to me? Does it confuse you? Don't worry. I'll tell you about it later.

The fact that I couldn't be assigned a job because my dossier was missing did not spare me from being persecuted during the Cultural Revolution. I was sent to a "study class for ten kinds of people,"[3] where, of course, no dossier was required. It was called a "study class," but there was nothing to study. Instead, we were criticized, denounced, humiliated, and beaten up.

However, during the Cultural Revolution, I didn't have as hard a time as many others. First, being a Rightist for so many years, I was considered a "dead tiger." All I was asked to do was stand beside the main targets of attack, such as capitalists and active counterrevolutionaries, when they were denounced at mass meetings. Secondly, my past experience of being struggled against had taught me how to deal with the situation. I pretended to be humble and honest so as not to attract the accusers' attention. The important thing was to do the right thing at the right moment. I could not appear to be too warm and attentive. Nor could I be too cold and passive. I had to present the image that I was "under great pressure." But, on the other hand, I couldn't afford to be too weak. Otherwise everyone would think they had a right to bully me at will. I must say that it was more difficult to perform right in daily life than it is to act on a stage. However, I did manage to do the best I could, like a good chef who knows how to cook his dishes at the desired temperature. Moreover, I had two other advantages, of which I made good use. First, I was well educated and good at calligraphy. Therefore I was asked by the neighborhood committee to write wall posters and slogans. Second, I had an old bicycle that I loaned to the Red Guards. Whenever it was broken, I repaired it and gave it back to them. Don't laugh. At that time, I felt very grateful just having anything to do, especially something that would make them happy.

People in the "study class" were beaten up every day. The Red Guards were so moody and emotional that they beat people at will. I was probably the only one who escaped such beatings. I must attribute that to my experience at the GG Farm, where I learned how to deal with adversity in adversity. In Chairman Mao's words, it was "learning warfare in warfare."

Recently I read a newspaper article, in which a youngster asked us Rightists, "Why didn't you stand up to fight against them?" I want to tell him that if he were locked with a tiger in a cage, he would be the first one to wet his pants!

I worry a lot that people are not blaming the dictators but their victims. A few years ago, I thought that the Cultural Revolution could never occur again in China. Today I have to think otherwise. Look at what's happening: the "model plays"[4] have regained popularity; Chairman Mao is once again regarded as a god; even Hao Ran,[5] author of the notorious novel *The Golden Road*, which glorified the Gang of Four's policies, is demanding a "fair treatment." History will repeat itself if it is not properly judged. Otherwise, why are you writing this book?

During the course of the Cultural Revolution, I was being tossed around like a toy. Whenever a new campaign started, I would be dragged out and struggled against. Otherwise, no one cared about me. I was totally forgotten.

In 1969 the whole country was mobilized to prepare for a war against the Soviet Union. It was decided that people had to be evacuated from big cities. Using that as an excuse, the neighborhood committee wanted to send me back to the village in Anhui Province, where my ancestors had lived. Their real intention was to take over my house. But ever since my grand-parents left the village many years ago, I had no more relatives living there, and so I couldn't go back. However, they found another excuse to kick me out. They sent my wife to the Z Village in the western suburbs in the name of "transferring a cadre to a lower level." Thus, as her spouse, I had to go with her.

Due to my experience at the GG Farm, agricultural work was no big deal to me. And because the political move-ment was not as intense in the rural areas as in the city, I found a haven in the countryside. I often found time to lay on our brick bed reading books and listening to the sounds made by chickens, pigs, birds, and cicadas. With simple food and fresh vegetables, I felt as if I was living in a dream world, like a hermit in a haven of peace. It wouldn't have been too bad if it had gone on like that for the rest of my life.

In 1973, because of a new policy by the central authorities, all the transferred cadres were recalled back to the cities. Again, I ran into a lot of trouble registering for my res-idence. Without a personal dossier, I was still considered a vagrant supported by my wife. How could a man in perfect health stand being supported by his wife? Since I had no income, we could hardly make both ends meet during those years. We used to have many books at home. But in 1968 the Red Guards took away all thirteen shelves of my books and piled them in the basement of the Institute. These books had been passed on to me by my father. Many of them were rare editions of ancient books, including many precious rubbings from stone inscriptions. The Institute basement was damp, and many books became moldy. Even worse, the basement storage place was next to a toilet. When the Red Guards went to the toilet, they would often tear out pages to be used as toi-let paper. The books were all ruined. Can you imagine that such things could happen in a country with 5,000 years of civ-ilization? If there had been a little respect for civilization, such a barbaric and ridiculous thing as the Cultural Revolution would never have happened!

The hardest time I had was right before the end of the Cultural Revolution. At that time, I felt as if it would never come to an end. As the saying goes, the darkest moment is right before the dawn.

When Deng Xiaoping[6] reassumed office, the local People's Political Consultative Conference (PPCC)[7] decided to resume research in the fields of history and literature. Since they knew about my situation, they asked me to give them a hand in checking out materials, copying documents, and running some errands. I was paid twenty yuan a month, which made me quite happy. Finally I had something to do to earn an income.

One day, when I was on my way to deliver a message by bike, I passed the sign of Xinhua Bookstore,[8] which reminded me of what happened in 1949. At that time, the Joint Publishing House in Shanghai was recruiting staff members. Among the 4,000 applicants, I scored the highest mark in the recruiting examination. Then, because of my excellent performance there, I was later transferred to the publishing house headquarters in Beijing. During the "Movement Against Three Evils and Five Evils"[9] in 1951-1952, many teachers at Yenching University were driven out of their classrooms. I was recommended by the Joint Publishing House to teach at this famous university. I was only twenty-six years old then! When we are young, we have the ambition for a successful career. As time goes by, some quit due to the lack of talent; some wallow in degeneration. However, I was pursuing my career in high spirits. Why should I take the hit because of political movements?

The Anti-Rightist Campaign was indeed a disaster. Most people who were labeled Rightists had voiced criticisms or suggestions to the leadership. But I had done nothing. I didn't write any big-character posters, nor did I criticize anyone. Who could have the heart to throw me into a miserable well and cover it with a huge rock? Even my wife was not spared. For all these years, I have never understood why it happened.

Lost in my memory of the past, I became too weak to ride the bike. Putting it aside, I sat on the sidewalk, buried my face in my hands, and burst into tears.

You are a sensible person. I want to ask you a question that has confused me for a long time. I thought I had found the reasons for my tragedy, but I am afraid that I can be too subjective. I don't want to wrongfully accuse other people. Therefore, I have never told anybody about my thoughts. But I would like to ask you to help me analyze the situation. You can probably tell me whether I am on the right track. And I will make it as simple and clear as I can.

In 1957 X was the president of our Institute and a member of the Leading Party Group of the Cultural Bureau. Mr. A was the director of the Cultural Bureau and the deputy secretary of the Leading Group. The two people were not on good terms with one another. X was much more talented and had a sharper tongue. Mr. A was a little intimidated and feared that X would take his position. Therefore he decided to get rid of X once and for all during the Anti-Rightist Movement. To achieve his purpose, he decided to accuse X of heading a so-called anti-Party clique together with the vice-president and me. When Mr. A failed to find any evidence against me, he took my comments on artistic issues as evidence. In order to completely defeat X, Mr. A went after me and labeled me an "ultra-Rightist."

Do you agree with my analysis? Say something, please. Don't just look at me like that. Or just nod or shake your head. Well, I know it won't help to know your opinion. I have suffered twenty-two years of bitterness. No one can change that. Now I'm over seventy.

There are times when I want to find out who stabbed me in the back, so that I can be more at ease with myself. But sometimes I am afraid to learn the whole truth. If I am right in my analysis, then I was merely a sacrificial victim of other people's power struggles. Life is a one-shot deal. But all I did was serve as a pawn in other people's fighting games. Whenever I think of this, I really want to take my life again!

Let me now return to 1979. I was busy with my own rehabilitation. One day I ran into Mr. A on the road. He had completely changed. Although he was arrogantly powerful during the Anti-Rightist Movement, he did not escape the more severe persecutions of the Cultural Revolution. When I saw him, he was ill and maimed, sitting in the sun with a walking stick. He raised his hand to say hello. I got off my bike and walked up to him. We had not seen each other for more than ten years, and he had lost all his radiating vigor. He was now only a weak and helpless old man.

"How are you doing these days?" he asked.

I told him I was being rehabilitated. He asked me whether I needed his help. I shook my head, figuring that he was the one who needed help.

Unable to make up his mind, he suddenly said to me earnestly, "I'm sorry."

Shaking my head, I said to him, "Let bygones be bygones." As I was going to say good-bye, he stopped me, saying with even more earnestness, "I am very, very sorry!"

I had nothing to say to that. Not long ago, Mr. B sent someone to give me a message, saying that he was too ashamed to see me, but that he wanted to say "Sorry." The messenger emphasized that Mr. B was quite earnest.

Honestly speaking, I was a bit touched by their sincere apologies. I guess artists are too easily touched and fooled by such feelings. Yet, when I calmed down and looked at my wife, who is now almost eighty years old, with all the sufferings carved on her face, I really wanted to yell at them: "How can it be possible to settle our twenty-two years of suffering by just saying you're sorry?!"

Did we suffer for twenty-two years just for them to say "sorry"?

God has never said confession can wash one's sins clean.

—*AUTHOR*

FOOTNOTES

1. In early 1957, just before the Anti-Rightist Movement, the Communist Party encouraged the intellectuals to voice suggestions and criticisms to the Party's work. The movement was known as "speaking out freely and airing views fully," or "Letting One Hundred Flowers Blossom." Those who did follow the Party's policy soon became the victims of the Anti-Rightist Movement.

2. Personal dossier is a file that keeps a person's school and work records, along with comments by his teachers and supervisors. Every Chinese has such a dossier, which is kept by the person's work unit. It follows the person when he or she changes their job or residence.

3. During the Cultural Revolution, those who were branded the enemies of the people included landlords, rich peasants, reactionaries, bad elements, Rightists, capitalists, and counterrevolutionaries. They were also called "cows, demons, snakes, and monsters."

4. Model Plays refer to the eight operas and dances that glorified the Communist revolution. They were the only plays allowed to be shown during the Cultural Revolution.

5. Hao Ran is the author of the notorious novel *The Golden Road*, which glorified the extremist policies of the Cultural Revolution.

6. Deng Xiaoping was the general secretary of the Party when the Cultural Revolution began. He was purged twice by Mao Zedong during the Cultural Revolution. After Mao's death, Deng eventually emerged as China's paramount leader.

7. CPPCC is an organization made up of members of democratic parties who support the Communist Party.

8. Xinhua Bookstore is the official chain bookstore responsible for the distribution of books in China. It has branches all over the country.

9. "The Three Evils" refer to corruption, waste, and bureaucracy; "The Five Evils" include bribery, tax evasion, theft of state property, cheating on government contracts, and stealing economic information.

Confessional

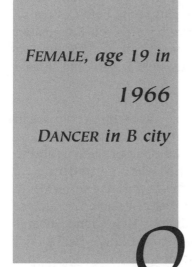

FEMALE, age 19 in

1966

DANCER in B city

O H, author, let me ask you something: why is it that people can only live once? Who made it so? If people could have more than one chance to live their lives, I am sure they could live righteously, intelligently, and truthfully. Why is it, then, that you can only live once—a life full of irremediable guilt that only weighs more heavily the longer you live? In the end, it is not death that calls you deep into the earth, but the heaviness of your own heart that crushes you into the ground. How I wish I could live my life over again! Let me explain.

　　If you owe an obligation to a living person, you can always think of some way to square accounts. But what if the person you have wronged is already dead? Then you are doomed never to make amends. You must bear the guilt for the rest of your life and carry the weight of your debt like a heavy cross. Author, isn't it your duty as a writer to soothe the wounds of the human heart? Tell me, then: when a person meets with such suffering, how is she to free herself? Well, you don't have an answer? Some people say that because life is a one-shot deal, it is destined to be tragic. What do you think? That means that if tragedy is decreed by heaven, by fate, then all we can do is submit. And to submit is to endure, to endure until the day death settles everything, right? You must think that I'm deliberately mystifying things; that I've got us stuck between a hammer and an ax, trying to stump you by asking questions that can't be answered. But I'm not! I don't know why my emotions have gotten the better of me so suddenly again. Actually, ever since that time on Babaoshan Revolutionary Cemetery,[1] I've been much calmer. That time on Babaoshan? Yes, that was the time we held a memorial service for my poor father.

Let me go back to the beginning. I was thirteen years old when my father was labeled a Rightist. I was studying at the dance academy. The class I was in was one of the best in the country. It produced topnotch dancers. I was a gifted dancer.

What can a thirteen-year-old know of her father? How could I have known that during the War of Resistance Against Japan,[2] he had been a member of Guilin's New China Theater Troupe, an arm of the Communist Party, where he worked passionately to promote the Resistance? Nor did I know that when the Resistance forces retreated from the Guilin Front, he moved with the troupe to distant Kunming, where, often suffering from malnutrition, he nonetheless worked tirelessly on stage to rouse the masses to defend our country. As far back as I can recall, I was always passed back and forth between the arms of his colleagues, whom I called "aunts" and "uncles." They were the ones who taught me to sing. I was like a little kitten basking in the affection of everyone around me. And Dad, he was the best, and he loved me the most. I could tell from the way people looked at him that they liked him, trusted him, and respected him. I could tell that he loved me the most from the expression I saw in his eyes when he looked at me—fondness, encouragement, trust. On occasion, those eyes flared with the kind of passionate love that inspires others. This was a kind of intuition, which is a child's only measure of the world, and it happens to be the most accurate.

Think about it: if someone had said my dad was a bad man, how would I have reacted? Of course I would have resisted the idea wholeheartedly. But soon afterwards, I believed as completely. Why? Because I was too simple, too pure, too naive. After all, I was only thirteen, and all my teachers thought I looked much younger. Once we had class in the courtyard, practicing some basic techniques, and I couldn't stretch my leg out straight. The teacher was furious. He snapped his whip in the air to frighten me. But, far from being frightened, I caught on my tongue the flecks of sweet pollen stirred up by the whipcrack. Because I had that endearingly innocent quality, and was a talented dancer, I was everyone's favorite student. Therefore I was often chosen to participate in the important foreign affairs of our country, presenting visiting dignitaries with bouquets of flowers. I remember in 1959, when Chairman Mao visited Zhongshan Park,[3] myself and a little boy were chosen to present him with bouquets. Chairman Mao took the flowers from me, and then shook my hand. That night I wrote in my diary, "Today I gave flowers to Chairman Mao, and as I held his big, pale hand, I was truly happy." To put it crassly, I was in an extremely privileged political position.

But that all changed suddenly one day. I remember that day clearly: I was on my way to present flowers to Chairman Kim Il Sung of North Korea. I was already dressed, my hair combed back and held at the nape of my neck by a red-and-white polka-dot ribbon tied in a butterfly knot. All the teachers were ooing and ahing about how pretty I looked, and I was extremely excited.

Just then, my head teacher called me into his office and told me with a grave face, "You won't be going today. Something has happened at your home."

"What?" I asked. This was completely unexpected, like thunder out of a blue sky. I was even less prepared for what he was about to say.

The head teacher asked me, "Do you know what a 'Rightist' is? A counterrevolutionary, an enemy, a bad guy.

Your father has been designated a Rightist."

"My father is the best person in the whole world, Teacher, you must have heard wrong," I said. My whole body trembled, and my voice quivered as well.

He was remarkably patient with me, spelling it out slowly: "You know I am very fond of you. You must listen to me. Your father used to be a good man, but he has changed. He has been obstructing the Revolution in his workplace. He would never let you know of his activities. Why? Because you are a good child, and he was afraid if you found out, you would turn against him. Haven't you seen counterrevolutionaries in the movies? Some of them start out as revolutionaries, but then become traitors, real scoundrels. Do you understand? Yes, you understand. I dearly wish your father hadn't changed, but he has. And now you must make a clean break with him."

Crying, I believed him. It was that simple. From that moment on, I completely severed relations with my father. From the time he was made a Rightist until the day he died, I never saw him again.

If only this all transpired now, I never would have believed such a crock!

But it happened in the 1950s, a time when Chinese people in general were politically naive and obedient. Many adults believed in such accusations, and some sought divorce so as to make a clean break with their Rightist husbands or wives. How could such an unworldly girl as myself know any better? Time and again I have interrogated myself and my motivations: was I afraid of being implicated, afraid of being disgraced? Did this fear lead me to act against my conscience and sever my relations with Dad? I must say it was not so in the beginning.

At the time, I acted out of a sense of pure moral integrity. Once I had a dream that Dad, dressed in enemy uniform, was chasing me, and even shot at me. That's how I felt about him at the time.

I wrote Dad a letter. I did not write a salutation at the top of the letter because then I would have had to call him "Dad," and I felt that calling him that would have shamed and humiliated me. Instead, I wrote these stern and ruthless words: "You have already become an enemy of the people. Now you must do your best to reform yourself. Not until you have earned your right to return to the midst of the people will I again call you 'Dad'."

I later found out that by the time Dad got this letter he had already been sent to a labor camp in the Great Northern Wilderness. But think about how much pain that letter must have caused him! I didn't find out until much later how Dad ended up being labeled a Rightist. During the Anti-Rightist Movement, the chief editor at the publishing house where Dad worked was named a Rightist. Dad was a good friend of the editor's. When the Party leaders told Dad to give evidence against his friend, Dad refused to say a word. He held his ground for more than a year. In the end, they made him a Rightist too. In a society that did not tolerate a man's integrity, Dad was vilified and trampled on by his peers. His only reward was the steel blade of my letter thrust through his heart. I was the one who hurt him most cruelly. I was the most heartless of them all!

The strange thing was that he didn't seem to hate me in the least. It was as if he never felt the pain I inflicted upon him. Up there in the Northern Wilderness, he heard that I was dancing in a production of "The Mermaid." Somehow he managed to get hold of a copy of *People's Pictorial*[4] magazine, and he pored over one of the production photos with a magnifying glass until he found the image of my face. I have heard that that was the only comfort he found in his wretched, bitter existence in the distant border area. He showed that photo to virtually everyone there; some people, I am sure, saw it more than once. He kept the magazine pressed under his pillow for two years until, during the natural disasters of 1961, he starved to death there in the Northern Wilderness. When they lifted his corpse off the bed, they found that magazine under his pillow. Its pages were fuzzy from wear, but that one photograph was preserved without a wrinkle. I heard that from Mom.

Mom also told me that Dad's life in the Northern Wilderness was one of pain and exhaustion, poverty and illness; that he only received eight pounds of rice per month, that he got pneumonia, that he died of starvation and was buried in his worn-out sleeping mat. My mother went to the Northern Wilderness herself to get his things. He had just a few items of ragged clothing and a couple of tattered hats, plus an old enamel mug and basin. Aside from that, his only other possessions were the magazine and a diary. In his situation, he could never have dared write down his true feelings; the "diary" was actually nothing more than a collection of memoranda and daily accounts. But in the middle of those pages was written one line born of irrepressible emotion: "I've found her in the *People's Pictorial*. She's grown even more lovable. As I write, I am shedding tears of excitement!" Those were his last words to me.

His last words—one line, thin like a whip that lashes me each time I repeat them.

I turned fifteen the year he died. We had been apart for two years: one of us cold and unyielding, the other steadfast in his love. After that first letter, I never wrote to him again, much less visited him.

I often ask myself whether my behavior during those years was simply due to a combination of naiveté and a revolutionary education. Was there no selfish motivation, no fear of political oppression or guilt-by-association or a fall from grace? I dare not admit that there was, for if I did, my heart would have burst with shame. But I have to say there was.

The sky fell down around me when he was made a Rightist. From that moment on, all the important official ceremonies took place without me. Originally I was told they would bend the rules to allow me to join the Communist Youth League[5] at age fourteen, but afterwards it was never mentioned again. Each time my classmates went to dance in a major performance, I hung around the courtyard all alone. For the first time, I felt deeply the wounds of political discrimination. The kind faces of teachers who used to be nice to me suddenly changed, as quickly and completely as actors in Sichuan Opera change their masks. They did everything to force me to expose Dad, but what could I expose? Because they couldn't get anything out of me that they could use for their own political ambitions, the teachers started to cold-shoulder me, hate me, and squeeze me out.

But how could I have abandoned Dad, at a time when he needed me the most? In a world that was enveloped by a blinding blizzard that froze heaven and earth alike, I was the only one from whom he could draw a little warmth.

Right now, if I could exchange my life for his, I would not hesitate to die. But why did I desert him for fear of pressure at that time? I loathe those four words "make a clean break." They are like a knife that shredded our lives and cut up my relations with Dad. And the irony is that I am the one who held that knife in the first place.

The more clear-headed I become, the more it hurts. The more it hurts, the clearer I become.

I have changed a lot due to the death of my father. I turned inward to face myself, instead of outward to face the world.

I started to hate myself, doubt myself, deny myself, even fear myself. I felt as if a stray dog had bitten my conscience in half. I was on the verge of mental and spiritual collapse. The only thing that kept me going was my hard work, because one of Dad's fondest hopes was for me to become a first-rate dancer. I dedicated myself to dancing, determined to be the best, so as to make up for my guilt.

When the Cultural Revolution started, my family was completely broken apart. Mom was sent to the countryside, along with my brother and sister. I was left alone in the world, with no one to lean on. As I said before, by this time I was no longer interested in the outside world. I felt no fear during the Cultural Revolution, much less cared about anything. When the Red Guards said Dad was a counterrevolutionary, I'd say he was a good man, almost wishing they would beat me to death. To be beaten in defense of my father, and to die and be reborn, seemed to be the only way my conscience would be calmed. The Revolutionary Faction in our dance company, who were jealous of my talent, labeled me a "white expert."[6] They barred me from the Model Play Troupe. Since there were literally no performances other than model plays, I was in fact out of a job. But I still trained vigorously, thinking that if I stopped, all that remained on earth of my father's hopes and dreams would die as well. I trained every day and did sit-ups in bed at night. When I took the trolley, I never sat down, but practiced my balance in the jolting vehicle.

The Cultural Revolution amounted to an unprecedented destruction of the entire Chinese society. The large scale persecutions made me more clear-headed and, thus, even less able to forgive myself for betraying my father. Although I must have appeared somber and strong when I was out in the society, at home I was extremely weak. I missed Dad, and the feeling grew with the passing days. If someone dropped by for a visit and began speaking of Rightists, the Northern Wilderness, labor camps, or criticism and struggle sessions—even if they never mentioned Dad—I would break down, sobbing uncontrollably. I would cry and cry until I could feel only emptiness, a void that nothing could fill.

In 1975, organizers of the Guangzhou International Trade Fair[7] came to our troupe to select dancers to perform for some foreign guests. Since I was the best in Chinese folk dance, they had no choice but to send me. They emphasized that they sent me because they wanted to give me a new chance, and that I would be subjected to their control. I thought here at last was my chance to make good for what I'd done to Dad. I performed the "Red Silk Dance," and at each show I was a roaring success. With each curtain call, as I turned to face the ovations of the audience, I felt I was facing a pitch-black, icy-cold shadow, facing the absence of my unreachable father, and it was to him that I bowed. In my heart I told him how I missed him, loved him, asked for his forgiveness. I felt that finally I had a chance and a way to redeem myself. It was a desire that had been suppressed for too long, and its sudden release proved too much for me. Excited, almost beside myself with joy, I danced madly, losing myself in the dance, until my body and spirit gave way. Suddenly my heart started palpitating, my pulse sometimes reaching 140 beats per minute, and I fainted. Afterwards I was bed ridden for several months, and everyone said I was just not myself. The doctor said I could no longer dance; but how could I stop dancing? While I was recovering, I drilled in secret, practicing some simple steps, and silently begged my father to protect me, to help me stand up again, to help me return to the stage, to give me another chance to redeem myself. My guilt still pressed on me like a stone slab.

In 1979 Dad was finally rehabilitated.

When he died, he was only forty-five, a man in his prime. My memory of him is one of vigor and vitality. If he had been alive in 1979, he would have been just over sixty, but I believe his enthusiasm and his love of life would have remained undiminished. At age sixty he could have been enjoying some of the best years of his life. Instead, he was long since dead and buried. What a tragedy.

Some friends and colleagues of Dad's from the publishing business decided to organize a memorial service for him at the Babaoshan Revolutionary Cemetery. I was asked to write an eulogy. Because there was so much I wanted to say, I accepted. When I picked up my pen, a thousand emotions welled up from within me, a mixture of grief and anger, a desire to vent and avenge and accuse. But when I read the eulogy there in the cemetery, I was curiously calm. I had not expected so many people to attend the memorial service. The hall was full. Many of them were well-known writers and publishers. They listened as I spoke each word:

"Dearest Dad—"

At last I had called him Dad. It was something that had lain like a stone in my heart for twenty years. At last, in front of such a dignified and impressive crowd, I proudly and confidently called him "Dad." I was not excited, though. Instead, in an unusually calm voice, I continued reading:

"Today, standing here, I am not sad, nor am I happy. I am only filled with a deep regret and resentment.

"I hate myself for being too weak-willed. My weakness made me submit to the pressures of the outside world. Weakness made me not dare to comfort you or love you at a time you needed me the most. Weakness made me do nothing but watch while fate delivered you into the hands of misery.

"I hate myself for being too ignorant. Ignorance allowed my consciences to be tricked. To this day I am unable to forgive myself. Why did I believe the lies that denounced you as an enemy of the people? Dad, do you still remember the letter I wrote you back then? There was no salutation to begin that letter. I wrote, 'Because you are an enemy of the people, I cannot call you Dad.' Although that must have hurt you deeply at the time, you still pored over the *People's Pictorial* with a magnifying glass to find my image in a production photo of 'The Mermaid.' You wanted to see me. My good father, my dear Dad, I know you would never blame your ignorant thirteen-year-old daughter, but as I grew with time, my own anguish deepened, and I became less able to forgive

myself for the pain I inflicted upon you. It tormented my conscience. Not daring to love is a human tragedy itself. It can
transform the purest love into the most ignorant hatred. This
reversal of love and hatred is cruel. Dad, you were tormented
to death in just such a situation.

"Some people are in no need of a soul, but I believe that
someone as honest, kind, and sincere as you must have a soul.
You will not be forgotten. That lonely soul of yours should be
comforted. Dad, would you feel comforted to know that so
many of your friends and colleagues took it upon themselves to
gather here to remember you? Dad, I love you, I miss you—did
you hear me? I am sure you did! Dad, may you rest in peace."

The whole time I was reading this eulogy, the entire
hall was silent, silent enough to hear each muffled but irrepressible sob. Me, I didn't shed a single tear. I heard my own
unusually clear and steady voice, sending each word straight
into that big, wide space of the mourning hall. I could even
hear my own breathing between the sentences. I felt as though
my body were in heaven, amidst the glorious brilliance of the
spirits, speaking these words directly to Dad. I felt his dense,
warm, and expansive presence. And I felt that he truly forgave
me, and that we had returned to the very beginning. At that
instant, I felt I was purified, awakened, and rescued by an
unbetrayable truth and a whole-hearted love, which took me
from a boundless bitter sea to a bright and speckless sky.
Never in my life had I been so free, so relaxed, so serene!

Ever since then, I've felt much better.

But if you think I freed myself so easily, you are wrong.
Earlier I told you, if you owe an obligation to a living person,
it's a cinch to repay; but the person to whom I owe a moral
and emotional debt is, after all, my deceased father. I have
always wondered what he must have felt just before he died.
His beloved daughter had "made a clean break" with him: how
could he not have felt the pain that was caused by the betray-
al of a loved one, and the cold sadness of his world? Whenever
I think like this, that dark shadow of bitter regret begins to roll
in on me. Perhaps that is something from which I will never be
free as long as I live.

Chinese religion does not have the concept of confession. Without it, though, the longer people live, the more ruth-

less and exhausted they become. People who have a spiritual life simply cannot live without confession. My heart has become my own confessional. Whenever I get to this point, I retreat into my dark and tranquil confessional, and whisper to myself.

Oh, author, this is the way I see life: There are countless possible paths to take, but each person can only take one path. Once you've made a wrong choice, even if you discover your mistake and try to correct it, you cannot possibly recover what you lost along the way. Of course, nothing can be defined as completely positive or negative. What the cruelties of life and society have taught me is this: never again be naive; never again act against your conscience. I would rather pay a heavy price for following my heart, than to suffer the grief brought upon by an insincere act.

These are the rules I made for myself when I walked out of Dad's memorial service at Babaoshan.

Confession can free us from our demons.

—AUTHOR

FOOTNOTES

1. The Babaoshan Revolutionary Cemetery is located in the western suburbs of Beijing. It provides funeral service mainly for Party cadres.

2. The War of Resistance Against Japan lasted for eight years, from 1937 to 1945.

3. Zhongshan Park is a public park next to the Forbidden City.

4. *People's Pictorial* is a popular monthly magazine.

5. Communist Youth League is an organization, affiliated with the Communist Party, for young people who are not old enough to join the Communist Party.

6. White Expert referred to people who focused on professional study, but ignored political studies during the Cultural Revolution. They were often criticized for their lack of political consciousness.

7. Guangzhou International Trade Fair is the major annual trade fair in China for international commerce.

I've Become a Different Person

我變了一个人

MALE, age 27 in

1967

**ELEMENTARY
SCHOOL TEACHER
in T City**

*I*n every person's life there is one date they remember. Besides their birthday, I mean. Of course you remember your birthday, 'cause with no birthday there'd be no you. But I'm talking about something different, like the day of your first kiss, your wedding, your divorce, the day your parents died, stuff like that. Days that your life hinges on. I have one of these days. It's April 4th.

April 4th is a bad-luck day. Napoleon was defeated on April 4th, Ali Butuo was hanged on April 4th, Zhang Zhixin[1] was executed by a firing squad on April 4th. April 4th also happens to be the day I was thrown in prison, April 4, 1970.

I was sentenced to twenty years, so my prison term should have been up on April 3, 1990. When they sentence you to many years like that, they always let you out on the day before the anniversary date on which they locked you up. Otherwise, they'd have kept you in one day too long. So, as you might guess, I was headed for trouble on the fourth.

Even now, when April 4th rolls around, I feel like death is hanging over me. My whole body aches, I get chills, and I don't dare think about anything.

April 4th is like a nail that once nailed me to a cross. Now I've been taken down from the cross, but that nail is still in me. It still drives, hard and fast and deep, into my psyche.

I was in jail for ten years, all the while not knowing why I was there in the first place. When my verdict was read aloud in court, I was so shocked I asked, "Are you talking about me?" It wasn't until after I was released that I found out what had happened. But it turns out that not knowing was better, since then at least I had the suspicion that they must have some reason, even if it was just that I stepped on an ant or something. But once I knew the reason of my conviction, that was it. I was done for. I felt hollow, as if I had stepped off the earth and was floating in some cold and boundless universe.

Ten years was like a knife blade that sliced me in half—one half the past, one half the future, two halves that could never be reunited into a whole. There's no way you can comprehend this feeling, to be cut in half at the waist, and still be alive.

I used to be such an idiot, one who seemed to be living in a dream.

My life story couldn't be simpler. Go on, write it down—born in '41. Primary school, then middle school, and graduated from high school when I was eighteen. I didn't go to college, but willingly accepted the Party's assignment to teach at a primary school. Up until then, I'd never left school, like a little stream that flowed unsuspectingly straight, without any twists and turns of its bed. This little stream was so clear you could see straight to the bottom. I lived honestly and cleanly. But it seems that God was arranging trouble for me, having me born into a capitalist family.

My father was a big capitalist, the president of a salt company. After Liberation he didn't work anymore. He liked antique books and art, and he stayed at home reading all day or messing with calligraphy and painting. He rarely showed his face outside the house. Because he was so well-known, he was made a member of the Chinese People's Political Consultative Conference. They gave him a Mao suit to wear, and before each meeting they'd send a car around to pick him up. When the car arrived, he'd change into the suit and hobble off to the meeting, leaning on his cane. The paintings and calligraphy that he collected were all famous masterworks; he spent nearly all the money he'd earned in his whole life on his art. He had a lot of famous artist friends, like Zhang Daqian and Qi Baishi.[2] Zhang Daqian even painted a picture in honor of my birth—a little stone-green snake lying on a cinnabar-red rock, because I was born in the year of the snake. After Liberation my father donated his whole collection, piece by piece, to the government. These included a couple of stunning paintings by Ba Da Shan Ren and Hui Nantian,[3] both the finest of fine art! There was also one by Wen Zhengming,[4] from the Song Dynasty, with calligraphic inscriptions by each of eighteen scholars of the School of Wu, and one by Zhu Zhishan,[5] who was known as a master of *kai-shu*[6] style calligraphy. On the back of this painting there's an inscription of about a thousand characters by him in cursive style. All these paintings and more were donated by my father. He did it for two reasons. First, he really wanted to do a good deed; and second, he wanted to buy some political capital. At that time all the big capitalists thought like that.

I inherited that kind of thinking too, which sort of complicated my otherwise simple honesty. On the one hand, I piously went about my self-remolding. There was a problem with my "bloodline," so I quite happily gave myself a "transfusion," and did my best to act correctly in all situations and at all times. On the other hand, I was quite attentive to my own "safety coefficient." Confucius wrote, "I daily examine myself on three points," and every day I examined my actions, wondering if I had said or done anything that might have displeased the leadership. If I had, I believed that each wrong act or word would make my coefficient take a nose-dive. But if I had said or done something that day that gained the praise of the leadership, then my coefficient would jump, and I would feel comfortable and safe. This method actually got me good results. In school I was admitted to the Communist Youth League; after I got out of school and was working, I was made a member of the League Organizational Committee, chairman of the union, and a member of the "core group." This was an unexpected honor, and I was really flattered that the leadership would allow me such a privilege. So I became more indebted to the Party and even more politically conscious. Let me give you an example. I liked history and was a big fan of fine arts, and there was this elderly gentleman with whom I wanted to study classic texts and calligraphy. But first I took the initiative to report this to the committee and get their approval before I went to learn from him. In another instance, I had this light-blue, Western-style suit that I had only worn once. During the Lantern Festival,[7] a bunch of friends and family were coming over to celebrate. I put on the suit and looked at myself in the mirror. It looked pretty good. But later I realized that this was just a manifestation of the hidden bourgeois consciousness that flowed in my veins. I realized I had to nip this evil in the bud. So I put the suit back in the closet and left it there until it was confiscated in a house raid during the Cultural Revolution.

I had discovered a lifestyle that suited me: Being diligent to win the praise of the leadership at work, plus wearing the simplest and most modest clothing possible, plus speaking and acting cautiously, equals the safety coefficient. Then using this safety coefficient, plus studying literature and painting in my free time, equals my entire life.

When I got home from work each day, my greatest joy was reading, memorizing classical poetry, and practicing my calligraphy and painting. I'd open the black lacquer cabinet and, one by one, take out the precious, ancient works of art, and intoxicate myself with the intricacies of brush and ink. Young people today would probably think I led a pretty pitiful life. It was pitiful! It was as pitiful as a chicken awaiting slaughter. But the most pitiful thing about it was the fact that I thought my life was really pretty good, quiet and full. Look, this is some of the calligraphy I wrote then: "tranquil," "refined," "circumspect"—that was me. Here's a photo of me—really "literary," don't you think? And sort of reserved? Ha! what a goof.

On August 23, 1966, the Red Guards started doing their search-and-confiscate house raids. I was at school writing slogans on posters to promote Mao Zedong Thought. At the time, I was still a member of the "core group." Suddenly an old classmate rode up on his bike and told me, "They're raiding your house." Then, just as suddenly, he turned around and rode off. At that moment I felt the sky cave in on me. After the raid, I was put in with other people who had problems, forced to confess my family history, and criticized. Every last thing had been confiscated from my house. All those priceless works of art, the paintings by Shi Tao, Gao Fenghan, Ren Bonian, Ren Fuchang,[8] had all been burnt into a pile of ashes. Do you know what it feels like to be completely deprived of your life? In a flash, my entire life was gone, like a fish that has been suddenly yanked from the water and left gasping on the bank. What safety coefficient? All that was just me fooling myself. Safety coefficient = zero! I was left holding this big huge zero, and nothing else counted. It was all completely meaningless.

I was now a member of a family with nothing to its name. All that was left of my home were a couple of people, my parents and brothers and me, and all that was left of me were my bodily functions. All day I was made to read *Chairman Mao's Quotations*, make self-criticisms, and endlessly repeat my confession of my problems. My name often showed up on big-character posters. At first I was afraid to see my name up there, but, by 1968, I had gotten used to it. Those colleagues of mine who were free of problems wouldn't give me as much as a smile. When they called my name, they used the same cold tone of voice they might use to call a mule or an ox. But I was used to it all. There was nothing in this world that I couldn't deal with. When I saw group after group of people being beaten, arrested, jailed, or committing suicide, I thought, "safety—now that is freedom." I mean, the only concrete, practical kind of freedom was to be safe and sound and problem-free.

I thought I had achieved that kind of "freedom" easily. But then one day I was arrested.

After I figured out what was going on, I wasn't the least bit scared. The reason for my arrest was that, in 1967, during the worst of the chaos, the father of one of my brother's friends, who was the Party secretary at a middle school in Beijing, was labeled a "Capitalist Roader." He was struggled against so harshly that he couldn't take it any longer. He left Beijing to hide until things died down. Seeing he was in trouble, I let him stay at my house for a while. I'm a pretty good cook, so sometimes I'd have some old classmates over for dinner. About a week later this guy went south to Yangzhou to stay with relatives. After the worst of that movement was over, he returned to his school in Beijing. He was pretty savvy, and in order to rally the masses he sold me out—he accused me of harboring a "black organization" in my house. Ungrateful? Well, I don't blame him for that, because at that time, "ungratefulness" was to be expected.

I thought, in this case, the odds were in my favor, because even if you told me to organize something, I wouldn't have the guts to do it. They investigated me for quite a while, but couldn't come up with any proof. So they just issued a verdict, saying I was one of those "sons and daughters of the exploiting class who could be re-educated with a little pushing and pulling," that I should be "dealt with according to the Internal Contradictions Among the People,"[9] and they let me go. Oh, and they gave me a Mao pin. It was one of those Mao pins issued by the Municipal Revolutionary Committee, and they only gave them to people who belonged to the "revolutionary masses." It was like a badge of citizenship, or like the ID cards we carry around these days. Happily, wearing my badge, I met a girl and married her.

On my wedding day, as I looked at my wife, I thought, from this day forward, whenever I do as much as take a deep breath, I'd better think hard about whether I'm breaking some rule. Otherwise, I'd never be able to face this woman who just agreed to spend the rest of her life with a poor sucker like me. But I hadn't realized that April 4th, that bad-luck day, was waiting for me. Suddenly some men from the Revolutionary Committee of the Public Security Bureau came and carted me off to prison. This time I was scared. I hadn't committed any crime, so why'd they nab me and throw me in jail? Could it be that they've got the wrong man, I wondered. But I didn't dare ask, because in those days there was no such thing as getting the wrong man. Back then, men weren't much different from chickens or cats. How could you grab the "wrong" one?

In prison, we all had to wear the blue prison uniforms and shoes. There was a huge pile of shoes there. I just picked a pair that fit my feet. When I put them on, I noticed that #171 was inked on the tongue of both shoes. My heart nearly stopped when I realized that my prisoner number was also 171. I was destined to be there. This was a sign.

Of course, I still hoped for some good luck. I knew I had not committed any crime. Who could have expected that life would be so grim as to take away even this hope?

I was interrogated six separate times. Each interrogation was conducted in the middle of the night. They asked me very strange questions. They kept asking me over and over again to turn in my pistol. I thought they must have got it wrong, that it was not me they wanted. I told them, even if you wanted me to go out right now and get a pistol, I wouldn't know where to go to get one. I've spent my whole life in school. When I graduated, I got a job teaching. Except for in the movies, I've never even seen a gun.

After the six interrogation sessions, they suddenly stopped. It was as if it had been an episode too weird even for a dream.

While in prison, I was ordered to study political propaganda materials every day. The furnishings in this prison were pretty unusual. In the middle of each cell was a string of long, low benches. During the daytime, prisoners would sit on these benches reading Mao's works and other revolutionary propaganda; in the evenings, they spread wide wooden planks on top of the benches and slept there. On the door were a couple of palm-sized little windows that could slide open and shut—they were the observation holes for the guards. As soon as one of the little windows slid open, all the prisoners would immediately sit up straight and act serious. Then the little sliding windows were replaced with mercury mirrors. The mirrors were scored with lines, the mirror side facing in, so the guards could see into the room, but the prisoners couldn't see out. Pretty slick, huh? Once they did that, none of the prisoners dared to slack off, ever. One time I went over to check myself out in the mirror. It nearly got the pants scared off me. I looked awful—sickly pale, and my cheeks were all caved in, like two big ditches on either side of my face. My beard was so long, I hardly looked human. Only later did I find out that I had tuberculosis.

I thought that as soon as they figured out that I didn't have any gun, they'd let me go. It had to be a case of mistaken identity, unless someone framed me. But who? I've never been the type to offend people. Who would be so hard-hearted as to set me up? Besides, that case with the Beijing schoolteacher had already been closed.

One day, they suddenly brought me up again for interrogation. Again came the questions about the pistol.

This time I got aggravated. I said, "I have absolutely nothing to do with any pistol."

This was the first time in my whole life that I had ever dared talk back to the authorities. Who'd have thought it. Instead of getting pissed off, the interrogator mellowed a little. He said, "Don't be too quick to dismiss this matter. Let me give you a little hint: start thinking about toys."

Well I thought that was really weird—in such a serious, life-and-death kind of situation, what's he doing talking about toys? I said, "I've seen toy pistols, yeah, but think about it, I'm a teacher, I can't carry a toy gun around with me all day!"

The interrogator was really patient that day. He said, "Calm down. Think a little harder. What else do you carry around with you."

I thought again, and then I remembered! I'd had a little pistol-shaped ornament on my keychain, about two centimeters long. A friend had given it to me. It was made in France. It was copper inlaid with silver, really pretty. I said, "There was one. A little pendant on my keychain."

The interrogator said, "Exactly. Why didn't you confess to that earlier?"

I was stunned. Had they really thrown me in prison on account of a keychain? Did they really think I could have used such a little thing to commit a crime? I mean, every house has a kitchen cleaver, so should the whole country be thrown in jail? I stared at him with my mouth agape, speechless.

He said, "I just want you to write about this problem."

Problem? My sky went black with clouds; my brain spun. But I wrote down all the information I could think of about who had given me the little keychain, which years I carried it, and when it was confiscated during a house search. He also told me to draw a little sketch of it. He read the "account of the problem" that I had just finished writing, nodded, and praised me, "What a good attitude you are demonstrating!"

From the time I was arrested until my sentencing, they had asked only about this pistol. They never asked about anything else. I'd been locked up already for eight or nine months.

At first I thought, when this matter was cleared up, they would let me out. As the days drew on, I became puzzled as to why I hadn't been released. After some more time, I felt sure that something wasn't right. I had a sense of impending disaster. I felt as if I had been gripped by some strange magic hand. Whose hand it was I had no idea. It was just a feeling. I couldn't escape it.

Sure enough, on November 26th—it was snowing lightly that day—someone called, "Number 171!" As soon as I left my cell, a bunch of armed police officers in full uniform appeared. They tied me up with a rope and threw me in the back of a big truck. On board the truck were a number of other prisoners. We were all being taken to a big theater for a public sentencing. When we got to the theater, I was ordered to stand at the head of the line. This was the position reserved for prisoners with the heaviest sentences, usually the death sentence. I thought, that's it, it's all over for me. Nothing I could say or scream would help me now. I was a chicken on the chopping block.

That day there were two little incidents that were really remarkable. While they were tying me up, one young cop reached inside my sleeve and pinched my wrist, saying "If the rope's too tight, just say so." And then, as we prisoners were sitting in back of the open-bed truck bouncing down the road, we kept getting hit by branches. It was this same young cop who said to me, "Duck your head, careful of the branches."

Back then, any sympathy for a prisoner was absolutely forbidden, but he wasn't the least bit secretive about saying this
stuff to me. So I thought, I must be headed for execution,
because the only time they're nice to a prisoner is right before
they shoot him. Only later did I find out that the cop did it
simply out of the kindness of his heart. It's too bad that, in the
state I was in then, it was impossible for me to look at him so
that I could remember his face.

The court pronounced me guilty on three counts:
extremely reactionary thought; attacking the command of the
proletariat and the policies of the Cultural Revolution; and
using my home as a base to receive enemy radio broadcasts,
voice grievances on behalf of Liu Shaoqi,[10] and plot to organize a counterrevolutionary clique.

Any one of these three crimes was punishable by
death. As I drifted in a space of nothingness, I heard them
yelling from the stage, "Sentenced to twenty years in prison!"

Only twenty years? Ah, my life was given back to me,
I was going to be OK. At that point, twenty years in prison did-
n't seem like much.

After the sentencing, I was sent to XXX prison to serve
out my term. First they put me through re-education. They
asked me what I had to say. I said, "I just wonder, is this verdict really about me? I've never done even one of the things I
am accused of. And how come you've never interrogated me
about them?"

Asking that question counted as "stubborn resistance," and I was sent to a special study class, called the
"Flying Blood Study Group." If you didn't admit your guilt,
they would beat you, and your blood would fly. That's what
the name meant. Intense, huh?

But to be honest, I was never beaten, because my
tuberculosis had already advanced to the point that I was spitting blood. Every day I wore two gauze masks and carried
around a sealed plastic cup that I used as a spittoon. In the
space of an hour I'd cough up a cupful of blood. Every time I
coughed up blood, I thought that this would be the last time.

They kept me locked up there for four months, but still
there was no way I would admit to these crimes. One day an
army representative and the Discipline Section chief called me

out to speak with me. I put on a quilted jacket, cupped my spittoon with both hands, and sat down on a bench.

The Discipline Section chief said, "Today, if you have something to say, just say it. Whatever you want to say, it's all right."

I said, "Why was I sentenced for crimes I was never interrogated about? You said I listened to enemy radio broadcasts, but during the Cultural Revolution our house was searched so thoroughly that they confiscated everything but the floorboards. Where would I get a radio even if I did want to listen to the enemy? If you want to convict me for that crime, you'll have to send me out to commit it now! How can I admit to it? You tell me." When I finished speaking, I coughed, but the coughing made my throat tickle and I had to spit blood.

The section chief gave me a cup of hot water to drink. He shuffled through the papers in my file, and then pushed it over to the army rep, and without turning away from me, said to the rep, "Look, again with this."

The army rep looked at it, and didn't say a word. The two of them were quiet for the longest time. Then the Discipline Section chief said, "There are some discrepancies in your verdict that we are powerless to correct. Anyway, this is not the time to be solving that problem. You must first get beyond this difficulty of admitting your guilt. What do you think should be done about it? Let me suggest a solution: starting today, don't bring up this problem again, OK?"

I said, "I'm not the one who brings it up. It's brought up to me every day."

The section chief replied, "All right. Starting today we won't bring it up either. But let me ask you, do you still have bourgeois ideas? Are you able to criticize your own thinking?"

I replied, "Yes, I do, and I can."

He then said, "Good. Now go back to your cell and prepare a self-criticism. And be quick about it."

Next day, the prison authorities called together all the prisoners to listen to me criticize my bourgeois thought—my family background and my desire to establish myself as an expert instead of as a revolutionary. Then I moved on to label my crimes and criticize myself according to Party principles.

Afterwards, the Discipline Section chief expressed his opinion: "His self-criticism was very thorough, digging out the roots of his crimes. Let's hear your suggestions about him. Has he dug deep enough?"

Well, if the section chief just said it was thorough enough, do you think anyone would dare say it wasn't thorough enough? So this self-criticism was allowed to stand as my admission of guilt, and I was returned from the "Flying Blood Study Group" to the regular prison. I'd been released from a prison within the prison. Although I had not left the encirclement of iron bars, still there was a huge difference. It was like I'd been raised up from the eighteenth level of hell to the fifteenth level.

I'm really grateful to that Discipline Section chief. At that time, and in that place, it was a real display of humanitarianism. Not long thereafter, he was transferred to the City Public Security Bureau, and later he was instrumental in getting my verdict overturned and getting me out of jail. But I'm getting ahead of my story.

When you're sentenced to twenty years in prison, it's almost impossible to imagine the day you might actually walk out of jail alive. Not to mention the fact that my TB had already spread throughout my whole body. I had pulmonary tuberculosis, lymphotuberculosis, gastrotuberculosis, and epididymal tuberculosis. If TB was radioactive, I'd have been a walking nuclear arsenal. I must say the prison doctors did their best to cure me. But after seven days of not coughing up blood, I went out to dig air-raid shelters. Why? I can't exactly say. It wasn't because I wanted to demonstrate that I was trying hard to get out early, nor quite because I wanted to drive myself to an early grave. I felt like I had already attained the Buddhist spiritual ideal—all is empty and void—and I was really quite calm at heart.

You want to know what kept me going during that time, what was the mainstay of my spiritual well-being? I didn't have a mainstay. Although I was a political criminal, I really didn't have the slightest comprehension of politics. The political criminals of those days weren't people who went out and committed some "crime" for the sake of politics. They were the sacrificial objects that politics demanded. I didn't even understand why I was in jail. Where would I have gotten any spiritual support? Live or die, I just let nature take its course.

My wife divorced me; my mother came to visit me; I never shed a single tear, never was the least bit moved. It wasn't that I was actively trying not to be moved. Weird. I just wasn't. It was just as well. In jail, any emotions, hopes, or beliefs you might have became ways of torturing yourself. I stopped believing in anything. When your life is like that, what's the point? My only diversion was writing calligraphy. I wrote out all the poems I had memorized. I asked my family to send some special paper that I sewed up into a book, and then I filled each page with different styles of calligraphy. I called it the "Book of Contentment in an Ancient Timbre."

This contentment didn't mean I was happy with my lot. It didn't really deserve to be called happiness, because where there's happiness there must also be sorrow. Thinking about happiness is also a kind of aspiration. With the absence of aspirations, everything follows Nature. It is a state in which life becomes death, and death becomes life, in which life and death coexist. If I had not reached such a state, I would never have lived until today—so many people around me lost their minds or their senses, or died of disease, or committed suicide! Hm. All this stuff I'm saying, do you understand it?

After almost ten years in prison, the only thing that made any lasting impression on me was another prisoner. He had once been an interrogator for the Public Security Bureau.

He told me the reason he was in prison: Once he was given a really unique case, it was a case of gang rape. The defendants were a group of VIPs from various rebel groups. One of them was even a member of the Municipal Revolutionary Committee.

During the process of the interrogation, he discovered that each time the plaintiff told her story it was a little bit different, that the facts didn't line up with each other. So in his report to his superiors, he wrote, "Due to inconclusive evidence, this case should be dropped." Within a few days, a really high-ranking city official came to talk to him. He said that in view of the extenuating circumstances of the situation, the authorities had already decided which defendant should be found guilty of which crime, which ones should be sentenced to death, which one granted a stay of execution. The official demanded that he carry out their decisions. They told him he must not take any measures to the contrary. After this conversation, the interrogator went home and said to his wife, "I might have to leave home for a while. Don't ask where I'm going, and don't ask anyone for information about me." He took a bedding roll to the office, opened the file on that case, and wrote in big letters, "Spare their lives!" Then he sat on his bedroll and waited. Immediately he was arrested for engaging in counterrevolutionary activities. Even before those "gang rapists" were convicted, he'd begun serving a seven-year prison sentence.

Well, I used to think my case had been unfair, that it didn't have a leg to stand on, and I used to try to figure out what was really going on. After I heard his story, though, I didn't even try to figure anything out anymore.

In a world like that, what is the meaning of "injustice"?

Injustice didn't even feel like injustice. Now, that's the extraordinary thing. And the days passed smoothly enough. So that that old saying really felt true: "one day in jail equals three years on the outside." Before I realized it, the Cultural Revolution came to an end.

One day in 1977, I was taking some air in the exercise yard, greedily basking in the sunlight, picking lice, and plucking my beard. The big iron gate that opened into the yard had a machine gun mounted on top of it and two little gatehouses on either side. From inside the glass window of one of the gatehouses, I heard someone calling my name. I went over and a man came out. It turned out to be that Discipline Section chief who had rescued me from the "Flying Blood Study Group" several years before. He looked left and right to make sure we were alone and then said, "Let's take a walk." We walked for a long time before he said anything. He just kept rubbing his hand over the heavy flesh of his face; the stubble of his beard rasped loudly under the pressure of his hand. When we had reached a safe distance away from the people in the exercise yard, he said: "Hurry up and write an appeal. I'll come pick it up tomorrow morning, right here." Then he walked away.

Dumbfounded, I just stood there. See, this was an interesting turn of events, huh? I wrote the appeal and, next day, stuffed it into his hands. I actually wasn't terribly excited by this turn of events. A stone dropped into a dried-up well won't make waves.

For nearly a year after I gave him that appeal, nothing happened. If, from the day I handed him that appeal, I had started being optimistic, hoping night and day for a reprieve, wouldn't I have just been torturing myself for nothing?

By this time I had already stopped doing heavy work. I worked in the prison architecture studio as an assistant to a prisoner who had been an architect. I could draw, so I helped him with sketches. Suddenly one day, someone from the Discipline Section came and said to me, "Go gather your things. Your family has sent someone to pick you up."

I went to the Discipline Section and saw my brothers there waiting for me. When they saw me, they were overjoyed. The judge read the ruling on my case. It was just a few sentences: "The defendant's words and actions during the Cultural Revolution were not sufficient grounds to charge him with the crime of counterrevolution. In light of the recent appeal and re-examination of the case, the defendant is declared not guilty and is hereby released." Then the judge imperiously handed the ruling to me, along with a small sum of money and some ration tickets.[11] He also gave me the papers I would need when I went to get my residence card, went to the grain shop to get my grain rations, or when I reported to my work unit. That was it; I was out. It was as simple as the day I went in, and just as mystifying.

On the road home, the sight of people coming and going was like a vision from another world, familiar yet strange. I bet someone returning to earth from a trip around the universe would feel like this too. When we arrived home, I found the warmth and smell and everything just as it used to be. All the little details of the house triggered my memory, bringing back things I had long forgotten, until I was really rather moved. After all, I was just a normal person, not an immortal. But I didn't cry. It's not that I was hardhearted, just that my emotions had been blunted. I'm sure my calmness somewhat surprised my family. Perhaps it was precisely because they sensed how completely I had changed, from the inside out, that my entire family burst into tears.

After about a week, a messenger came from the court to give me a summons. It was blue. It told me to show up at the courthouse, and then, "You may take a leave of absence from work, but do not misunderstand: the leadership wishes to speak with you."

As soon as I entered the court building, "the leadership" was unusually enthusiastic. He came up and patted me on the shoulder, saying, "Ah, you're here! Come, come, this is the first time we've met, we must have a good talk. Otherwise, you might go to your grave without understanding why!"

Puzzled, I waited for him to talk. He said, "Do you remember the February 21st Speech[12] during the Cultural Revolution?"

"No, I don't," I replied. In the beginning of the Cultural Revolution, I could never keep straight who was struggling against whom, nor did I really care.

He said, "After the February 21st Speech, Jiang Qing[13] criticized the military control commission here, saying, 'You have not conducted your class struggle well. The sons and daughters of capitalists in Shanghai and Beijing have been organizing counterrevolutionary cliques, and they have been seized and swiftly dealt with. Your city is full of capitalist offspring, how could there not be even one counterrevolutionary clique?' So the military control commission immediately went out and arrested a bunch of the children of big capitalists. You were targeted because that school Party secretary from Beijing made accusations against you. But during the investigation, they couldn't find a single shred of evidence of any relations between you and any others, so you couldn't be called a counterrevolutionary clique. But neither could you be released. They had to make some sort of report to their superiors. So you were found guilty of 'plotting to organize a counterrevolutionary clique.' That way it counted as a clique, even though it wasn't actually a clique. And that's why you didn't have any co-defendants. That's the truth behind your situation."

I'd gotten used to not knowing. Now, the more I knew, the more I was at a loss.

He continued: "I came from Beijing, and I was even worse off than you. You were in jail ten years, and I was in for eleven, but I got out a few months earlier than you. The central government sent me here to investigate unjust, false, and misjudged cases. In the process of my investigation, I found there were two really odd cases, one of them being yours. There wasn't the slightest correlation between the contents of your file and the final verdict. After I read the appeal you wrote a year ago, I had your case cleared up as quickly as possible. But let's forget about it all. The past is the past. You're still young, you've got a long life ahead of you, right? Whatever you do, don't go blaming your work unit. Even they never figured out exactly what happened in your case. If you're smart, you won't go making any trouble about it. I say all this from the bottom of my heart. Are you willing to take my word on this?"

His enthusiasm was almost passionate. Ten years ago, I might have hugged him for joy. But at that point I just gave him a little smile. Hey, I'd started letting nature take its course a long time ago.

Being in prison and being on the outside are the exact opposite of each other. On the outside, you look forward to good things and not to bad things. But on the inside, you look forward to the bad things and not to the good, because if good fortune finds you, it's time to start worrying. For example, if they tell you to change your clothes, you're going home for a visit, that's good, right? Wrong! It's probably because your father's died, or your mother is critically ill, or there's something up with your wife. On the other hand, if they are really ruthless to you, and 'struggle against' you day and night, then you're fine, that's normal—'cause they sure didn't put you there so they could buy you drinks. But if you're on the outside and you're 'struggled against,' then that's certainly something bad.

Or again, when the doors of a prison are locked, that means there are people inside; but when they are open, you can be sure there's no one in there. Yet isn't it just the opposite on the outside? When the door to a house is open, there's sure to be someone inside, and it's only locked when there's no one home. Otherwise why would thieves all be such good lockpickers? Another thing is, the locks on doors outside of prison are all on the inside of the door, while locks on doors inside a prison are all on the outside. It really is all turned around, isn't it?

In jail, if they think you're well-disciplined, you get to sleep on an open plank bed. When there are a lot of people, everyone's crammed onto one long platform, with at most seven inches of space per person. If you have to get up in the middle of the night to pee, your spot will be gone by the time you get back. But if they think you're a troublemaker, or a dangerous type, then they'll make you sleep alone in a single room. That's the opposite from what you'd expect.

As to meals, in prison you never get to eat your fill; hunger is a strong and constant feeling. While in prison, I could eat four steamed cornmeal buns at one sitting and still not feel full. When they're dishing out food at mealtime, your eyes bug out of your head with hunger; but if they really let you eat your fill one day, you'd know something was up. Such special care would mean you're about to be executed.

The weirdest thing is, after I was released, I kept having this dream that I was in jail and couldn't get out, I'd keep banging against the bars. But while I was in prison, I never once had a dream that I was stuck in the slammer. You can go anywhere in your dreams—to mountains or famous temples, anywhere in the world, wherever you think would be nice. Some dreams I had in prison I can still remember clear as day. For instance, once I dreamt I was standing in front of the entrance to the Daybreak Movie Theater, and I got on a big bus. I knew everyone on the bus, though I had no idea who they were. The bus started moving, and on both sides of us were gardens and Western-style houses, really elegant, really pretty—oh man, there were houses with pointy roofs like in fairy tales. Houses of all kinds, with the lights lit up. It was really gorgeous. I walked towards a little corner, with green grass and narrow lanes, and it was pretty dark, but I could make out the shape of a Chinese-style pagoda. It was an odd architectural style, like two halves of two separate pagodas stuck together, with big columns and lattice-work fans. Inside they were selling food, all of my favorite foods, and I ate and ate, and it tasted so good... But after I was released from jail, I couldn't have this kind of dream no matter how hard I tried.

Even today, good news makes me nervous, and bad news doesn't. When people told me they'd like to exhibit my calligraphy in galleries nationwide, I'd get that nagging whisper in the back of my head telling me that something bad, some kind of trouble, would follow.

It's not that I'm numb; it's just that rarely will anything get me excited. Let's say you get all excited about some good news—but how can you be sure it's really good news? Then again, let's say you get all worked up over bad news—but if it's really bad news, what can you do? And what can it do to you? Look at me, all those years on the outside worrying about my "safety coefficient." By all appearances it seemed like my coefficient was really high, but in the end it wasn't worth crap. If you want to know what people really think about you, wait until you're arrested, then you'll find out. By the time you're released, the policies have changed, and everyone has a smile for you. Great, huh? But they're phony. So.....so what? So my old classmates now call me headstrong and reckless. They say I let my temper govern my actions and words, and that I'm inconsiderate of others. I'd agree with that. I've had quite enough of taking others into consideration. Now, I am the only one I listen to.

My ex-wife has already remarried. She has a child, not by her husband. I was arrested forty days after we were married, on April 4th, that bad-luck day. The child was born in late October. My ex-wife says she adopted it, that it's not mine. I think the child looks a lot like my sister, but I don't want to go into the matter too seriously. Sometimes I go to visit her and the kid, and we get along like old friends. The kid and I have a sort of unusual bond. Of course, a bond doesn't mean anything, I'm not asking it to mean anything. The fact of the bond itself is enough. The way things are is precisely the way they were meant to be.

Ever since I got TB in prison, I've been completely impotent. Other guys in jail would have involuntary ejaculations, or they'd jerk off, but not me. When I first got out, I didn't have the desire to remarry and raise a family. I thought I'd be content to go through life like a monk in the layman's world. Later on I met a divorced woman, and I told her up front that I couldn't do it. Who'd have thought? It turned out she'd had a miscarriage which led to an infection, and she had to have an operation in which they'd plucked all the various female organs out of her, so that she didn't have the desire for that sort of thing anymore either. So we got together. Without that little complicating factor, we stay out of each other's hair, we live in peace together, and we take care of each other. Oddly enough, we're even more inseparable this way. Now we've really reached a state of desirelessness. They say we're a match made in heaven. But no, more literally, our match was created right here on earth.

One day after the Cultural Revolution was over and things were getting back to normal, I was going through the confiscated items the government had returned to me, and I came across some calligraphy I had written before the Cultural Revolution. It really astonished me. It seemed like the words were written by me, but then again it seemed like they were written by someone else. Only then did I realize how completely I had changed. I had become a different person. No matter how I might try, I'd never be able to hook up where my old self left off. I'd never get back on that path. And I wasn't in the least bit sad. As far as I am concerned, being sad is just you helping fate hurt you. Why should you sit around making things harder on yourself? You're better off accepting life the way it is now. Don't hurt other people, and don't hurt yourself.

I only believe that no one will ever change me back again.

The God who created humans was once defeated by the Cultural Revolution.

—*Author*

FOOTNOTES

1. Zhang Zhixin was a woman cadre of the Propaganda Department of Liaoning Province who openly defended Liu Shaoqi and opposed the policies of the Cultural Revolution. She was labeled an "active counter-revolutionary" and was executed on April 4, 1975.

2. Zhang Daqian and Qi Baishi are both famous modern Chinese artists.

3. Ba Da Shan Ren, also named Zhu Da, and Hui Nantian were Qing Dynasty artists.

4. Wen Zhengming was a Ming Dynasty artist.

5. Zhu Zhishan is a well-known Ming Dynasty calligrapher

6. Kai-shu calligraphy is a style of calligraphy that is easier to read than many other styles.

7. The Lantern Festival occurs on the fifteenth day of the first month of the lunar calendar. The Chinese celebrate the festival with lion dances and other festive activities.

8. Shi Tao, Gao Fenghan, Ren Bonian, Ren Fuchang are all Qing Dynasty artists.

9. Based on the theory of Mao Zedong, there are two kinds of contradictions: one among the people, the other between the people and the enemy. While contradictions among the people can be dealt with leniently, those between the people and the enemy must be solved with fierce struggles.

10. Liu Shaoqi was the President of China when the Cultural Revolution began. One of the main reasons Mao Zedong started the Cultural Revolution was to get rid of Liu, who was persecuted and died in humiliation in 1969.

11. Due to insufficient supplies, rations tickets were required to buy food, cloth, sugar, meat, and other daily necessities for several decades after 1949. It was not until the late 1980s when the government stopped issuing such tickets.

12. On February 21, 1968, Jiang Qing made a speech in which she accused people in the field of art and literature of holding underground meetings and attempting to seize power from the Central Cultural Revolution Group.

13. Jiang Qing was Mao's wife and the head of the Gang of Four. She was arrested after Mao died.

It's Hard to Explain

说不清楚

MALE, age 32 in

1966

HIGH SCHOOL TEACHER in U City

I HAVE a tragic temperament. What I mean is that I seem to have been born with a certain gullible quality that has always steered me straight into tragedy. And what's still more tragic is that, even when I recognize my own gullibility, even when I know I've been duped, I can never quite explain exactly how it happened. I get really distressed about this, and make things even harder on myself. I hate my temperament, but I'm stuck with it. Because of it, I even thought about suicide at a very young age.

Once when I was little, I saw that my sister-in-law was really tired, so I went to fetch water for her. How small was I then? You know how two water buckets are attached to a long bamboo pole by a hook and two rings? Well, when I shouldered the pole, the bottoms of the buckets scraped along the ground. When the buckets were full of water they were so heavy that they hurt my shoulders, and I didn't walk so much as I staggered. Anyhow, to get to my sister-in-law's, I had to pass right by our neighbor's front door. As I staggered past their door, one of the grownups came out and said, "What a strong young man you are! And it's so good of you to take the time to fetch water for us. Here, let me take it, let me take it...." As he spoke, he took the water bucket, lifted it, and dumped the water into his own water vat.

And me? I stood there like an idiot. I was too embarrassed to say, "This water wasn't meant for you." If I had said that, I would have felt, as we say in our dialect, "short-faced," and it would have made me look bad. But inside, I knew the score—he was taking advantage of me. So if I knew it, why didn't I say anything? It would have been a most common-sensical, ordinary thing to say. So why couldn't I say it? At the time, I just didn't have the words. After all these years, whenever I think about that little incident, I don't hate my neighbors—I hate myself. That's precisely the gullible quality I am talking about! In later years, if I came to grief, or was put at a disadvantage, or was wronged somehow in politics, it was because I lacked this concept, or language, or mindset. Exactly what it was I lacked, I still can't explain.

That was the first time I was conned, and the first time in my life I'd ever found something hard to explain.

On the road into our village there was a man with a wheelbarrow who had stopped to sell fresh sweet melons out of baskets. There were several people standing around, buying and eating the sweet melon slices.

Slices of sweet melon cost five cents apiece. I handed over my five-cent note, got a slice of melon, and stood to one side to eat it. As I was eating, the melon-man said, "Hey, Little Walnut (my nickname was Walnut), did you pay for that melon you're eating?" I guess he'd forgotten that I had paid.

I told him I had. The melon-man pointed to the box holding the money he'd collected, and said, "Which one is yours?"

The box was full of five-cent notes. I saw one that looked like it might have been mine, and pointed to it, saying, "That one."

Who'd have thought, a guy standing nearby eating his melon said, "No, that one's mine."

I panicked. Once I got nervous, all the five-cent notes in the box looked exactly the same to me. So I just picked a different note and pointed to it, saying, "This one."

Would you believe it, another customer piped up: "That one is mine, see, it's got a little rip in the middle. Hey kid, don't go trying to eat melons without paying."

This time I'd managed to put myself in the position of a con man. Now the melon-man, the melon-buyers, and the melon-eaters were all accusing me, and I couldn't say a word. It was as if I really had cheated the man out of a slice of melon. My face was burning, I was so flustered.

There was a kind old woman from my village whom I called Third Grandma. She spoke up on my behalf: "You, melon-man, why are you being so hard on him? He's just a little kid. Can you think of any little kid who doesn't love sweet melons? Maybe this kid's parents didn't give him any spending money. What's one slice of melon to you? Just look at what your mean words have done to him now!"

This kind of sympathy was even worse! It just confirmed my status as a "con man," as surely as if a verdict had been passed by a judge. Sympathy can ruin you, too.

At the time I felt that it wasn't fair, but I never even thought about our family's reputation. A few years later, my mother and a neighbor got into an argument, and the neighbor cursed her, "Your family is a bunch of melon-stealers!" Only then did I discover that I'd earned us such a bad reputation. I was so angry I just jumped up and down in place, crying "ah, ah," but still I couldn't explain. I was so upset I ran to the well and rammed my head against its stone base. If it weren't for my sister-in-law who grabbed me just in time, it would have been all over for me. That's what I was talking about a minute ago, when I said that I had thought of killing myself as a child.

Let me tell you another story. One autumn day I was carrying a basket along a road by a little stream when I saw something stirring up the mud in the stream bed. I put down my basket, took off my shoes, and waded into the water. When I bent down to touch the thing, I discovered it was a crab. Being just a kid, I couldn't catch the tough little guy—when I tried it just tweaked me with its pincers. At that point, Bighead Li, the horsecart driver, passed by, and I yelled, "There's a crab!" He said, "Don't move, I'm coming!" He stopped his cart, waded into the water, and snatched up the crab on his first try. He lifted up the big, live crab and laughed, saying, "This'll go great with some wine!" Then he got back on his cart and drove off.

At the time I didn't think anything about it. Again, it was because I didn't have that concept, or the words—"Finder's keepers!" That's how simple us country kids were. In our eyes, there was no such thing as a bad-guy. But thinking about it years later, I get really angry. Wasn't that like stealing candy from a baby? I certainly learned something about Bighead Li ... but I always feel like there's some deeper lesson here. What is it? I still can't quite explain. You shouldn't trick a little kid like that. If you do, once he grows up and figures it out, you'll have to pay the price. It's not revenge I'm talking about, necessarily. It's more like you will be exterminated in his heart. That's a fate worse than death!

The things that have been deposited in my soul by countless generations of ancestors are both too many and too few. After some hard soul-searching, I can come up with only two words; but these two words nearly fill my soul to the brim. They are "ren" (tolerance) and "shan" (goodness).

What is ren? The character for ren is the character for "heart" with a "knife" written over it. So if someone sticks a knife into your heart and you still don't make a sound, that's ren, that's tolerance. And shan? The ancestors say that human nature is essentially shan, or good.

Later I discovered that ren is a very stubborn characteristic. To this day I have been unable to rid myself of it. But shan is weak: with the slightest change in circumstances, I find myself acting in a way quite opposite to shan. I understand clearly when it was that this started to happen.

At the time I was a teenager, and I went into town to play. In the middle of the empty square they'd set up a stage, as if there was going to be a performance of some kind. At the foot of the stage, vendors were selling deep-fried tofu, candied calabash, roast sweet potatoes, and all kinds of snacks. Then folks came in droves from all the work units in town to engage in a singing contest, half of them singing "Unity Is Strength" and the other half singing "Hey La La La."[1] But as soon as the mayor got up on stage, the atmosphere changed. He was wearing a felt hat and a traditional-style cotton robe, and he spoke as if he was yelling, bending at the waist with each phrase. Suddenly I saw, in an empty area to one side of the stage, five solitary wooden stakes driven into the ground. The person standing next to me told me that the stakes were to tie people to, before they were executed by a firing squad. I immediately remembered a popular book that had been circulating around our village. There was a drawing in this book of an evil demon tying a person to a wooden stake, and then cutting out his tongue—and I was terrified.

It wasn't long before a big horsecart brought the criminals into the square. They were all tied up, and affixed to their backs were signs made to look like the arrow-shaped tokens of authority that were used by the imperial army in ancient times. At the top of each sign, the man's name was written in black ink, and then either struck through or x'ed out with red ink—I couldn't see clearly which, but I just remember feeling it was blood, blood red. That was the first time I associated the color red with terror. In later years, the sea of red that was the Cultural Revolution made my heart shudder. But the roots of that fear were planted in me at this time.

When the prisoners were pulled off the cart, their faces were awfully pale, and their eyes and eyebrows looked extraordinarily black, probably in contrast to the whiteness of their faces. Instantly all the kids in the square were so scared they all ran yelling for their mommies and daddies. Maybe these criminals really had committed all sorts of crimes, and deserved to be executed. But I felt for them, probably because I was still a child and my essentially *shan* nature was still intact. Then when a young man jumped up on stage and screamed accusations at them, beating them with his belt, I felt even sorrier for them. But as the young man kept beating the criminals, the whole audience began to scream, "Beat them! Beat them!" This chant got louder and louder and clearer and clearer. Everyone raised their fists in unison and leaned forward. Over a thousand people assumed this same position. Before I knew it, I found myself with my fist raised, screaming along with the crowd, "Beat them, beat them, beat them!" As I screamed, I could feel my own hatred growing. Almost instantly, I felt my blood begin to boil and my chest fill with rage.

Later, during the Anti-Hu Feng Movement,[2] when they started to criticize Hu Feng, I really hated him. Then, when I heard they'd captured him, I felt sort of sorry for the guy. Every political movement after that was the same: each time there was a criticism session, I felt true hatred; but as soon as they started to "struggle against" the person, I'd get all sympathetic for them. It was always this kind of back and forth tension between hatred and sympathy. What do you think that's all about? I myself can't explain it.

How I got labeled a Rightist is even more impossible to explain. The reason was simple, even a little silly. I was a freshman in college. It was the mid-50's, when the Party encouraged people to air their views freely. Some classmates were talking about this worker who was really nice, but his boss was a real tyrant—the boss had lost some stuff and said it was the worker who'd stolen it. One day, the worker disappeared. Later people found out he'd killed himself. The students were really upset and wanted to have a memorial service for him. I was the first one to agree with them, because I felt a good person had been unjustly hounded to death, and that it was our responsibility to redress such an injustice! Actually I didn't even know the worker in question. His suicide happened the year before I got to school.

Perhaps the reason I thought the memorial service was a good idea was because of my essentially *shan* nature, or because of my willingness to fight for a just cause. But the Party branch did not agree. A few days later, the *People's Daily* newspaper published an article titled "The Working Class Speaks!" That was the start of the Anti-Rightist Movement.

And because of the incident with the memorial service, I was labeled a Rightist. Yes, it was a simple, silly thing. But even so, it became the root of personal and family disaster for decades afterwards.

I don't want to talk about the physical suffering I endured after I was named a Rightist. I was made to carry heavy burlap sacks, to do hard labor, and I was beaten. But none of this really added up to much. The spiritual torture was far worse than the physical torture. For example, I never heard or cracked a joke the whole three years I was in college. What flavor has a life without jokes? People really need humor. Without humor, people can't get along well with each other. In the cafeteria, when students lined up to buy food, everyone would tease and laugh with each other. It was really fun. But once people knew I was a Rightist, their faces immediately dropped. Sometimes I wanted to tease someone, or to have someone tease me, but that was impossible. No one dared to be that way with me, and I didn't dare to be that way with anyone else. Contrary to what you might think, not being teased is evidence that a person has lost his or her social rights, including the right to self-respect and dignity. Can you imagine that? How deep is this kind of anguish!

Since no one paid attention to me, I fell in love with novels. The characters in novels didn't care if I was a Rightist or not. I could crack all kinds of jokes to myself about the characters in novels, and it wouldn't matter. Novels back then were mostly about good people doing good deeds. Looking back on them now, they seem rather shallow. But at the time, they were really inspiring. One night in study hall, I got so much into the novel I was reading that I forgot I was a Rightist. Just then, the Party secretary came in, because he had an important announcement to make to the students. Suddenly he yelled, "All the Rightists get out!" Only when I heard him say this did I remember who I was. We Rightists shuffled out of the room, flustered and awkward, barely daring to whisper to each other. That really hurt. Speaking of hurt, it is only now that I recognize this hurt. At the time, I felt that I really was a Rightist, a sub-human, a third-rate citizen. When I left the room, it was as if I was throwing myself out.

At first, we Rightist students got along pretty well among ourselves, because we had a common ground of experience. But people were always doing their best to abuse us, and slowly we stopped respecting each other as well. Each of us lowered our own expectations of ourselves. For example, we studied just enough to pass, wore ratty clothes, swore like sailors, and didn't care about anything. When we cleaned the bathrooms, people would come in and do their business and saunter off without flushing, and we had to clean up after them. We were supposed to clean up other people's shit, and still take ourselves and our lives seriously? I now can really understand why prisoners fight so much among themselves.

I don't want to talk about how they tortured me, but there is one thing I'd like to ask: I know how I became capable of being ruthless, but how did they get that way? Do they themselves know? I mean, surely they weren't born so ruthless. I bet they themselves can't even explain it.

I must confess my guilt to you. Because of my position as a Rightist, two of my brothers died. Altogether there were five of us brothers. The ones who died were the third and fourth.

I'll tell you about my third younger brother first. I regretted telling him about my being a Rightist. Shortly after I was made a Rightist at school, I went home during winter break. Carrying around this Rightist label, my heart felt sort of queasy. Think about it. I was the only college student in our family. My family was especially good to me. And the better they treated me, the less I dared tell them that I was a Rightist. Finally I couldn't stand it any longer, and I told my third brother. He had a really bad temper, was ferocious and hot-headed. He was a clerk in the local commissary. After he heard about me, he was always in a foul mood and kept trying to pick fights with the commissary director. The director said, "I'm going to make you a Rightist if you keep on like this." My brother said, "I don't believe you." But finally they really did make my brother a Rightist.

He was only eighteen. Go find an eighteen-year-old these days. What are they like? These days, eighteen-year-olds are even smarter than adults. But in those days, eighteen-year-olds were just children. Hit them, and they'd get more obstinate. Once when my brother was chatting with some other young Rightists, he said, "We've got no future here. We should get ourselves a little boat and escape." Someone reported this, and he was seized and made kneel on the counter of the commissary every day while they "struggled against" him. They hung a big lightbulb just above his head that baked him until he was drenched in sweat. Later he was tied up and dragged to the Public Security Bureau where he was accused of being "a traitor and a defector." Traitor? He was a kid shooting off his mouth. Even if he'd gotten a boat and made it to the Bohai Sea,[3] he'd have been capsized by the first wave that came along. And besides, would he have known where to go in such a big ocean? Nah, he was just letting off a little steam.

Just thinking about the image of my little brother being tied up and dragged away... I really can't bear it. Even though I didn't actually see it happen, I can imagine what it must have been like. I realize that it was my telling him about being a Rightist that destroyed him. I never saw him alive again.

In 1960, when I graduated, I was sent to teach in an elementary school at the county seat. At that point, my brother was already in prison, but hadn't been sentenced yet. I couldn't go visit him, because I was a Rightist and he was a counterrevolutionary. If we had been allowed to meet, who knows what crimes we might have perpetrated. One day, my mother's toothache was acting up, and I took her to the county hospital. As we were eating lunch in town, one of my uncles from the village came riding up on his bike, and announced, "Your brother is back!"

My heart brightened: my brother is back, that's great, he's been released. But my mother's face darkened immediately, and she said, "He's dead, let's go home!" She was really something. How could an old lady from a tiny village have such an accurate judgment? At the time, I still didn't believe her. I gave my uncle a few *mao*[4] and half a kilo worth of ration tickets to thank him for his trouble in looking for us. At the time, a few *mao* and some ration tickets was quite a lot. I put my mother on the train, and then went back to school to ask for a leave. Then I hurried home. When I arrived, my brother's body was laid out on a plank bed. His head wasn't much more than a skin-covered skull, and I had to look long and hard before I could recognize him.

I heard that he'd arrived home on a donkey cart at nine that morning. He was lying in the cart on a pile of dirty straw, covered with an old, worn blanket, with his feet sticking out. He'd originally had a pair of padded cotton trousers that my mom had made especially for him. They were huge, reaching up almost to his chest, and down to cover the tops of his feet; and they were made of thick cotton, because Mama was afraid he'd freeze. But someone had taken those good trousers and given him a pair of kid's pants. His calves stuck way out from under the trouser legs, and his butt stuck out from the top. It was the middle of winter. How could he not have frozen to death? They say that when he got to the door of our home, he was still breathing. His wife asked, "Is there anything you want to tell your family?" and she gave him a sip of warm water. But he was dead before he could swallow the water.

My mother told me that when she touched my brother's stomach, she could feel his backbone. Where were his intestines, his stomach, all the stuff that was supposed to be in his gut? He was wearing a worn out old sweater, covered with sorghum husks and red dust. What was that red dust doing on his sweater?

Oh, I thought of something else. This is also something I'll regret for the rest of my life. A guilt that will never leave me. My father found a letter taped to my brother's stomach. It was a gorgeous letter. No author could have thought it up even if he'd tried. It was great literature. I bet even Tolstoy and Cao Xueqin[5] wouldn't have been able to write such a letter. It was from my brother to his wife, Guiying. Listen to this. He wrote:

Guiying,

I am really starving. Please hurry and bring me something to eat. I want steamed bread, steamed rice, vegetable balls, pancakes and crullers, steamed stuffed pork buns, noodles with meat sauce, deep-fried fish, deep-fried shrimp, deep-fried nuts, steamed crab, stewed pork, fried eggs, stir-fried tofu, potstickers, dumplings, steamed sweet buns, stir-fried nuts, stir-fried liver, sauteed pork with scal-

lions, soy sauce beef, pig head meat, mutton fondue,
twice-cooked pork, stewed chicken, stewed duck,
stewed pork knuckles, fried pork strips, fried pan-
cakes, twice-cooked pancakes, stewed tripe, braised
mutton, braised beef, braised pork, braised duck. . .
If you don't have any of these, just bring two sweet
flourcakes instead. But hurry up! Hurry up! I beg
you!

On the bottom was written his name. Such a long menu. Can you imagine what state he must have been in when he wrote it? To this day, whenever I go to restaurants to eat, I can never look at a menu, because all menus are like my brother's last will and testament. Once a friend invited me out to dinner and gave me the menu to order from. I suddenly said to him, as if I'd gone nuts, "If you make me look at a menu then I'm not eating!" He was really confused.

Speaking of my guilt, when my brother was in prison, my mother brought him something to eat each time she went to see him. I always sort of resented her doing this; I thought that prison must be the one place where you can't starve to death. It was right in the middle of the Three Disastrous Years,[6] you know? Our family had to scrounge just to find enough for ourselves to eat, and if we kept sending him food, what would be left for us? Although I never stopped my mom from taking him food, and never said anything about it, still I had these thoughts in my heart. When I saw the letter my brother wrote, I felt guiltier than hell. If I'd known how hungry he was, I would have starved to death myself in order to let him eat his fill. After all, he suffered and died all because of me.

I still remember very clearly my father reading this letter out loud. My brother's body had been moved onto the *kang*.[7] I sat on the edge of it, with my mother, my sister-in-law, and my two other brothers standing at my side. My father was crouched by the head of the *kang*, leaning on it. At the head of the bed was a small oil lamp. As my father read each item of the letter aloud, my heart was pulverized. When he finished, he held the letter up to the flame and burned it. Then he leaned his head against the edge of the *kang*, his shoulders heaving, as if he were in pain; but he made no sound. Tears fell from our eyes, but none of us made any sound either. A person had died unjustly, and we didn't even make a sound. How could that be? How could we have tolerated it? What do you say?

My older brother worked in the Public Security Bureau of another county. He inquired and was told that my brother had been allowed to eat only one bowl of sorghum per day. Then he'd been yoked up like a beast of burden, whipped, and forced to pull a grindstone, making a kind of red dust. Finally I understood why there were sorghum husks and red dust on my brother's clothes. We had no idea what the red dust was used for. But we did know that my brother had been beaten, starved, and tortured to death. So my older brother filed a complaint against the prison warden. Soon thereafter the Cultural Revolution began, and instead of the warden being punished, my brother was accused of attempting to reverse a verdict on behalf of a counterrevolutionary. He was criticized, struggled against, and lost his job. The disasters in our family came one after another, and I was the root of them all. But my parents and my brothers never once blamed me, never even said one bad thing about me. The less they blamed me, the more guilty I felt. Sometimes I wonder why they didn't blame me. Perhaps it was *ren*?

I don't mind having to tolerate misfortunes that other people have brought upon me, but I can't stand having brought misfortunes on other people.

Ren is the first law of survival that my ancestors taught me. But who taught them? Which ancestor was it who invented this law and caused it to be passed down through the ages? When exactly did people start tolerating? I once asked a historian, and he laughed at me, as if this were an ignorant question of no academic value. I asked him, is your job just to mess around with dead legacies? Why don't you do some research on the deadly, living legacies that still oppress our people after thousands of years?

If we're talking about things that can't be explained, this is the biggest one.

Let me tell you about my other little brother, my fourth brother. Our family was really poor in those days. In good times, a strong worker could earn at least fifteen cents per day; but in bad times only seven or eight cents. To help out, my fourth brother went scavenging for some kindling wood to sell. This was a people's commune, though. Every blade of grass on the ground belonged to the commune's production brigade,[8] so "scavenging" was actually stealing. The production brigade leader found out about my brother's scavenging and made my brother parade around the streets with the kindling on his back. Why did they treat him so harshly? Was it because his older brother was a Rightist? But my younger brother was so poor, there was no way he could get married. So he went out and stole. He went to nearby Whitestone Village and stole a bunch of brooms off the roof of their production brigade. He took them into the town market to sell. But he was too honest to be a good fence; while he was selling the brooms at market, his nervousness showed in his eyes and gave him away. Those city folks were sharp. They noticed this and grabbed him and asked about the brooms. He got scared and confessed the whole story. They took him into the local police station. After a couple of days in custody, he managed to open the window of the cell and escape. No one paid much attention to a petty thief who'd escaped, but a few days later someone discovered his body in the gutter next to the railroad tracks, stiff as a board and covered with bugs. Some people said he deliberately lay down on the tracks, hoping the train would run him over; others guessed he'd been trying to jump onto the train to get away, but missed and fell onto the tracks instead. I know in my heart, he wasn't trying to escape: he wanted to die.

Our family was so poor we didn't have a shred of respect in the village. His brother was a Rightist, and he himself had become a thief. Let's not even talk about him getting married—he couldn't even live with himself. And how could he explain this to our parents? Death was the only solution. But there weren't any injuries on his body, which was weird. If the train had hit him or run over him, there would have been major injuries. This is another thing that's hard to explain. What? Ask a doctor to do an autopsy? Easy for you to say. In those days, if someone like us died, it was the same as a stray dog dying. Who'd care enough to do an autopsy? Dead is dead: dig a hole and bury the body, and that's that.

So that's how my two brothers died because of me. And they both died as criminals: one a counterrevolutionary, the other a thief. My parents ended up with three bad sons: a counterrevolutionary, a thief, and a Rightist. You tell me what kind of family that is?

At the beginning of the Cultural Revolution, the Party secretary at the school where I taught told me to speak the truth to Chairman Mao, to confess my problems, to hide nothing. I thought and thought and finally remembered a "problem:" once, when I was correcting a student's homework, I'd meant to write "use Maoist thought to criticize bourgeois thought," but I'd made a mistake and wrote, "use Maoist thought to criticize Maoist thought." The student had brought the corrected homework to me and said, "Teacher, you made a mistake." I was so scared I broke into a cold sweat. I corrected it right away. Luckily this kid was really nice, and didn't tell anyone about it.

I told the Party secretary about this incident, and confessed my crime to Chairman Mao. Actually, if I had kept my mouth shut, no one would have known about this incident. What was wrong with me? No one pressured me into confessing this. Why did I have to say anything? Did I trust them? Did I think I wasn't in enough trouble? Was this "crime" weighing on my mind? Was I just born with an especially spineless character? I can't say why I had to confess this incident. This is the reason I've always suspected there is some kind of tragic element lurking in my blood.

That is how I became an active counterrevolutionary, because I had the gall to oppose Chairman Mao. I was criticized and beaten until I couldn't stand it any longer and ran home and hid out in my village. Later two factions at the school joined together and sent people to bring me back from the village to continue my sessions. Let's not talk about the sorrows of the flesh; talking about that is pointless. As soon as the flesh stops hurting, you forget about it. But the pain in the heart cannot be forgotten. A lot of the time you don't know exactly what the pain is about. It's impossible to explain. If some day you can explain this pain and talk about it, then it will stop hurting. The pain is there only because you can't explain it.

In the big earthquake in 1976, our whole county collapsed. The train couldn't get through, and I had to run a dozen or so miles to get home. By the time I got there, our village was rubble and corpses. The corpses were all relatives and friends. I knew them all. The earth god and the village god, though—heavenly beings that we earthly people created—were good to us. They didn't take a single member of our family. We set up a big tent in the wide, empty field outside the village. We weren't sure if the tent was to live in or to shelter us until death arrived. The hardest part of those days was finding anything to eat. The production brigade used big loudspeakers to order everyone around: "Comrade poor peasants, come to the production brigade office to pick up your emergency rations."

The "emergency rations" consisted of a few crackers. Everyone went to stand in line, but the production brigade said the crackers were only to be given to the poor peasants. People like us who had "problems" were not allowed to receive any crackers. My wife went, but they sent her home empty-handed. As other people walked past our tent, I looked at their expressions. The poor peasants were carrying bags full of crackers in both hands, looking so haughty! And people like us hung our heads silently and pathetically. Such a simple thing had clearly divided people into two classes. Villagers who had crackers would never give you any, you had to slink off to one side like a dog. But neither would they eat in front of you. Why do you think that was? Because they were afraid you'd ask for some if you saw them eating? Because they felt bad about eating when you had nothing? Or because they were afraid they wouldn't be able to withstand the urge to share a little with you, and then would be punished by the production brigade? It's hard to explain. That's even worse than the hunger.

I went to scrounge for food in the rubble that had been our house. After scrabbling around for a while, I came across a plaster bust of Chairman Mao. In those days every house had one. There was a kid in our village who went to rescue his mother from under a pile of rubble. Just as he found his mother, he also came across a bust of Mao. He first rescued the bust, and then went back for his mom. This action was praised by the authorities in the commune. But the bust I pulled out of the rubble was handicapped; it was missing an ear. I got worried. I set Mao on brick and said to him, "Now, sir, what do you think I should do with you? Our family doesn't have anything to eat or a place to live, how can we accommodate you? And you're missing an ear. If they say I knocked it off on purpose, our family will be even worse off. Tell me, what should I do with you?"

I thought of a risky plan. First I hid that bust, and then I dug a really deep hole in the rubble. At dusk, after I made sure the coast was clear, I sneaked back into the area and buried it. If someone found out about this, they would have strung me up! Was I a criminal? That night I was too frightened to sleep. My heart was pounding for days. Later, I always regretted it, and hated myself for doing such a thing. For a long time afterwards, this criminal feeling weighed on me.

Me. What the hell is wrong with me?

After the Cultural Revolution ended and my Rightist problem was settled, I did everything I could to clear my third brother's record and his reputation. I couldn't allow his departed soul to bear the label "criminal" for all eternity. But this problem was kicked up and down the bureaucracy; I spent three years on it, and must have walked three thousand miles altogether in an effort to clear his name. Yet no one would explain the problem to me. It wasn't that they couldn't explain, but that they wouldn't explain. Especially one detail—when my brother arrived at home, gasping his last breaths, it was nine a.m. on January 15, 1960. But his arrest warrant was also dated January 15th, and on it was also a note, "Sentence commuted because of illness."

According to the warrant, then, it was on January 15th that the Precuratorate had notified the Public Security Bureau that it was to place my brother under formal arrest. The PSB chief would have to sign the warrant and then go to the prison where my brother was being held. Once he saw that my brother was half-dead, he would have written "sentence commuted because of illness," and sent my brother home. That all would have taken quite a long time. But my brother arrived at home at nine a.m. on the 15th, which meant he would have had to have left the prison no later than eight a.m. That would have left no time to take care of the paperwork. How could these two things have happened at the same time?

The Cultural Revolution was over, and no one wanted to take responsibility for what had happened then. I think that is why, even if they could have explained it to me, they didn't. To this day, I still have two such brothers: one a counterrevolutionary and one a thief. And they've long since become ghosts. In those days, even a living person didn't count for much; a dead one was worth less. My mother died of illness, but I think it was depression that caused her illness to become critical. And all this was because of me. Even though my case was cleared, and I turned out all right, do you think I can live a happy life? Guilt is a stubborn thing. It stays in the heart, and can rise up to torment you at any moment. No one will ever know how weary my life has become.

I want to write a "Family Lesson" to leave for my children. My "Lesson" will not contain a single sentence that can explain anything. It will only relate these unforgettable matters to them, and leave these unanswerable questions for them. Young people these days certainly have more brains than we did. If they can explain all this, they'll be able to prevent it from happening again. If they can't, or don't, it will be hard for them to avoid repeating my experience—unable to voice their grievances, fooled and bullied at every turn, able only to await their tormentors. They will have inherited this tragic temperament that will keep steering them straight into tragedy, even into tragedy's deepest abyss.

Is it that the personality is tragic, or that tragedy chooses such a personality?

—AUTHOR

FOOTNOTES

1. "Unity Is Strength" and "Hey La La La" are two popular songs after Liberation.

2. Hu Feng was a writer and literary critic. In 1955, he was denounced for his views on literature and art. He was arrested as head of the Hu Feng Counterrevolutionary Clique.

3. The Bohai Sea is off China's east coast, at the west end of the Pacific Ocean.

4. In Chinese currency, one *mao* equals ten cents.

5. Cao Xueqin was the author of *A Dream of Red Mansions*. He is considered one of the greatest writers in Chinese history.

6. In the three years from 1959 to 1961, China suffered serious economic difficulties, mostly due to the Great Leap Forward of 1958. Agricultural production was down. Millions of people died of starvation.

7. A *kang* is a wide brick platform, heated from beneath by a built-in hearth and covered with mats and bedding, that serves as a bed in many rural Chinese homes.

8. Production brigade was a production and administrative unit under the commune system. It was dissolved after China started its economic reform in 1979.

The Dear Price of Worship

NARRATOR & VICTIM ONE
*FEMALE, age 21 in
1967
COLLEGE STUDENT
at B City*

VICTIM TWO
*Male, age 25 in
1967
CADRE of Writers'
Association in
B City*

PART I:
THE AGONY OF WORSHIP

I DON'T have a great deal of esteem for writers, because while they tend to think of themselves as unusually profound, very often their works turn out to be pretty shallow. For instance, one writer has described worship as the most unselfish of feelings. After reading that, I had to conclude he'd never worshipped anyone in his life.

Worship is the act of giving your heart and soul to the person worshipped. If it is too easily offered up or carelessly lost by the worshipped, all that remains of the worshipper is an empty shell, an abandoned carton of the self with no hope of replenishment.

Worship is the most dangerous adventure in the world. It amounts to a pledge of one's life. For this reason, I read very little and prefer to rely on my own experience of the world rather than the specious profundities of writers. Do these words offend you? Do you agree with what I say? Are you being honest? Anyway, I don't care if you are being honest because I have a story to tell you.

II

The person I worshipped most was Mao Zedong.

And not only me. Go ask anyone of my generation who they worshipped when they were in their twenties. I can assure you, you'd get the same answer from everyone—Mao Zedong. Let me give you one small example to show how pure and innocent the worship was.

Li Min, one of Mao's daughters, was my classmate in college. Mao's birthday was on the 26th of December, and one year, on the night of the 23rd, nine coeds living in the same dorm got together to discuss sending him a birthday gift through Li Min. Some suggested weaving a long scarf and embroidering it with large characters reading: "Long Live Chairman Mao!" Others proposed sending a bouquet of colored, silk-embroidered flowers, with each of us contributing a special one. We chattered on about this past midnight. We were so highly stimulated by our discussion that the room looked like a galaxy of eyes pulsating like stars, but still we couldn't come up with a gift that appropriately reflected our ardor. Worship is always difficult to fully express.

"How about taking a photo of all of us together and sending it to my father with a letter?" Li Min finally suggested.

We all applauded her idea. If he had a photo, Chairman Mao could look at each of us and get to know who we were.

After class the next day, we sneaked out of school one by one and met at a photographer's studio. Things you really enjoy are always more fun if you make them a secret. At first the photographer wasn't sure he could finish the job on time, but, when he found out that we wanted to send the photo to Chairman Mao, he quickly changed his mind. He took on the job as if it were a critical political mission and gave us the photo the following day.

The other girls asked me to write the letter to Chairman Mao. It was the most difficult letter I'd ever written, and I stayed up almost all night just to pen a few decent sentences. The floor was covered with rejected drafts. Of course the brilliant words I'd wanted to use only came to me after I'd given the letter to Li Min.

A week later, Li Min returned and told us Chairman Mao was quite pleased with the photo, and had even pointed to my image and made a comment about how young I looked. According to Li Min, while the famous poet, Guo Moruo, was visiting her father to congratulate him on his birthday, the Chairman put the photo under the glass cover of his work desk. Li Min's news couldn't have made me happier. I could now be with Chairman Mao every day, and he could look at me every day! After that, whenever I gazed at his picture hanging above the classroom blackboard, I felt his warm and kindly eyes shining on me like the sun, instilling in me immense spiritual energy! It was no wonder I was one of the top students at my college.

III

At that time I also worshipped another man.

During the Socialist Education Movement[1] we were both sent to the No. 3 State Cotton Factory to write a history of the factory. Writing a history about capitalist excess and proletarian suffering was expected to give us a deeper understanding of the class struggle. The man I worshipped wasn't from our college. I was a sophomore studying Chemistry at Beijing Normal University, and he was a senior at Peking University, a very devoted student of Chinese literature. He was of average height, thin, always simply and neatly dressed, and he impressed me as being steady and reliable, clear in his thinking, and very gentlemanly. To a young science major like myself, he had the look of a refined scholar. He was also the leader of our writing team. Although he didn't talk a lot, he was very solicitous of all of us. Whenever we were hungry because of working late, he'd surprise us with some tasty snacks he'd prepared himself; and on the weekends when we had time to relax, he'd take pleasure in pulling from his pockets a bunch of movie tickets and handing one to each of us. He

acted as if he were an older brother, and I, being quite unso-
phisticated, appreciated being treated like a younger sister.
But after we'd finished our project and he accompanied me
back to school, carrying my luggage up to the door, his eyes
had a strange look I didn't understand. "Can I see you again?"
he suddenly asked.

I didn't know what he meant and answered like a simpleton: "Why not? Come whenever you like."

Yes, I was very naive at that age. Of course, I knew
about love from the books I'd read, but the idea of being infat-
uated with anyone seemed strange, distant, and unrelated to
me. I have no idea how it happened, but he gradually captured
my heart, as if it were the most natural thing in the world.

As we got to know each other, I found out he was very
poor. His family lived in Nantong City in northern Jiangsu
Province, an area that had been the revolutionary base of
General Chen Yi[2] and the New Fourth Army.[3] His uncles had
all been involved in underground communist activities. After
his father was killed by the Japanese, his widowed mother
raised him and several brothers and sisters. His middle school,
high school, and university education had been sponsored by
the government who provided him a monthly allowance of
$19.6 yuan. I found his family background highly admirable.
It helped him attain unusually important positions, such as
director of Foreign Students at Peking University, and caused
everyone to regard him as a promising young revolutionary:
exactly the kind of person I was attracted to. The "Graduate
Job Application Form" he gave me to read was filled with
exhilarating sentiments and vows. His desire to be sent to the
aboriginal forests, remote mountain villages, or barren fron-
tiers and prairies to offer his life for the benefit of the revolution moved me so deeply I cried out to myself, "I'll follow you
wherever you go."

Thus it was quite a surprise that after his graduation,
he was assigned to a position only a few blocks away from
me. At first when he told me he was going to "Wangfujing,"[4] I
had no idea in which remote corner of China it was located.
He laughed and said: "The only place in China that has a
Wangfujing is Beijing." It turned out his work unit was the
China Writers' Association, which was located on Wangfujing

Street. His classmates all envied his good luck. But the Association was such a bastion of ideological prominence that only politically correct and academically excellent students like himself could be assigned there.

To ensure that my studies weren't disrupted by our relationship, I restricted myself to meeting him only once every two weeks in Beihai Park.[5] Each time we met, I spent most of the day listening to him. He knew so much I felt my knowledge increasing by leaps and bounds, and I imagined how wonderful our future life together would be. My political ideals fused with his image, forming a vivid, resplendent whole; and I was often intoxicated with my good fortune and happiness.

IV

I finished my graduate admission tests in May 1966, and was confident I'd scored high. But then, in June, the Cultural Revolution broke out and the students at my college went mad, running around screaming, "smash to bits the old graduate education system," and throwing all our test papers into a large brass urn. I climbed up to the third floor of my dormitory and, from a window, watched them burn test papers just as the peasants had burned land deeds during the Land Reform Movement.[6] I knew the country was in for trouble again. The suddenness of it terrified me. The succeeding chaos was even worse, and one by one members of our University's Party Committee were subjected to struggle sessions.

The effect of the struggle on the Writers' Association was even more profound. All famous writers were "black listed," and many middle-ranked cadres also found themselves in hot water. He was the only one who was believed to be politically clean, and was elected leader of a revolutionary organization. Perhaps because of his family background and experience, he remained comparatively calm, maintaining his refined manner in the midst of all the turbulent activity. He told me again and again, "Trust the Party, close ranks with the Party organization, pay close attention to Chairman Mao's new instructions, and follow the main line; but by all means, never blindly follow others in their condemnations." No matter how appealing the slogans at our college were, or how confused I became, as soon as I saw him I immediately regained my composure. I truly believed that our political innocence and loyalty to the Party would prevent us from being shipwrecked by the tumultuous Cultural Revolution.

Taking advantage of the campaign to exchange revolutionary ideas, I returned to my hometown in Sichuan Province and told my family about our relationship, which made them very happy. My mother bought him a sweater, a pair of cotton trousers, and several pairs of socks. She neatly packed them, together with some of our village's best tangerines, into a small suitcase I carried on the crowded train back to Beijing. After I returned to my dorm room and cleaned up, I quickly went off to see him with my suitcase in hand, my mind filled with the image of his smiling face as I gave him the gifts my parents had sent.

V

Before I arrived at his room, I ran into one of his former Peking University classmates in front of the living quarters of the Writers' Association. He'd always been quite friendly when we'd met before, but this time he seemed cold and distant. After giving me a quick greeting, he abruptly walked away, making me think something was wrong. Years later I decided this fortunate omen helped me endure what was to follow.

When I entered his room, I found myself face to face with a man who'd substantially changed. I couldn't tell whether his expression conveyed abnormality, fear, misery, or even madness, but it was unforgettable and shocked me to the bone. His hair was completely disheveled, his face furrowed with lines. The moment he saw me, tears began to stream down his face. Even before he spoke, he handed me a printed, small-character poster, from which I only read the first two lines: "Down with those who dare to oppose Chairman Mao! Down with counterrevolutionary XXX!" Could it really be true that he was the counterrevolutionary XXX? I was too dizzy to read any further. I felt my body weaken and heard my suitcase drop to the ground with a thump.

A moment later he explained what had happened.

In his undergraduate years, whenever he'd read Chairman Mao's works or poems, he'd freely written out comments in the margins, most of which were from a literary perspective: for example, "good or excellent," "so so," or even "not very good," or "wrong." At the time he didn't regard what he wrote as having any importance, and soon forgot the content. One day one of his dorm mates happened to leaf through his books looking for Mao's quotations, found his comments, and disclosed them to the Writers' Association. It became an extraordinary event, and immediately caused a big stir.

I was stunned by what he told me. All I could think of saying was 'how could you have done such a thing,' but the words never left my mouth. I tried to pierce him with my eyes, hating him. I quickly picked up my suitcase and decisively walked out of his room—I was going to leave him!

Of course he followed me out, insisting on using his bike to help me with my suitcase, and we rode all the way across the city without exchanging a word. The solid and unshakable bridge that we'd formed had snapped at the center, and the surging, tempestuous current overwhelmed us. Without hesitation, I turned my back on him. But what did he do?

When we reached the gate of my college, he said: "What I did was regarded as an offense to Chairman Mao, and my situation is hopeless. Although I am in love with you, I'm not worthy of continuing our relationship, and think we should end it and not see each other any more. But even so, after you graduate and are assigned to a job, please leave your address with my older brother in Nantong City. Alright?"

He'd never behaved so awkwardly in front of me, and, to be honest, I hadn't really listened to what he was saying. After returning to my room and throwing aside my suitcase, I went straight to bed and didn't get up for three days. My mind was a cauldron of turmoil—oh, how I hated him. How could he have written such nonsense about Chairman Mao's works? It seemed so contrary to what he had usually told me: how the Communist Party had nurtured and educated him, how devoted he was to Chairman Mao, and how he was ready to offer his life with unswerving loyalty to the cause of revolutionary literature and art. I felt deceived and betrayed. I wondered if I'd been bewitched by him, and I began to believe that he really was a counterrevolutionary hiding behind the flag of the revolution. I went over and over in my mind everything I could recall him telling me in the two years I'd known him, scrutinizing every word for counterrevolutionary insinuations that could have influenced me. And I came up with nothing. I had never been so tormented. Could I have been deceived by him so profoundly that I had lost the ability to grasp how he had done it? I decided to take part in the Writers' Association's criticism meetings and hear what others had to say about him so I could see his real face.

On the fourth day after I left him, I finally got out of bed and made my way to the Writers' Association.

VI

In those days, I was possessed by two forms of worship: one for Chairman Mao, the other for him.

My worship for Chairman Mao involved the lofty worship of an ideal image, whereas I worshipped him as the flesh-and-bones man with whom I was in love. Yet the latter was based on the former, a worship so powerful it engulfed everything. The relationship between the two seemed crystal clear.

More concretely, my worship of Chairman Mao was unconditional, but my worship of him had limits. If he really had been against Chairman Mao, I had to cut him out of my life. That was why I had so resolutely walked out of his dormitory room. But it was no easy matter to expunge such a forceful presence from my heart. And it was harder to explain the unforgivable thing he had done.

VII

The five-story Writers' Association building seemed to reach up to heaven itself. On the outer wall hung huge posters denouncing him. An eerie chill passed over me as I began to climb up to the assembly hall on the fifth floor where the criticism meeting was being held. A number of people in the Association knew who I was, and though they tried to ignore me, they did show a certain respect for my persistence and honesty in pursuing the truth. Throughout the ten straight days I attended the meetings, I sat quietly in a corner seat in the last row of the assembly hall, intently listening to all the speeches criticizing him, and carefully reading what was written about him on the big-character posters lying in the middle of the aisles. I found nothing in them that differed from what he'd already told me. I found some criticism of him well justified, but all the truculent talks about class struggle seemed excessive and unconvincing. Indeed, I felt I had the purest motives of all those present.

After the series of meetings ended, he was suspended from his position and demoted to work as a janitor at the Writers' Association. I didn't go see him right away because I still hadn't made up my mind about him. Although the matter he was condemned for took place in his undergraduate years, and it was the only incident for which he was criticized, I still hadn't formed a definite opinion about his character. Overcome by worry and doubt, terrible emotional conflicts and ideological struggle, I couldn't find a moment's peace. Nobody could help me resolve this problem, and nobody would. So I decided to go to Nantong City, his hometown, to look into his background and see if he'd been honest with me about his past.

VIII

Coincidentally, it was then that the "January Storm"[7] broke out, and large numbers of students flocked to Shanghai to exchanges revolutionary ideas. I went along with my classmates and asked to stay on a few more days, making up a story about my aunt being ill. Then after my classmates left, I bought a boat ticket to Nantong City. When I got off the boat, I followed the directions he'd given me earlier and soon located his hometown's commune. I presented a letter of introduction showing I was a member of the "Jinggang Mountain Red Guards of Beijing Normal University,"[8] a letter specially prepared for exchanges of revolutionary experiences, and told them I was checking up on someone. It surprised me that his family was so well known there. Right after I mentioned the family's name, the leaders of the commune told me he came from a revolutionary family, that his father had advocated fighting the Japanese and had been killed by them, and that his two uncles had been senior underground Communist Party members before Liberation. Everything they said was consistent with what he'd told me, as if an exact print of the original. This softened my feelings about him.

I decided to find his older brother, a teacher at the commune's elementary school. When I met the brother, I sensed he was a simple and honest man, thinner than his younger brother but with similar facial features and gestures. I didn't know how to introduce myself, but his wife recognized me immediately—their family had a photo of me—and gave me a warm welcome. The villagers' earthly kindness deeply moved me. The following morning the older brother took me to see his mother, to the house where he was born and raised, carrying me adroitly on his bike some twelve miles along a muddy, zigzag path through the rice paddies.

She must have been told that I was coming, because even from a considerable distance, I could see her standing at the entrance of the thatched hut village. I'll never forget that scene. Her hair was knotted at the back of her head, and she wore a dark blue, muslin jacket and a pair of baggy slacks that ended at her calves, revealing her ankles and a pair of small feet that had once been bound. She was exceptionally tall and thin, stood very straight, and had deeply furrowed cheeks that looked as if they'd been sculpted. What should I call her? Without thinking I cried out: "Mom!"

The old woman extended her long, thin, trembling hands, and began caressing me with great tenderness. It was genuine maternal love. Of her five children, he was the most promising—attending a university in Beijing, assigned a good job in that great city... Could she ever have imagined her son would become a counterrevolutionary? Naturally I didn't say anything about that, and explained that he'd been very busy and had asked me to visit.

His mother summoned all his brothers and sisters together and slaughtered a chicken in preparation for a special meal. The news of my arrival spread like wildfire around the village, and everyone—male and female, old and young, carrying children or leaning on canes—came to take a look at the future daughter-in-law coming alone to visit her husband's family before the wedding. I was probably the first female college student from Beijing ever to come within thirty miles of this village, let alone visit it. The villagers all hovered around me, gawking and smiling, and asking all sorts of questions. I felt as if I'd already become one of the family.

His mother held me in her arms for much of that night, expressing a mother's profound love for a son by talking on endlessly about his childhood. Without consciously being aware of the change, by sunrise I no longer believed he was a counterrevolutionary. As we parted that morning, his mother gave me some peanuts as a gift. I carried the peanuts back to Shanghai, and without stopping immediately went on to Beijing to see him. When I placed the small bag of peanuts in front of him, he was smart enough to figure out what had happened and began weeping, feeling contrite about dragging his elderly mother into the mess he was in. I'd never seen him cry like that for anyone.

It was then that I decided to resume our relationship and was determined to take the big step of marrying him.

We were married on December 1, 1967.

One could hardly call it a proper wedding night: the two of us sobbing in each other's arms until daybreak...

IX

After we were married, my college assigned me to a position in Yanbei Prefecture, a remote area of North Shanxi Province, but due to the violent armed fighting there, I couldn't go to that prefecture and remained at home without much to do. It appeared that his "problem" had been put off "for resolution until the later stages of the Cultural Revolution." The movement had definitely lost its way and was floundering in the dark.

One day I went over to the Academy of Sciences to read the big-character posters, just about the time General Yang Chengwu[9] was championing his slogan, "Establish the Absolute Authority of Chairman Mao," and posters conveying that idea were everywhere. For some inexplicable reason, I felt quite tense that day, sensing something terrible was about to happen. I went home and waited until dark for my husband to return, but there was no sign of him. A little later the door was suddenly flung open and he was marshaled in by two people from a rebel group within the Writers' Association. "We need to search his books again," one of them said. They looked everywhere, confiscating all the works of Chairman Mao on his bookshelves. "We're planning to organize a meeting to criticize him tomorrow morning, and he won't be coming home for a few days," they informed me. Then they took him away. I sat blankly on my bed, making no attempt to follow, feeling as if the great disaster I anticipated had just struck, and that this time his leaving was final. How empty and large the room seemed without him.

I sat up all night. The next morning I went to the Writers' Association. As before, I climbed the five flights of stairs and took a seat in the assembly hall waiting for the meeting to begin. Due to the pernicious effect of General Yang Chengwu's propaganda, the atmosphere at the meeting was more tense than it had been at previous meetings. Nevertheless, this time I wasn't participating to determine whether he was a counter-revolutionary, but was there to be with him. I wanted him to know that he wasn't alone, and that we would bear this together. I was emotionally tied in knots, and the thunderous shouting of the participants seemed distant and apart from me. When the meeting was finally over, the rebel group wanted to talk to me in another room, and even called in some of my classmates to persuade me to break with my husband. But I had already made up my mind that I wasn't going to say a word.

All of a sudden, I heard a lot of rushing around and noise outside, as if something had happened. A terrifying thought came to me. He may have jumped from the building! I leapt from the sofa and tried to run out of the room, but several people blocked my way. Nobody had to say a thing. I knew what had happened, and I remained standing where I was, dazed and wooden-like. The criticism meeting resumed a little later, but quickly transformed into a condemnation meeting. I could hear the slogan shouting intensifying, alternately growing louder and softer, distant and close—one minute like thunder crackling, the next like a remote whisper. I lost all feeling. I felt as if my body and mind had ceased functioning: I couldn't cry, I couldn't laugh, I couldn't do a thing.

Before I knew it, a group of people had surrounded me and were talking in the clever way Writers' Association people did when they didn't want to say anything directly. They apparently feared that they might shock me into madness. Lost in a sea of fishlike eyes and wriggling lips, I didn't respond at all. I thought this might be how it is when someone is about to die.

They didn't let me return home that day, and instead sent me off to the home of the wife of an old writer. That woman had "made a clean break" with her accused husband. The Writers' Association also sent a female cadre with me, apparently fearing I might do something stupid. The truth is I couldn't have done a thing, and I felt like an imbecile who understood nothing. I couldn't think, lost all sense of time, and even had no idea whether my husband died or not. I'd become an insentient lump of flesh that could scarcely move.

Later I found out he had jumped from a fifth-floor window, his lifeless body becoming a devastated heap of blood and broken bones. He'd been born into a family with a good class background, had consistently received preferential treatment, and, as a consequence, couldn't bear the condemnation and abuse brought by the Cultural Revolution, an attack on his self-esteem that only suicide could dispel. The Writers' Association sent a telegram to his older brother asking him to come to Beijing to arrange the funeral, but he refused to see his brother's corpse for fear that he might collapse at the sight of it. Two weeks after the funeral, his older brother came to see me.

I was feeling particularly strange the day of his brother's visit, still in the dazed state in which I had been for many days. But the moment I saw his brother, all the details of what had happened surged into my mind. For the first time since his death, I felt unusually clear-headed and energetic, like someone who had just returned from the dead. Only then did I fully comprehend that my husband was gone. I jumped into his brother's arms and wept profusely.

His brother seemed much thinner than before. His enormous eyes were flooded with tears, with an expression very much like my husband's. I felt all the ways my husband had looked at me were now reflected in his brother's eyes, and, at that moment, it was a miracle I maintained my sanity. It might have been better if I had lost my mind, because then I probably wouldn't have experienced the abuse that was to follow.

Already feeling empty and bereft, I got rid of our place and sold everything we had—furniture, pots and pans, kitchen utensils—all of it for anything I could get. Since he'd been branded a counterrevolutionary who'd committed suicide to avoid punishment, I wasn't given any money for his funeral expenses, and his brother didn't have enough money to return home. I gave his brother half of what I had, and we parted in tears. I was so distressed, all I wanted to do was to get away— away from Beijing, away from the place where he'd taken his life, away from all of it. I wanted to make as clean and quick a break as I could. With my suitcase and bed roll strapped to my back, I set out alone for the unknown, to North Shanxi Province.

PART II: WORSHIP'S REWARD

X

LIFE HAS TAUGHT ME A HARSH LESSON: Naiveté is far more damming than stupidity.

After I reported to the Yanbei District Office in Datong City and learned that I had been assigned to teach at the No. 1 Middle School of Shanyin County, I immediately told the official in charge: "In view of my situation, I don't think I'm qualified to be a teacher." I then provided all the details. My full confession was a product of the lengthy education the Party had given me—nothing should be hidden from the Party apparatus—and I could only relax after spelling everything out clearly. I told my story in the morning. By afternoon all the other university graduates who'd reported to Yanbei were staring at me as if I were some strange being. I found their whispers and twisted faces oppressive, and, with my head lowered, I made my way back to the guesthouse where my roommate, a thirtyish-looking local woman, directly asked: "Is your husband dead?" Her question startled me. After I asked where she'd heard that, she told me that at noon the district official in charge of assignments had called all the college graduates together and warned them that I was dangerous and should be watched. It was obvious he'd disclosed everything I'd told the authorities.

I was afraid to leave my room, and sat in bed staring at the ceiling, unable to eat. I felt as if my life had ended, and I was only twenty-one.

The next morning I decided to go discuss the matter with the supervising official. As soon as I opened the door of the guesthouse, a young girl began screaming: "Counterrevolutionary! Counterrevolutionary! Black widow! Black widow!"

That was the last straw. I knew I had to leave the district quickly without any farewells.   Acting on impulse, I bought a train ticket for Xi'an where my older sister lived. The moment I got a look at her standard Party-member face, however, I knew I'd made a big mistake. I told her I hadn't gone to my assigned position and had come to visit her instead because of the fighting in Shanxi Province. My sister worked every day, giving me time to walk aimlessly along the streets of Xi'an and to stand among the bustling crowds. After I'd spent all my money, I had no idea where to go next. I knew I couldn't go to Sichuan Province to live with my parents. They had enough problems of their own. My father, an engineer in the oil industry, was also being denounced. In the midst of my confusion, I remembered the last words my husband's older brother had said to me before he'd left Beijing: "If things get too rough for you, come stay with us. As long as we have enough to eat, you will too."

I sold my watch, the only thing of value I owned, for seventy yuan, and bought a train ticket to Nantong City. At the station I wrote a letter to my sister, telling her all that had happened. Eventually she wrote back, telling me that after she read the letter, she stayed up all night weeping, and blamed me for not giving her the chance to console me when I most needed it.

XI

My husband's mother was staying at his brother's house when I got there. The moment she saw me, this tall, thin, elderly woman rushed out of the house quickly on her once-bound feet, stumbled and fell down in the dirt. I rushed forward to help her and quickly found myself locked in her arms, both of us choked with grief. Although we'd both lost the same person, at that moment it seemed as if we had suffered doubly.

"If you want to stay with us, we can go through this together," his older brother told me.

I decided to live with his mother in the countryside.

As soon as I entered the thatched hut where he'd been born and raised, a feeling of security enveloped me as if I were a small bird or wandering child returning to the nest. I no longer had any interest in my job, my salary, or my status as a university graduate. If I had to die, it would be here with them. From then on I worked with the villagers in the fields every day, digging up weeds, hoeing the ground, and harvesting the wheat. I refused to take any money for my labor. When his mother and I were together, I often had the illusion my husband hadn't died, and even that I was him, a fantasy that offered me great comfort. The villagers were very kind to me. They knew that something had happened, but never asked me about it. I was like a survivor of a violent storm at sea who'd managed to make it to land alive, and had found refuge on a sandy beach, feeling extraordinarily calm and relieved lying under the warm rays of the sun. At times the pretty landscape in North Jiangsu Province seemed like something from a dream. Gazing out at the billowing clouds and rain-soaked trees, the faint reflection of the rice paddies in the water, and the thick, yellow expanse of vibrant rape-flowers, I could imagine him as a child riding on the back of a water buffalo and playing with his friends in the fields.

After the Yanbei District Office discovered I'd disappeared, they started asking about me everywhere, calling Beijing, Xi'an, and Sichuan. When they finally learned I was in Nantong, they sent letter after letter urging me to return, the last one an ultimatum. Initially I was determined never to go back, but the Cultural Revolution eventually came to the countryside, and the situation became even more critical after the "Six-Point Regulation on Public Security" was issued. According to the regulation, I was a member of a counterrevolutionary family and had to be subjected to surveillance. One night his older brother sped home from the commune on his bike as if there were some terrible emergency. He quickly repeated to me what one of the village cadres had told him: "Your sister-in-law is a runaway member of a counterrevolutionary family. There's going to be a meeting tomorrow morning to denounce her, so you'd better get her away from here fast."

His mother got so angry, her cheeks began to tremble. "Let them kill me first," she said. Dead or alive she wouldn't let me go.

I knew I couldn't stay any longer. Aside from my own problems, his two uncles had been condemned as "traitors," and the family situation was becoming desperate. The denouncements in the countryside could be more violent than those in the city, frequently involving severe beatings with clubs. I was afraid to return to North Shanxi, afraid of the presiding official, and afraid of all those peculiar stares. The world seemed to be coming down on top of me. Not seeing any way out, I began to consider suicide. If I were dead, I could join my husband immediately: death would obliterate all barriers. Nevertheless, I couldn't implicate his family in a suicide at their home, and so I finally got his mother to let me leave after I told her I would go to Shanghai temporarily until things quieted down.

At midnight my husband's brother carried me away on his bike, ensuring that no one would spot us by circling in and out of the pitch-dark fields. We arrived at the Nantong docks the next morning. Only when we said good-bye did he discover that I hadn't brought anything with me. How could he have known that I'd decided to make my peace forever? We enter the world with nothing and leave it with nothing, and in either case, have no need of anything.

I boarded the boat, feeling relieved and unburdened.

XII

It's true that the desire to live is always strongest just when you've decided to die. After the boat had been put out to sea, I began pacing up and down the slippery deck. The sky seemed unusually dark and the fog was so thick the boat seemed unable to push its way through. In the distance all I could make out was the shadow of an occasional vessel, a whistle announcing its presence, or the sudden appearance of a seagull before it disappeared into the damp ocean mist.

The more desperate I became, the more I thought about continuing to live, though hating myself for my cowardice in fearing suicide. The ship's sound system fortuitously echoed a line from "The White-Haired Girl,"[10] one of the model plays of the Cultural Revolution: "I refuse to die! I want to live!" These words rang out so sharply and clearly they pierced me to my very core. I remembered the humiliations the white-haired girl suffered—banished to the forests and forced to live like an animal on a diet of wild fruit—and how she still retained the will to survive. If she could live, why did I have to die? Suddenly my whole body reverberated with the words: "I want to live!" Although I didn't know what I had to live for, this was the first time in my life the words "will to live" held any real meaning for me. Excited, enraged, confused, and bewildered, I finally reached Shanghai and pushed my way through the crowd leaving the ship: I returned to Shanghai, I returned to the world.

A refugee from the Cultural Revolution had been saved by one of its model plays. How absurd! And what about my former worship? It had already become an obscure thing of the past.

XIII

After I returned to the Yanbei District Office, they sent me to O County to work as a teacher as punishment. This was the poorest and harshest area of North Shanxi Province. Although O County was shut off from the outside world, I discovered that the more remote a place was, the faster news traveled there. When I arrived, everyone seemed to know about my circumstances. Even the beggars along the street had nothing better to do than point their fingers and make remarks about me. Right away the Political Affairs Section of the County Military Control Commission[11] informed me: "We've reviewed your case and decided to send you to the Dingjiayao Commune to teach in the middle school. Remember, you're supposed to be undergoing re-education by the poor and middle peasants, so watch what you say and do. And anytime you leave the area you have to check with us for permission." This kind of talk no longer made any impression on me. I nodded indifferently.

The next morning I found myself on a cart belonged to the Dingjiayao Commune Supply and Marketing Cooperative, which would take me to the school. The cart made a trip to the Commune every other day, carrying sweet herbs dug up by the mountain people, an assortment of agricultural products, and other bare necessities. I threw my suitcase onto the cart and jumped in. As we left the county seat, I was struck by the beauty of the day.

We traveled along the Shanxi-Inner Mongolia border through a chain of soft, dull hills. There was no road per se, only the imprint of two shallow wheel tracks left by other carts. The old driver spoke a local dialect that I couldn't completely understand. Over the twenty-five or so miles we traveled, I hardly saw anyone. It almost felt like we were the only two people in the world. Oddly, leaving human society for this vast, empty, supremely quiet, and undisturbed terrain didn't make me feel lonely at all: just ahead were three horses and the back of my driver; all around me was a bounteous and hospitable natural realm; and my ears were alive with the musical sound made by the cart brushing against the tall grass. As the cart rocked back and forth, almost without conscious awareness, I found myself singing one song after another until I'd sung every piece I knew. I felt as if I hadn't a care in the world, and I enjoyed the moment to its fullest, not worrying about what lay ahead. I even wished the journey could stretch on endlessly for thousands of miles, for several decades.

Late in the afternoon we arrived at a high pass in the mountains. I was taken aback when the driver told me this was where I was to get off. Two rows of isolated, empty, brick houses stood below the dark shadow of the mountains with no other sign of village life. Before I could protest, the old driver told me, "This is the school." Then he turned me over to a deaf and dumb old man who came out of one of the doors. The old man heated a stove and made me some steamed potatoes and a bowl of salt water for dinner. After I'd finished, he led me to a small, cold, and gloomy brick hut, which he indicated was where I would live. How could there be a school without a principal, any teachers, or students? I felt confused and afraid, imagining I was entering a labyrinth with no way out. That night, my first in those desolate mountains, I became very frightened in my empty hut. The pleasure of the day's soulful journey was nothing more than a memory. I badly needed female companionship and finally ran over and knocked on the old man's door to ask if there was a woman I could talk to. But no matter how much I shouted and gestured, all the deaf and dumb man could do was wave his hand to signal that he didn't understand.

It's well known that the Buddhist Hell has eighteen levels, and I wondered whether I'd somehow ended up in the very lowest. All night my heart cried out: Life, do you have anything worse to offer? Could you give me a taste of the worst first?

XIV

My living quarters were on the site of the Commune's Revolutionary Committee, the front row of houses occupied by the Committee's chairman, vice-chairman, secretary, a messenger who also acted as postman and pharmacist, a veterinarian, and the deaf cook—most of them old men. The Commune had planned to use the back row of buildings as a middle school serving all the village elementary schools in the area, but due to the chaos caused by the Cultural Revolution, children weren't interested in attending. Consequently, all the buildings were empty. "Go out to the villages and mobilize the students," the Chairman of the Revolutionary Committee told me. "If you enroll one student, teach one; if no students show up, then you have nothing to do." He must have sensed that this suggestion was upsetting to me, so he added: "Superintendent Wang's in charge of the schools in Huchaigou valley. Go find him and do whatever he tells you."

I ran alone more than seven miles along a mountain road until I reached Huchaigou, imagining Superintendent Wang would understand my situation, but quickly changed my mind when I saw him. Superintendent Wang was a short, bearded man whose icy stare imparted immense hatred, and who made it evident that he wanted to put me in my place right away: "I know exactly who you are," he said. "You're here primarily to be re-educated by the poor and middle peasants; and, when you have a chance, to run a middle school and mobilize students to attend it."

He didn't say another word, conveying the impression that it would be just as well if I failed. How could I mobilize the students in a commune stretching out over such a large territory? Fortunately, the commune secretary was a kindhearted man, who sketched a map of the area for me. After that I began wandering from village to village through the vast, inhospitable wilderness, knocking on every door like a beggar trying to find students for my school. Before I had a chance to enroll even one student, however, I received a notice ordering all the county's six hundred teachers to convene immediately in the county seat to organize study teams. The Campaign to Clean-up Class Ranks[12] had begun. Another disaster was imminent.

XV

The Movement to Clean-up Class Ranks came on with such ferocity I knew I couldn't avoid it. I decided to go see the Political Commissar of the County Military Office who was in charge of political campaigns in the educational department. I told him everything I had been through, but this time I wasn't the naive person who had opened her heart to the authorities at the Yanbei District Office. This time I knew I stood to be persecuted, which made me curiously unafraid. I would tell them everything. If that led to my execution, I hoped it would happen soon. To my surprise, the Commissar seemed truly moved by my story. I asked, "Should I discuss these matters at the study sessions?"

"It's not your problem, so it's up to you; in any event, our county will not be too concerned about it."

I understood why he responded so cautiously. He was in fact implying that I didn't have to say anything about my past. I was relieved to know how this important official viewed the matter. But, when I participated in the study sessions, I still felt like I was entering a meat grinder. Seeing that I was remaining silent, Superintendent Wang tried to put pressure on me by making a show of attacking someone else in my presence in order to scare me. But I was determined not to suffer again for my naiveté and earnestness, and just gritted my teeth. I didn't say a word.

The condemnations in this remote and impoverished area were much more brutal than they would have been in the big cities. Sometimes the leading county officials were brought in for criticism meetings with heavy manure buckets tied around their necks with iron wire, and, while they were subjected to verbal abuse, their tormentors threw rocks at the buckets causing the dung to splatter all over their bodies. A number of the victims couldn't stand such degrading treatment and tried to commit suicide. If there was nothing around to kill themselves with, some would even grab their chopsticks when they were eating, shove them into their noses and slam their heads so forcefully on a table that the chopsticks might pierce their brains. Others would simply jump into a latrine and suffocate to death.

Two weeks later, at the instigation of Superintendent Wang, I became one of the principal targets. The tension drove me into a state of panic. One day, when we were all inside studying Chairman Mao's works, Superintendent Wang noticed me sitting on a bed and abruptly yelled at me, "Stand up!"

I immediately stood up on the bed.

"Who do you think you are, standing up so high," he shouted. "How dare you stand higher than the wall portrait of Chairman Mao?"

I jumped to the ground and retorted, "You asked me to stand."

The superintendent was really put off by my answer and kicked me all the way to the door. All I could think of doing was rushing out to find the Political Commissar, who I regarded as my protector. "Thinking about running away, are you?" the Superintendent said, grabbing me. The slaughter was about to begin.

I still don't know how, but from somewhere inside me I summoned up the courage to reply, "Isn't the Political Commissar of the County Military Office the highest ranking official in the area? Go ask him what he thinks and, if he wants me to talk, I will." Although I really didn't expect this challenge to bother Superintendent Wang, it did. For a moment he didn't know what to do. In fact, nobody knew how the Commissar would respond, and I had no idea if he would protect me. The one time we'd met he'd tacitly expressed a measure of sympathy for my predicament and spoken a few ambiguous words, but we were now going through a very stormy period where sympathy was a fragile and unreliable commodity. In any event, my fate was in the Commissar's hands.

Surprisingly, when they went off to the County Military Office to ask the Commissar about me, he told them, "Since her records haven't arrived, there is not much we can do about her now." Because of his attitude, I escaped further persecutions. A little later, a group of university graduates from the study team who had no political problems were sent to do some physical labor in the villages. The commissar ordered me to go with them. Thus I unexpectedly got away from the movement's implacable, onrushing wheel. I felt immensely grateful to the Commissar and considered him the most noble man on earth. I had no idea he had an ulterior purpose.

XVI

After I returned to the Dingjiayao Commune, I was continually busy rushing around from village to village in those barren mountains, trying to mobilize students to attend school. You can imagine how it felt for a young woman to be walking alone in that wild, dreary wasteland. I was afraid of running into anyone, and afraid of not running into anyone; afraid if I ran into anyone he'd be a thug, and afraid if I didn't run into anyone I'd get lost. Once I did lose my way and accidentally walked across the Shanxi border into Inner Mongolia where I was detained for an entire day as a spy. In the winter, on the snow-blanketed ground, I'd often see the footprints of wolves, leopards, and other predators out prowling for food. To boost my courage, I'd often sing non-stop at the top of my voice, sometimes even crying while I was singing and having no idea why. Perhaps because they were moved by my sincerity and tenacity, I finally mobilized twenty-eight students, and the fact that they all boarded at the school dispelled some of my loneliness. I served as principal, teacher, and the attendant who rang the bell for class to start. I'd wake them every morning at five, when the mountain air was fresh and chilly, then lead them to the empty playground, where all of us would face the rising sun and hold up our Little Red Books as high as we could in a salute to Chairman Mao. I have to confess, I felt this to be a sacred mission. Was it worship? That I couldn't say for sure, but I deeply needed some sort of spiritual support and encouragement to fill the void within me. Actually, during that period, there were times when I considered myself relatively happy, particularly at the great progress my impoverished school kids were making in their studies. Sometimes, while working until midnight correcting their homework and preparing for class, I'd be frightened to death by a yellow weasel making a scratching noise on my paper window curtain. On those occasions, my students became my teacher and instructed me to extinguish the oil lamp as soon as I heard the noise and the weasel would go away. My students and I became very close. Whenever they noticed I wasn't eating properly, and we were out in the fields digging up sweet herbs, they'd forage for wild bird's eggs and stuff them into my pocket. Once I reached into my pocket for a handkerchief and instead felt a sticky, fleshlike thing, and was so startled I screamed. It turned out to be a baby chick that had hatched in my pocket. This caused them to roar with laughter. They truly were an immense source of comfort and pleasure for me.

On the day of the Dragon Boat Festival,[13] each of my twenty-eight students brought me a piece of yellow cake filled with potatoes, bean curd, and steamed goat meat. Then another political rectification campaign was launched, and Superintendent Wang brought all the primary school teachers in his jurisdiction to our village for a meeting. While looking at the yellow cakes, he pointed his finger at me and said, "We no longer have visible counterrevolutionaries; but there are still those who hide behind the red flag for the purpose of desecrating that flag, and who inveigle the students in an effort to create successors. This is the latest form of counterrevolutionary activity under the new situation of the class struggle."

After I heard that, I decided the only alternative I had was to go out to one of the villages to teach elementary school. Superintendent Wang immediately approved this suggestion, informing that village's poor and middle peasant Revolutionary Committee to keep an eye on everything I did.

Although I'd lost almost all my interest in life, I also discovered I could either spend my days trying to keep my spirits up or walk around depressed. Once, after looking at an ashen face staring back at me in the mirror, I quickly washed, looked again, and discovered the same pasty features with lightless eyes. I was only twenty-four.

XVII

One day a piece of good news descended from heaven: The county authorities had reassigned me to teach chemistry at the county middle school. After I began, a cadre in the Political Department of the County Military Office told me the decision had been made by the Political Commissar, and then, after hemming and hawing for awhile, he finally explained the Commissar hoped I'd marry his brother-in-law, a mine worker in Datong City, a man who had a deformed leg. It was at this point that I suddenly realized why the Commissar had given me special protection during the Campaign to Clean-up Class Ranks. And just as I was thinking myself lucky to escape from Superintendent Wang's control, I'd fallen into the more powerful hands of the Commissar. Fortunately, the principal of the county middle school, a 1965 Shanxi University graduate, was an honest man who'd been through some rough times himself. He was sympathetic with me and introduced me to an elementary school teacher in another county, also a university graduate who had been assigned to this remote area. After overcoming numerous difficulties, I married him instead, and, because of that, was transferred from O to K County. Although my marriage and transfer greatly offended the Commissar, it put an end to the ten-year period of misery that is still agonizing to recall.

XVIII

My husband is an honest and considerate man who treats me well. Nevertheless, I rarely feel the passion for him that I did for my first husband. That was my first love, pure and innocent. It also possessed the sanctity of worship and lifelong devotion. A person can only worship with such intensity once in a lifetime, and, when such love is shattered, it is nearly impossible to restore.

After the Cultural Revolution had run its course, the authorities rehabilitated my former husband and arranged a memorial ceremony. Ten days after the news reached Nantong, his mother passed away. I know a good deal more about life now and will never worship again because I've endured the annihilation of worship and the worship of annihilation. The fact that I've survived both has been the most memorable experience in my life. That, of course, is perhaps the most tragic thing as well.

The worshipped destroy the worshippers by killing their souls.
—AUTHOR

FOOTNOTES

1. The socialist education campaign was also known as the "Four Clean-ups Movement." It was designed to rectify things in the political, organizational, and ideological spheres during 1963-1966.

2. Chen Yi was one of China's ten marshals. He led the New Fourth Army in guerrilla warfare against the Japanese invaders.

3. After the Communist Party and Kuomintang agreed to join forces in fighting the Japanese, a branch of the former Communist army was renamed the "New Fourth Army."

4. Wangfujing is the busiet commercial street in downtown Beijing.

5. Beihai Park is a public park in the center of Beijing.

6. After the founding of the PRC, the Communist Party conducted a land reform movement to re-allocate land in the rural areas.

7. In January, 1967, rebel groups in Shanghai, headed by Wang Hongwen, seized power from the Shanghai Municipal Party Committee. The incident set off a nation-wide campaign by rebel groups to seize power from existing authorities.

8. Jinggang Mountain in Jiangxi Province was one of the earliest revolutionary bases where Mao Zedong fought guerrilla warfare against the Nationalist army. Because of its revolutionary history, many rebel groups and Red Guard units named their organizations after it during the Cultural Revolution.

9. General Yang Chengwu was a supporter of Mao. He was acting Chief of the General Staff of the PLA when he was accused by Lin Biao and Jiang Qing in 1968 of "forcing his way into the office of the Central Cultural Revolution Group" in 1968. As a result, Yang was removed from his position. He was later rehabilitated.

10. *White-Haired Girl* was one of the model plays during the Cultural Revolution. It was an opera about the sufferings of poor peasants before Liberation.

11. The Military Control Commission of the People's Liberation Army was established in various work units to take effective control of the Party and government organs. It often put itself above the rule of law.

12. Clean-up Class Ranks was a movement intended to root out class enemies shortly after the Cultural Revolution started.

13. The Dragon Boat Festival occurs on the fifth day of the fifth month of the lunar calendar. It is widely celebrated in China with dragon boat races and the offering of food to China's earliest known poet, Qu Yuan.

The Story of a Smile

MALE, age 30 in

1968

MANAGER of a trading company in S City, F Province

O RIGINALLY I intended to use this "story of the century" as the basis for a novel. And the wonderful ending I happened onto last night would have provided me with a coup de grace for an unparalleled farce. It's a shame I can't write it. One reason for this is that I'm related to the would be protagonist, and the other is that the story, without the slightest embellishment, tops the hell out of anything written by the absurdist masters, Becket and Ionesco. I'm also convinced that none of the stories in your *Ten Years of One Hundred People* can measure up to mine. So I've decided to let you have it. You're fortunate that luck always seems to come your way, whereas, in my case, when it finally does arrive, it departs too quickly. However, that's neither here nor there. Can we agree that you'll give me a good story in exchange for mine? Can we enter into a gentleman's agreement? Just kidding. I don't want anything in return and will gladly give it up without offering the slightest resistance, because your *Ten Years of One Hundred People* doesn't hold a candle to the story I'm about to tell. Now let me begin.

I

I believe what a psychologist once said: "The smile is the most plastic expression of human emotion." There are only a few ways in which sadness or anger can be expressed on one's face, but the variety of smiles is limitless.

Close your eyes for a minute and try to picture these expressions. For example, there's the broad smile, the narrow smile, the silly smile, the dumb grin, the uninhibited smile, the deranged smile, the sardonic grin, the suggestive smile, the smirk, the taunting snicker, the secret smile, the fatuous grin, the cold smile, the pained smile, the hustler's sneer, the false smile, the treacherous smile, the teasing smile, the seductive smile, and so on and so forth. Of course, there's also the tender and affectionate, the insinuating and understanding, the shy and bashful, the formal and perfunctory, the flattering and toadying, the awkward and embarrassed, the depreciating and contemptuous, the sad and grieved, the consoling and empathetic, the forced and reluctant, and, last but not least, the I'm-at-the-end-of-the-road smile. Yet there's still another category that includes the leer of the fox on the prowl as well as the eternal and immutable, and the blank and meaningless smiles; nor can we forget the weepy and sniveling smile, the smile of laughter and tears, and the smile that isn't a smile. And finally we come to the set of smiles that the eighth generation of critics have dreamed up in imitation of the most with-it technical, scientific jargon, such as the "marginal smile," the "interfacing smile" and the "multi-faceted, deep-dish, machine-processed smile." Oh, I see you're smiling too—yet another—the prankster's smile.

In the midst of the current mania for how-to-do-it books, it would make great sense for someone to compile a thick, unabridged Smile Dictionary as a reference book for psychologists, psychiatrists, officials who go around ass-kissing their bosses, and fledgling authors. But to get to the point of this story, although humankind is capable of infinite richness in the ways the mouth can be spread across the face, my brother-in-law totally lacks this ability. The weirdo can't smile!

The first one to discover that my brother-in-law can't smile must be a genius. And I can assure you that person was not my sister. As a math teacher in middle school, her primary interest has been in the numbers on either side of an equation, and being somewhat of a late bloomer, she didn't get kissed until she was in her late twenties. And myself? No, you're wrong. I'm no genius in the human relations department either. In China the people who are most sensitive to human relations are political cadres, not writers. Thus the first person to discover my brother-in-law was unable to smile was Mr. Wei, the political cadre at my sister's school. When Wei told my witless sister about this remarkable gift, she replied, "I've known him for almost a year and hadn't noticed. How could you have come to this conclusion after only seeing him once at my house? If you'd said he's somewhat on the dull side and doesn't like to talk, I'd agree with you. But saying he can't smile is nonsense! How can someone not know how to smile?"

At the time my sister was madly in love with him. The two of them were with each other every day after work like flies. It's a fact that when these superrational scientifically-minded people fall in love, compared to normal people like us, they do it to the extreme and totally lose control. Anyway my explanation of love is as follows: Since the peculiar character of love is to love what you yourself love, love is nothing more than the love of oneself. The beloved becomes the object of all one's fantasies and dreams; the smile of the lover becomes the smile of the beloved, and the feelings the lover attributes to the beloved, and which so deeply affect the lover, are really a manifestation of the lover's own feelings. I know I'm right about this. Otherwise, why would so many people give their lives for the sake of love? Once love ends, the life of the lover is over as well. And I also believe that the first time one falls in love is the only time in life when one is truly insane, lost in a world of absolute illusion.

It seemed as if Mr. Wei's assessment burst my sister's bubble. No matter how hard she tried, she couldn't remember my brother-in-law ever smiling. This blank spot in her memory made her quite determined to test his capacity, and his upcoming birthday provided a good opportunity. Since he was born in the year of the pig, she went to a toy store and bought a fat, funny-looking, toy porker with a whistle on its butt, which made a strange sound when it was pinched. She wrapped the pig in colored wrapping paper, put it in her pocket, and that evening went off as usual to the Sea-Heaven Gate Park to meet him. After they met, she led him to a spot under a bright, sunflower-shaped lantern so she could see his face clearly. "I have a special gift for you," she said, fixing her eyes on his face and anticipating that out of interest or curiosity her words would at least elicit a trace of a smile and the question, "what kind of precious gift do you have for me?"

Actually this was exactly what he said. But it was also the first time my sister noticed that his face resembled the surface of a frozen river. It was devoid of the slightest suggestion of a smile. What a horror. Was it true that he couldn't smile? Such an extreme conclusion required further evidence.

My sister kept her cool, took the gift from her pocket, and tried as hard as she could to stay up-beat. "Here. Open it up and take a look," she said. If he didn't smile after seeing the fat little pig, there was nothing that could be done. It would have been her fate to have run into one of the most enigmatic faces in the world.

As my sister later explained to me, at that moment she was so nervous that her heart felt like it was jammed in her throat, as if the package he was about to open contained a time bomb. And what my sister had refused to believe was possible was then made manifest. After he removed the beautiful floral wrapping paper and saw what was inside, the expression on his face was exactly that of someone who'd just opened a piece of junk mail. After pinching the pig and hearing its funny screech, any normal person would have broken up in laughter, but all he could do was repeatedly exclaim: "Hey, hey. Hey, hey. Very funny. Very funny." His stiff and lackluster face resembled two tightly locked gates cinched across by a piece of tape. It was obvious that her boyfriend was an expression-impaired person.

My sister returned home and cried her eyes out, her naiveté scaring the heck out of us and provoking intimations of all sorts of disasters. And when she finally did provide the details, we were all dumbfounded and didn't know how to comfort her. I couldn't believe he didn't know how to smile, but I found thereafter that whenever I ran into him and tried to induce some movement across his face, I had no success whatsoever. On particularly amusing occasions, the best he could do was grin and mutter "hey, hey, hey." Although the braying sound he made did approach a laugh, the edges of his mouth remained locked in place, his face an expressionless slab of frozen meat.

For awhile my sister saw little of him. I assumed she feared being with him, feared he wouldn't smile. And when he did happen to visit her during that period, she rarely looked directly at his face, causing some rather stiff encounters I can tell you. Whenever I'd try to crack a joke to break the ice, my sister would reluctantly glance over at him, apparently hoping to spot a trace of a smile on his corpse-like face. I considered advising her to give up on him, that continuing on as she was would only drive her crazy, and, in any event, spending her life with this weirdo would be a great waste. How could she find any joy in life facing this class-struggle puss all day long. Everyone knows that the most common expression of affection between two people is a smile. A smile is one of the most satisfying responses to one's lover, one of the best anodynes to life's problems, and an effortless way of communicating. But before I had a chance to convey these thoughts to her, I came to understand that the real problem was she couldn't break up with him.

In fairness, I have to admit that my brother-in-law is a very dependable guy, and also quite smart. He studied economics in college and was the top student in his class; and, in my opinion, his English is even better than his Chinese. As for character, there's no doubt he's very serious about his work, trustworthy, extremely punctual, and unusually neat and clean. Although he only has two shirts, they always look brand new and even the patches seem like they've been sewed on for decoration. My sister fell in love with all these qualities.

He's also an orphan, a fact of life that can lead to stunted emotional development. And when he was in college in 1957, he got caught up in a political movement when people were encouraged to "speak out freely and air views fully." I heard that he took some pretty hard shots for it. Since everything in life at that time was decided by political considerations, no appealing female would date him, so this chunk of barren land remained desolate. If he hadn't come from a family with the right class background, he never would have been assigned to work for an international trading company. When he came to my sister's school to do some extra-curricular English teaching, they met by chance and quickly fell in love. This love was like a seed dropped down into a bare and desiccated patch of tundra, miraculously sprouting up and giving life to the entire plot. His feeling for my sister seemed to be rooted in a passion springing from his gratitude towards her, which made her feel doubly loved, cared for, and appreciated. And I learned from their relationship that a woman needs more appreciation than a man. One day they decided to go to the theater and agreed to meet inside. That evening, while my sister was having dinner, a bad snowstorm swept over the city. Hearing a knock on the door, she opened it and saw that it was him.

"Why are you here?" she asked. "Didn't we agree to meet at the theater?"

"Don't forget to wear a gauze mask to keep yourself warm," he replied. Although these words were spoken without the slightest trace of a smile, I did notice her face light up as she returned to her room to take a mask from her drawer. This is precisely the kind of treatment women want.

Nevertheless, despite his solicitude, after my sister came to believe he couldn't smile, she did consider ending the relationship a number of times. But her resolve never lasted more than three days. Inevitably she came up with some pretext to call and arrange to see him. One of the signs of true love is when two people constantly resolve to break up, but never quite seem to get around to really doing it. Therefore I changed my approach and tried to bring them closer together. In private I asked him, "Why is it I hardly ever see you smile?" a question I thought very cleverly phrased.

I was surprised to see him raise his eyelids in amazement, and in his typical, deadpan way, reply: "Hey, hey. That's a very interesting question." I concluded from his answer that he really didn't think himself incapable of smiling. It followed that since his peculiar talent wasn't due to illness, it wasn't related to any physical problem.

One day I read a book, the title of which now slips my mind, but there was a sentence about love that I remembered clearly: "Pay attention to the heart, not the face."

I left the book open to the page where that sentence was written and put it on my sister's desk, hoping she'd notice it. After she left for work the following day, I took a look at the book and saw she'd penciled in the words "Thank you" after the sentence. I realized that my sister had written these words for the author as well as for me, and it did happen that from that day on the awkwardness between them seemed to gradually disappear without any apparent conscious effort on their part. Later, after they married, my sister moved in with him, and they had a child. And whenever I visited them, I never had the sense my brother-in-law's impassive face had any negative effect on their relationship. In fact, his not smiling had some advantages: First of all, false smiles weren't a problem; and besides, whenever he did some favor for her and she wanted to show her appreciation with a smile, his expressionless response suggested his solicitousness was quite natural and should be expected. He even remained straight-faced when playing with his son. Sometimes I'd notice them rollicking around on his bed, his son laughing so hard he'd lose his breath, my brother-in-law, of course, looking like he was a member of a wrestling team. I also felt that my brother-in-law's somber face served as a quiet retreat for my sister, a safe haven to which she could withdraw from the world and enjoy the warmth and tenderness of their mutual love.

Having listened to this much of the story, I'd wager you're getting a bit restless—even thinking I've cheated you. I can hear your voice complaining: What kind of gem of the absurd is this? It's nothing but a typical love story. Calm down, my friend, calm down. All human beings are born normal; the absurd is imposed by life. In other words, absurdity is the essence of life.

II

I also believe what a philosopher once said: "Beware of anything that brings you happiness, because it will also bring you misery."

At one point of the Cultural Revolution in 1968, every work unit in the country participated in a campaign to "recall, set forth, and examine." Do you still remember the significance of the word "recall"? "Recall" meant to recollect peculiar events, that is, to remember any suspicious persons or circumstances, bring them to light, and search for clues to "root out the most deeply hidden counterrevolutionaries." For example, an old worker in a glue factory customarily greeted people by raising his hand to his eyebrow—a gesture similar to the way officers saluted each other in the former Manchurian Army. This gesture was "recalled" by someone and reported to the Special Investigation Team (SIT)[1] who found out the old man had been a military officer in the Kuomintang army in Manchuria,[2] and that he had kept this fact secret. The breaking of this case was regarded as a major accomplishment and the results were transmitted all over the country. For awhile, this provoked nearly universal probing of memories for strange occurrences. The wish to pull a bomb out from under one's bed became a common fantasy. Without warning, the day also came when disaster struck my brother-in-law. Someone at his company put up a big-character poster with the words: "Why doesn't he ever smile?"

This big-character poster had a far more shocking effect on the company than any million dollar export contract. Soon after it was posted, the more than two hundred company employees got together and searched their memories for impressions of my brother-in-law, and, of course, nobody could remember ever seeing him smile. The SIT quietly looked into the matter by interviewing his friends and neighbors, none of whom could attest that he'd ever smiled. This, of course, further aggravated the problem. And when it was my turn to talk to the SIT, I told them: "I've never seen him smile either, for he never smiled at home. Perhaps he just lacks the capacity for it."

"Don't try to cover up for him. Only dead men don't know how to smile," one of the team retorted. "We've questioned the teachers at his orphanage and his elementary and middle school, and his college classmates. They all claim that he knows how to smile, and, in fact, has smiled. Our dossier on him is full of evidence. The answer isn't that he doesn't know how to smile, but that his not smiling is politically motivated."

This suggestion astonished me. To tell the truth, I had no doubt the SIT had the evidence they claimed they had. How could a person not know how to smile? Therefore I began to wonder whether he'd been so abused in the Anti-Rightist Movement in 1957 that he'd undergone a complete transformation. I'd always known him to be a very introspective and withdrawn person who never talked about himself, and certainly not about his past.

The "right-deviationist" speeches he'd made in 1957, which were still in his file, were the evidence the SIT used to conclusively prove that the fundamental reason for his not smiling was his unbridled hatred for the new society. Nevertheless, they needed current evidence before they could brand him a counterrevolutionary. The fact that nothing in his work or speech directly confirmed their suspicion led them to conclude that he was one of those who had "taken deep cover;" and as such he was listed as a "key target of the movement," confined to his work unit, forced to confess his thoughts and to have his house searched. During their search, they confiscated his private letters and work notes, and even grabbed my sister's mathematics lesson plans. What they found in all these writings was nothing but a factual account of the events in his life, devoid of any mention of his feelings, not even those about the weather. Ultimately they tried to force a confession out of him. But being the person he was, he refused to admit he couldn't smile. And when they ordered him to smile, all he could do was grin mechanically as he had before, and mutter "hey, hey." At the criticism meeting, his mechanical grin and empty muttering had the unintended effect of turning the sessions into a comical mockery of their purpose with no value for the movement. Finally, one of the shrewder members of the SIT thought up a deft way to get at the truth, and asked him: "What are your feel-

ings about the Party and Chairman Mao?" After he responded
that he was extremely grateful to the Party and Chairman Mao
for raising him as an orphan and giving him a scholarship for
all of his schooling, the wily interrogator pointed to a portrait of
the Chairman on the wall and asked, "When you look at
Chairman Mao's portrait, should you smile or should you cry?"

"Of course I should smile," my brother-in-law replied.

"All right, then smile. Let's see if it's real or fake."

As my brother-in-law faced Chairman Mao's portrait
with the intention of smiling, he probably had no idea what
would appear on his face. I heard that when he put out his
teeth in an attempt at a broad grin, the convulsions in the
muscles of his cheekbones were so forceful that his eyebrows
began to tremble, and he seemed to be in great pain and was
frightful to look at.

"Is this how you treat our great leader? You call that a
smile? What a joke. That's no smile, it's a look of deep-seat-
ed hatred," the SIT members collectively screamed at him.
Now that they had their proof that he was an active counterrevolutionary, they could criticize and denounce him, taking
the movement to new heights of rapture. They were all filled
with such righteous indignation, it's a wonder they didn't eat
him alive.

For more than a year after that, my sister became a
member of a counterrevolutionary family, and my brother-in-
law's work unit constantly sent interrogators to her school to
force her to expose him. Although the school treated her well
and did their best to protect her, she was ostracized by many
of the people who had once sought her company, was continually depressed, and lost all interest in life. Once on a visit to
their house, I witnessed her suddenly slap her beloved son's
face, then break down in tears after he'd asked why his father
never smiled. It was the first time I'd ever seen her strike him.

Later, when the central authorities decided to re-
examine the old cases from the early stages of the Cultural
Revolution, my brother-in-law's case became a real headache.
The person assigned to examine the case questioned whether
a mere facial expression was enough to prove him guilty of
being a counterrevolutionary. After all, they couldn't take a
mug shot of his smile, as they might do in a murder case to

put evidence of guilt in his file. Some six months later, the authorities sent a Workers Propaganda Team[3] to help his company implement the re-examination campaign. By then, the SIT was quite happy to hand this hot potato of a case over to them.

In fact, it turned out that the workers were more clever than the cadres. After thinking about the problem for awhile, they came up with their own unorthodox way to resolve it. They called in my brother-in-law and ordered him to undress down to his underwear, which naturally scared him to death. But instead of beating him up, they asked him to raise his hands, as if he was a surrendering soldier. One of the team then began lightly running a piece of straw from a broom under his armpits and around his neck and the bottoms of his feet. My brother-in-law responded by grinning mechanically, making his typical "hey, hey" sound, and, with his arms and legs shaking wildly, finally yelled, "No, stop, stop, hey hey, it tickles, hey, hey, it tickles." But he never did stretch out into a smile.

The man from the workers propaganda team tossed aside the piece of straw. "What's the problem with the SIT?" he asked. "How could they accuse this man of refusing to smile? He simply lacks the capacity to do it."

As a result, the charges against my brother-in-law were dropped and he was rehabilitated. So as not to impugn the achievements of the earlier movement, the authorities concluded that, while they "had sound reason to investigate, since no highly incriminating evidence was found, the case could be settled in accordance with the principles governing contradictions among the people."

Although he was politically rehabilitated, he was transformed from an enemy who wouldn't smile to a weird person who can't smile. His fellow employees regarded him with great curiosity and interest. On any occasion when a smile was called for, all eyes would fix on his mouth. His colleagues, ironically, preferred not to see any spread of his lips, just to confirm that there really was this odd-ball guy they knew who lacked this most common of abilities. Of course, some wise guys at the company would sometimes put mice in his desk drawer or suddenly confront him with clownish faces, never giving up on the idea of manipulating him into a smile. They even gave him the nickname "Dead Face." And he knew about it. The man who couldn't smile had become an object of laughter. Although outwardly he maintained his composure, he became quite sensitive to that fact that his colleagues were deliberately insulting him. This exacerbated his already blank expression, his face taking on the look of an ice-covered rock. One day out of the blue he asked my sister, "Can you teach me to smile?"

With tears in her eyes, she replied, "I like you just the way you are."

From that day on, my sister rarely smiled herself. Most likely, she did this intentionally, not wanting to provoke my brother-in-law's feelings of inferiority. From my perspective, a family that doesn't smile is like a sky that's forever dark. Although the two of them were still devoted to each other, I always felt a gloom in their house that made their roof seem as if it was pressing down on them. I also lost my capacity to smile whenever I visited them. How strange. Why couldn't I smile? Once when I was at their house, I noticed a small table mirror that was broken in half. Inadvertently I looked into the mirror and tried to smile, but for a moment forgot how to move my facial muscles. The most I could manage was to open my mouth in an awkward grin. When I looked into the mirror again, I was confronted by a face with precisely the same expression as my brother-in-law's. How horrible and frightening.

III

I now believe even more in what an absurdist playwright once said: "Life is more absurd than the absurd arts."

Once the Cultural Revolution was kicked into the dustbin of history, life needed a new interpretation, including my brother-in-law's inability to smile.

A leader's capability was no longer measured by the number of people he could screw over, but by the amount of money he could earn. The international trading company's Party secretary was appointed its general manager, and he decided to set up a new branch to handle foreign and overseas investments, joint ventures, and exports. The branch needed a capable leader and the former Party hotshots, who were all well trained at organizing political movements but nothing else, were now obsolete. It was difficult to find the right person for the job, so the general manager started thinking about my brother-in-law as a possibility. He was a competent professional, and his foreign language ability was excellent, which would facilitate business dealings with foreigners. Nevertheless, objections were raised by the company's management, mostly due to his inability to smile. How could someone host foreign business-men if he couldn't smile? Although part of the management team thought he'd be a real dud in business negotiations, ulti-mately, he was found to be the best choice, and was appointed temporary branch manager.

In less than a year after my brother-in-law took up his new position, he had the business going in full swing. It turned out that what was most essential in discussions with foreign businessmen was one's ability to do business, not one's ability to smile.

Within several years, my brother-in-law became a successful executive, his branch of the company earning twice the profits as the rest of the entire company, an achievement the company's leadership could use for their own political promotions. As a result of his success, my brother-in-law's name frequently appeared on the front page of newspapers. He was elected a representative to the municipal People's Congress, made daily visits to the most luxurious hotels, and regularly hobnobbed with the most important city officials at their stately mansions. He also traveled abroad on business trips and moved his family into a deluxe three-bedroom apart-ment with all the latest appliances desired by an affluent fam-ily. Indeed, my sister took great pleasure in showing off the stylish new clothes and jewelry he brought back from his trips abroad. By then, it was no longer taboo for her to smile, and she indulged herself in this whenever she liked. As for him, he had his own private car, his western-style suit and hand-somely styled hair. The only thing that hadn't changed was his face, which still was incapable of forming a smile. Nevertheless, this wooden-faced man was warmly welcomed everywhere, received premier service with a smile at the big hotels he frequented for business purposes, and was greeted obsequiously by all his company's employees. Although this flattering treatment was partly due to his colleagues' wanting him to buy them gifts on his trips abroad, now that he was a VIP with power and big bucks, his subordinates felt it their responsibility to humor him, even if he couldn't smile. He was like a god among men, though perhaps even the great deity would have had trouble figuring out how he had suddenly become such a major celebrity.

Now I'm going to tell you about the weird thing that happened last night.

My brother-in-law, my sister, and their son were sitting in their living room watching a two-person cross-talk[4] comedy show on their 24" TV screen. All at once a sort of cackling sound came forth from somewhere deep within my brother-in-law's throat, a sound resembling the frightened clucking of a hen just before laying an egg. He continued making this "ge, ge, ge" sound for some time, as if something was caught in his throat and was causing him pain. My sister thought he might have suddenly become ill, but when she looked closer she noticed the edges of his mouth beginning to turn up, gradually pulled higher and higher by an invisible piece of string, his facial muscles twisting and contorting in the process, and his eyebrows, which had never before been affected by this kind of facial upheaval, looped in the shape of two small willow leaves. Suddenly their son cried out: "My daddy looks like Donald Duck!"

Their son's words had the effect of an explosive device. My brother-in-law immediately burst out in laughter, as if a long dead volcano had unexpectedly erupted. And his face was no longer contorted. There was no mistaking the genuineness of his laughter. Yes, he'd actually laughed. Later, my sister told me that, at that moment, his facial features seemed to be in full harmony, like a flower in full bloom with all its petals opening simultaneously, something none of us ever thought possible. Yet this display of genuine laughter so shocked her that she thought he'd gone mad. She asked him what was wrong. Apparently my brother-in-law's hands were shaking so much he couldn't reply, the two comedians on the television screen sending him into even greater paroxysm of laughter every time he glanced at them, his hands involuntarily covering his stomach, tears and mucous pouring down his face. My sister helped him into bed, and called me immediately. I rushed over and ran into their bedroom where he was twitching violently under his quilt as if he had a terrible fever. The bed frame was shaking and groaning from his convulsions. He continued to laugh as I raised the quilt to take a look, and his pillowcase was soaked with his tears.

"What's the matter with you? Are you ill?" I asked.

"I can't stop myself," he answered, continuing to laugh.

I gave him two tranquilizers, which eventually calmed him down and allowed him to fall into a deep sleep. Today my sister reported a miracle: a perfectly natural smile has appeared on his face. How strange and unimaginable. Can you tell me how this happened?

Even facial expressions were censured—a demonstration of the absolute authority of the Cultural Revolution.

—AUTHOR

FOOTNOTES

1. During the Cultural Revolution, Special Investigation Teams were set up in all work units to investigate people suspected of conducting counterrevolutionary activities.

2. Manchuria refers to the northeastern part of China that was occupied by the Japanese invaders between 1931 and 1945.

3. Workers' representatives were sent to schools and academic and technical institutions to assume administrative control.

4. A cross talk show is a popular two-person comedy act.

I Refuse to Admit
I was a Sacrificial
Object

MALE, *age 32 in*

1967

BUS CONDUCTOR
in T City

W HEN I wrote to you, I meant to throw a stone at you, not sure if you had the guts to write about me.

In the past ten years, many literary works have been written about the Cultural Revolution. Most of them are not completely truthful, and therefore not convincing. In these works, rebels are described as thugs—well built, inhumane, and merciless. It has become a stereotype, which makes us rebels laugh and somewhat angry. We are treated like slaughtered pigs with a seal on our butts. Anyone can take any piece he likes.

Why did I become a rebel? Of course there was a reason.

I was born in 1935. My family had been poor for many generations. When I was fourteen, I had to quit school because my family couldn't afford the daily meals. I found a job as an apprentice at a sewing factory. During the "Movement Against Three Evils and Five Evils," I stood with the Party and took part in fierce struggles against the factory owners, who were so wicked that, as soon as the movement was over, they declared that the factory was running at a loss and had to be closed. I was therefore out of a job. But their business never stopped. Their real purpose was to kick me out of the factory.

I looked for a new job and eventually became a bus conductor, earning 129 *jin*[1] of millet a month. Not bad. At the time, it was easy to find such a job. One could become a driver if one could lift a block of wood, or a conductor if one knew the simple arithmetic. The elder workers were mostly illiterate. New comers like myself were looked upon as scholars and were bound for fast promotion. I was good at writing and therefore became a special correspondent for the *Workers' Daily*. On the official stationery of the newspaper were printed two sentences: "To answer the call of the masses. To serve as the mouthpiece of the workers." Reading these words made me feel warm all over. At that time, the workers were having a hard time. The company leadership consisted of people with complicated backgrounds and they treated the workers unfairly. I stood on the side of the workers and wrote about the wicked things the leaders did. I considered it an act of loyalty to the Party. I was too naive to know that by doing so, I had alienated the company leaders and become a thorn in their side. While I was feeling good about myself, the leaders were plotting to get rid of me.

When the Rectification Movement[2] started in 1957, the company walls were covered with big-character posters. These were mostly composed of gossip, accusing one or another person of stealing small items or womanizing. I thought to myself: This movement was intended to help the Party rectify. What does all the gossip have to do with that? Therefore I wrote a big-character poster myself, saying: "It is true that airing different views is necessary. But don't forget Chairman Mao's six-point principles." To my complete surprise, this poster caused me to get into troubled waters. I was accused of making a sneak attack on the Party. Because of my poster, it was said, many counterrevolutionaries were not revealed. Every day they held meetings to denounce me. Since workers were not labeled "Rightists," they decided to send me to a labor camp to be re-educated through labor, with two years' probation in the company. And as a result, I could no longer be a special correspondent for the newspaper.

At the time, I really couldn't understand why my loyalty to the Party had been turned against me. Years later, when I was imprisoned during the Cultural Revolution, a fellow inmate who used to be a cadre at the Ministry of Finance and Trade told me, "Rectification was merely an excuse for outsiders. Its real purpose was to 'lure the snakes out of their hiding holes.' Because of your poster, all the holes were blocked. Of course you had to be persecuted." So I understood, but too late.

From then on, I became a little wiser. I told myself to shut up, work hard, and not make trouble for my parents.

When the Cultural Revolution began, things got much worse. The Red Guards turned everything upside down. I saw a person beaten to death on Fifth Street with my own eyes. A mass political debate was going on among the workers. Because of the lessons I learned from the previous movement, I kept my mouth shut and said nothing. However, everyone was required to speak at political meetings. The Cultural Revolution was intended to touch the heart and soul of each person. To stay silent was deemed an act of disobedience. When it was finally my turn to speak, I didn't know what to say, except to recite the official Sixteen-Point Directives:[3] "The focus of this movement is to rectify people in authority who are actually capitalist roaders within the Party." I didn't say a word that reflected my own thoughts, but merely repeated the Party line, which I thought was good enough to keep me from trouble.

I was wrong again. The next day big-character posters were all over the company accusing me of attacking the Party. I was locked up in a "cow shed."[4] Outside, the Red Guards were out of control. It was like the end of the world. I could only wait to die.

Up until then, the movement was manipulated by the official Cultural Revolution Group (CRG),[5] which was made up of leaders of the company. Soon after that, however, there was a sudden change at the top that completely altered the direction of the wind. The new directives from the central authorities accused the CRGs at various work units of taking a reactionary capitalist road, instead of Chairman Mao's revolutionary line. Their purpose, it was said, was to protect the capitalist roaders within the Party, alter the general direction of the struggle, aim at the masses, and attack the majority of the people. Chairman Mao issued his "Newest Instruction," saying, "There are thousands of points in Marxist theory. To sum it all up, it can be put in one sentence: It is right to rebel."

All of a sudden, the CRGs at various work units became the targets of the rebels. In retrospect, the real purpose of the Cultural Revolution was to get rid of Liu Shaoqi. Since Liu had supporters at all levels of the Party hierarchy, he could hardly be overthrown if his followers were not sidelined. That was why the masses were mobilized to rebel. But, at that time, no one understood such implications. It didn't take but a moment for the public to agree with the new policy, for it was absolutely correct that the masses had been oppressed, and, therefore it was right to rebel. In almost one breath, I wrote seventeen big-character posters, detailing how I was persecuted. In conclusion, I asked: "What was I guilty of?"

I was among the first people to rebel in our company. At that time the CRG was still in power. They sent pickets to arrest me. Someone in the company went to a nearby college and asked the student Red Guards to help me out. They came, I was freed, and in one blow, the CRG collapsed. I thought to myself, let's rebel! I had been pushed around for too long. But I wouldn't be manipulated anymore. It was right to rebel, and I had that right.

Here I need to mention those literary works again. They treat the rebels as thugs. Perhaps the authors were still sucking their mothers' breasts at the time all this happened. The fact is, at the start of the Cultural Revolution, it was the CRGs who were responsible for beating people and ransacking their homes. The earliest rebels were those who were persecuted in the first place. Otherwise, how could they rebel so ferociously?

At the beginning of the Cultural Revolution, the word "rebel" had a completely different meaning. It referred to counterrevolutionaries who tried to make a come-back. The new meaning of "rebel" was defined by Chairman Mao himself. Do you remember a photograph of Chairman Mao's, the one with a big red armband that said "rebel"? Earlier, he had a similar armband that said "Red Guard" when he reviewed several million Red Guards at Tiananmen Square. When Chairman Mao changed his armband to read "rebel," the word instantly took on a new meaning. It meant to rebel against the reactionary capitalist line. Only then did the workers begin to make their impact on society. That was how it happened, wasn't it? After all, we must respect history, right?

Chairman Mao was the red commander-in-chief. Wherever he pointed, we went. Without his command, how would we little people dare to rebel? At that time, all we had in mind was to have a red heart and a readiness to give our lives for the revolution. Every night we went out to put up big-character posters. There was no bonus, no pay. The only incentive was that we were happy to follow Chairman Mao to our deaths.

Thus as our fortunes changed for the better, our persecutors suddenly changed their identities as well by setting up their own rebel organizations. We became two opposition factions intent on fighting to the end. Both sides claimed to be defending Chairman Mao's revolutionary line, and each accused the other of opposing the red flag while holding one in their hands. Later on, people with different backgrounds started to join the faction, which made the situation more and more complicated. Since you are writing about the Cultural Revolution, you must truthfully record its process. Otherwise no one will believe you.

I was the leader of one of the first four rebel organizations in the city, the one named Trolley Bus Red Flag. I had 3,000 members under my command. The emergence of the workers overshadowed the young Red Guards. The workers became the center of society. At that time, rebel groups spoke for those who were persecuted at the start of the Cultural Revolution, opposed the reactionary capitalist line, and, therefore, gained widespread support. Our former persecutors were no longer popular.

However, every rebel group feared being defeated by the opposition faction, and did everything possible to prevail.

In the end, the fighting escalated into all-out war. As a result, people were not completely innocent anymore. To tell you the truth, I was very scared. Things were obviously getting out of control, and I knew that there would be repercussions afterwards. What was happening in front of me was so messy that I couldn't see any way out. I felt there was an irresistible force that was carrying me on a path to death. It was like riding on the back of a tiger. It would be worse to back off, though. The only choice was to fight to the end, therefore I had to strengthen my position. I would be untouchable only when I had enough power, and I was not the only rebel leader with this thought. We all felt much the same. Every group tried to strengthen its force by recruiting people. It didn't take long for different factories to combine forces and set up super-organizations.

I had a best friend with whom I had shared everything since early childhood. I told him, "From now on, we must separate and go our own ways. If you stay with me, neither of us will come to a good end." After that, I was alone and able to take on all responsibility by myself. If I had to die, I could die alone.

In reality, I knew I had to consolidate my forces step by step. I couldn't afford to make any mistakes. My group decided to unite with other rebel groups and set up a more powerful organization. There was one called Rebel Headquarters of Factories and Mines, which shared our views. After investigation, I found that some of their members had complicated backgrounds. So I abandoned them and sent people to other groups. We selected fifty-two groups, whose members had similar backgrounds and political views. Together we formed the Anti-Restoration Liaison, which became one of the most powerful rebel organizations in the city. I posted myself in the headquarters and worked day and night. Wherever fighting broke out, I sent support teams there. Whenever a major incident happened, I went there to solve the problem. I also sent people to Beijing to gather information, especially reports of the latest talks of top leaders. You couldn't do anything blindly. Otherwise, you would die before you knew it.

After the "January Storm" in Shanghai, a chain reaction was started around the country to seize power from the existing authorities. A high ranking official from the Central Committee was sent to T city to set up a Preparatory Committee to Seize Municipal Power. Their plan was to establish a revolutionary committee after seizing power, and then set up a red regime. At a meeting attended by leaders of various mass organizations, the official singled out the Trolley Bus Red Flag and two college Red Guard organizations for rectification. We knew that if that happened, we would be excluded from the red regime, which further implied that we couldn't avoid persecution. I said to the official: "You are only a new comer. There is no way you can get rid of us." Another rebel leader agreed and said, "If you do this, we will turn the city upside down as early as tomorrow." The official struck the table hard and said, "Whoever leaks out a word about this meeting must take full responsibility for its results." The meeting was over without any agreement.

We studied the situation carefully. If we were kept out of the revolutionary committee, we would be finished. We decided to rebel against the official. The next day we put up big-character posters criticizing him. At the same time we combined forces with other groups with similar views and set up a Preparatory Committee for a Grand Unification (PCGU). We were determined to fight head-on. The official had originally planned to seize power in three months and set up a revolutionary committee. We were determined to spoil his game. He bought out a rebel group and supported it with the army. In contrast, we were a group of nobodies, people with no official power. The pressure on us was enormous. We were prepared for the worst scenario, one in which we would use the river that ran through the city as a dividing line, take our people across that river and fight to the end. At that time, there was a rumor that Chairman Mao was ready to go back to Jinggang Mountain to engage in another guerrilla war if he were dethroned. Massive fighting erupted everywhere. The climax was the so-called "No. 609 Incident," which was well-known throughout the country.

No. 609 was a military plant, where the rebel group in power was our opposition. The incident started when a Red Guard Propaganda Team from the Industrial College, which was part of the PCGU, passed by the factory. The two sides shouted slogans and swore at each other. In the fighting that followed, all of our supporters were captured. When we heard that, all groups under the Grand Unification sent members to the plant in an attempt to take our people back. They didn't succeed. Instead, the leader of a rebel group from the Rolling Stock Plant was taken prisoner too. I arrived at the site the next day and was completely awed by the scene in front of me. No. 609 was completely encircled by our people. We set up an ad hoc command post and appointed several key leaders, including a Director of War, Logistics, Propaganda, and a Liaison. I said to our people, "No. 609 is a military plant, therefore we can't attack it. If we do, we will fall into the trap of our enemy." I issued several instructions: One, block all roads and bridges between the city and the suburbs, so that peasant rebel groups can't enter the city and further complicate the situation; Two, we will only surround the factory, not attack it; Three, we must maintain our superiority in numbers of people. At the time, No. 609 was beginning to bring in supporters from outside the factory. There were five truck-loads of them, about 200 people. We sent 400 people to encircle them. They brought in another 800, but we sent 2,000 more to surround this group. Outside the rear wall of the factory was the Tianjin-Pukou Railway. They planned to bring in supporters by train, but we sent people to block the railway also. Our strategy was to force them to surrender with encirclement.

That night, there was an incident with a rebel group from Dagang. It was dark, and people couldn't see each other clearly. One of our members was mistakenly identified as enemy and killed. When the incident was reported to the Command Post, the Dagang people lied to us, saying that the enemy had killed one of our fighters. People were immediately agitated. Thousands of them shouted that blood must atone for blood. An armed fight was imminent. People on both sides of the wall threw stones and bottles of sulfuric acid at each other. Relieving troops came in waves. Bulldozers were used. It was a bloody scene.

Adjacent to the factory was a mill plant, which was also occupied by the opposition. That night the Command Post decided to feign an attack on No. 609, while launching a full attack on the mill plant. The purpose was to occupy their outside post first. But, by the time our people arrived, the opposition had already fled. So we came back to attack the factory.

After Jiang Qing encouraged the rebels to engage in "verbal attack and armed defense," armed fighting became legalized and escalated. The situation turned into a real war. At the side gate of No. 609, our enemy used a bulldozer to force their way out, with people running behind the vehicles. In front of the bulldozer was a fender filled with sulfuric acid. When our supporters approached, the man on the bulldozer stepped on a button to spray acid. Many of our men suffered burned faces. The fighting became quite ugly. We had to adopt a new strategy by moving our people to the side and letting the bulldozer pass so we could beat the people behind it. The bulldozer was isolated. When our enemy realized that they had fallen into our trap, the driver tried to reverse the vehicle, but he switched to a wrong gear, and the bulldozer got stuck and stopped. Our people stormed it. The most hateful man was the one who released the acid, and it didn't take long for our group to attack him. Later we found out that he received over 270 wounds to his body. I could see from afar that the driver was still on the vehicle. Knowing that something terrible was about to happen, I rushed to the bulldozer and dragged him off the vehicle. As I did so, my left foot stepped on a broken acid bottle. I took the driver with me and went to the hospital to have my foot treated. Were it not for me, he would have had no chance to live another day.

The Preparatory Committee to Seize Municipal Power sent representatives to the site, but they couldn't solve the problem. Chen Boda phoned and ordered us to retreat. The Central Committee ordered the two sides to send twenty-five representatives each to Beijing for an emergency meeting. We decided to send twenty-three. But only five of us made the trip. Why? We were scared. We didn't know what the Central Committee had in mind, and were unsure of our own destiny. At that time, all rebel factions claimed to be defending the Central Committee, but all were afraid of it. The situation was so volatile that no one knew what would happen the next day.

Anyway, we went to Beijing and met with Jiang Qing, Chen Boda, Kang Sheng, Yao Wenyuan, Qi Benyu and Xie

Fuzhi.[6] We listened carefully and were pleased to be asked to come back another day to negotiate an "Agreement on Stopping the Armed Fighting." We returned to our city with the news, which ignited a bitter argument within the organization. Everyone wanted to go. Some groups said that we couldn't represent them and insisted that we hold another democratic election. We cast our votes and elected twenty-five representatives, including workers, cadres, and teachers, and I was one of them.

Why did everyone want to go? Because no one wanted to be left out. We had no official power in the first place and knew we would be more insecure if we were left out. To participate in a negotiation at the Central Committee level meant that we had made our mark at the very top, and that we would be treated more seriously from then on.

At the start of the negotiations, the two sides engaged in bitter wrangling over one specific sentence: "Do not loot guns; do not use guns." The phrase was drafted by the opposition, and I insisted it be reversed to read: "Do not use guns; do not loot guns." I pointed out to the opposition, "You have the support of the army and access to assault rifles. We have no official power, let alone guns. How can we open fire? This sentence is clearly intended to put pressure on us. It sounds as if we are going to loot weapons. If you use guns on us, we will try to take them from you, unless you promise not to use them." I was very uncompromising. They couldn't come up with a good response.

The vice director of the Preparatory Committee to Seize Municipal Power was also uncompromising. He said: "No more change: Do not loot guns; do not use guns."

I said, "Since you are unreasonable, we have to leave. Brothers, let's go." Everyone on our side stood up and left. The incident planted the seeds of hostility between me and the official. Eventually he became chairman of the Municipal Revolutionary Committee.

Although I appeared strong and uncompromising, to tell you the truth, I was very scared. He was a high ranking official. I was an ordinary citizen, a nobody. In his eyes I was like a small blade of grass, which he could trample under his feet whenever he chose to. All the power I had was temporary and would not last long. I had no choice but to act as tough as a dare-devil. Otherwise, I would have been crushed right there. But even my ability to act tough was temporary. I knew I would have my downfall sooner or later. I knew it all along.

In any event, the negotiations resulted in a peaceful settlement to the armed fighting. Chairman Mao approved the result himself, saying: "Very good. Do as decided." Many people on our side were elected to the Workers Representative Conference. Some were promoted to the Municipal Revolutionary Committee. I became a member of the standing committee, for which I was accused of climbing the official ladder. Some people likened me to a piece of porcelain. They said that I had changed from a civilian-made piece of porcelain to an official one. For me, it was not important to be an official, but it was important to protect myself. If you are at the bottom of the society, you are the safest when you stay at the very bottom. As you reach the top, you are safest when you get to the very top. That's how I looked at it. We were elated that we survived. We thought what was left could be resolved in "parliamentary struggles." We were also happy that the overall situation was stabilized, which was much better than expected.

What were the characteristics of the Cultural Revolution? It always made you feel that what was happening would stay that way forever. But if you really thought so, you were a complete fool. The Cultural Revolution was in fact characterized by constant changes and struggles. You went up, I went down; You lived, I died; You were happy, I was sad. My own tragedy started from there.

On February 21, 1968, I was suddenly told to attend an emergent meeting. But I was not told what kind of meeting it was, and where. We gathered at the Cadre's Club, where we got on the bus. The windows were heavily draped. We were ordered not to talk to acquaintances if we ran into any on the way. I looked around and saw a number of other buses loaded with people. Almost all leaders of revolutionary committees at various levels in the city were present. I sensed that something big was going on. We drove straight to Beijing, where we didn't stop. Instead, we headed for Changping and then back to Beijing. Finally, we arrived at the "August 1 Middle School."

Nearly all members of the Cultural Revolution Group of the Central Committee[7] attended the meeting. Premier Zhou Enlai[8] was there as well. But shortly after Jiang Qing started to speak, he left and never came back. Jiang Qing said: "I have evidence that some of you are having black meetings." This was the notorious "February 21 Speech," also known as the "Black February Incident." At that meeting, it was alleged that some people in our city were holding "black meetings" concerning art and literature with the intention of seizing power from the Cultural Revolution Group of the Central Committee, in other words, from Jiang Qing herself. The incident involved rebel groups in the field of art and literature under the Grand Unification. We had no idea what kind of meetings these were, or whether there were such meetings at all. Before we realized it, Jiang Qing declared: "The Grand Unification is an organization with serious mistakes." Following in Jiang's foot steps, Chen Boda went on to accuse ours of being a "reactionary organization." Thus the Grand Unification received a virtual death sentence.

On our way home, a leader of one of the rebel groups said to me, "How can we face our comrades when we go back? Let's rebel."

I replied, "Don't be foolish. We can't rebel now. If we do, we will be rebelling against the red regime and the Central Committee."

After we returned, we gathered leaders of all the rebel groups together. I said, "You may accuse me of being a traitor, or anything you wish. But the fact is that we are finished. From now on, I declare the Grand Unification dissolved." Without any further incident, not even a big-character poster, we disbanded, and the overall situation was stabilized.

Our opposition was surprised that such a powerful organization as the Grand Unification could be so easily subdued. Chen Boda said, "Why is it so quiet in T city? It was among the last cities to be liberated. Many landlords from other areas went there. It is a capitalist strong-hold. How can it be so quiet?" They had good reason to be surprised. The mere fact that an organization of tens of thousands of people was dissolved without a single incident was highly unusual. But we were not stupid. If we made any move, many lives would have been lost.

The Supporting the Leftist Team[9] summoned the leaders of the disbanded rebel groups to study sessions. They brought in a number of advisors to talk to us, trying to find out where everybody stood. One advisor said to me, "You must have had a tiptop advisor behind you to tell you what to do."

I replied, "Why do we need an advisor?"

He mentioned one thing: Once, before the Grand Unification was established, our opposition surrounded one of our groups inside the Industrial College. They demonstrated and shouted slogans, trying to start an armed fight. As soon as I heard about this, I went there and decided that we couldn't engage in fighting. I said that shouting slogans was a verbal attack. If we fought them physically, we would be responsible for the fighting. Instead, I sent people to surround the office of the Preparatory Committee to Seize Municipal Powers, where we also demonstrated and shouted slogans. As a result, those who surrounded the Industrial College retreated without any fighting.

He continued to say, "To tell you the truth, we have a record of everything you did. Tell me, who advised you to 'besiege Wei in order to rescue Zhao.'"[10]

I said, "No one but my own humble talent."

He said, "I don't believe you have such talent."

I told him, "It is not me who has the talent. You should read Chairman Mao's works. He taught me all the tactics of war."

Only then did I realize that they had been preparing to suppress us all along. They were, after all, experienced and shrewd.

As soon as the Cultural Revolution Group of the Central Committee turned against us, the Grand Unification was finished. All groups under it were disbanded, with the exception of the Trolley Bus Red Flag. It continued to exist because, first of all, I was still a member of the Standing Committee of the Workers' Representative Conference. Second, the elder workers at the company trusted me. They knew what kind of person I was. I used to write articles on their behalf. They remembered. However, the opposition was determined to kick me out of the Workers' Representative Conference and to disband our group at the same time.

Not long after that, rebel leaders in our faction were singled out for persecution. The man who had entered the

Municipal Revolutionary Committee was arrested and charged with "rape" on some fabricated evidence. The Workers' Representative Conference looked in my old dossier and found out that I was still under probation. They stripped me of my position, saying I was not qualified. For my part, I had been prepared for repercussions all along. I had never said anything politically wrong, or beat anybody, nor was I involved in affairs with women. There was nothing they could do to me. I returned to the factory to be a worker. Only this time I had to deal with endless investigations and testimonies. I knew almost everyone in the organization and had handled too many things. Whoever was involved in a case would ask for my testimony. I was a nobody to begin with. That didn't change when I reached the top, and it remained unchanged now that I had returned to the bottom. I believed everything about the Cultural Revolution was finally over. But I was wrong. I thought I had just returned to the bottom, but I didn't realize I was falling into an endless abyss.

One day people from the Military Control Commission of the Public Security Bureau came to visit me. They asked me about how people were beaten to death at No. 609. I told them what I saw that day, such as how the person on the bulldozer died. They took notes and left. I thought that was all. Two days later, three people came and asked me to go with them. I said I needed to use the restroom first. They sent one person with me. I thus knew something was very wrong. I accompanied them out of the factory and to a building used for the court. I was led to a small room behind the reception room. They told me, "We are pre-trial judges of the court and detectives from the Public Security Bureau. Let's study 'The Three Essays'[ll] together."

I replied: "I have already memorized 'The Three Essays.' I don't need to study them anymore. Just tell me what you want from me."

"There is something else that you didn't say about No. 609," they told me.

I gave them a firm answer: "There is nothing more." They kept me there for about a week, and then one day I was taken to another place where I was locked in a big room. It was a jail. I didn't know why I was there. I tried to remember every detail about No. 609. There was nothing new. I could only wait for them to tell me.

At one o'clock that night, four people came into my cell, including an army representative with a Shandong accent. It was the first time I had ever seen him. He was tall and looked fierce. He sat down in front of me. A secretary sat beside me, taking notes. The other two stood behind me. I felt something was about to happen, so I hurried to tie my shoe laces. I practiced *kung fu* and played basketball before, so I knew how to get prepared. The two people behind me asked what I was doing. I said my feet felt cold.

The army representative questioned me about No. 609. I have good memory, so I recounted every detail I knew. He asked about the back gate. I said I was never there, and that I only went to the front and side gates. He asked me again whether I went to the back gate or not. I said absolutely not. He became furious, saying, "You are not honest. I will make you change your answer."

I said, "No matter how I change, I must stick to the truth."

He struck the table hard and yelled, "You son of a bitch."

I raised my head and shouted back, "*You* son of a bitch. What right do you have to scold me?"

The man behind me then punched me in the neck. I reacted quickly. Without leaving my seat, I kicked him to the floor. The army representative jumped on me and grabbed my hair. It took all my strength to push him away. He fell on the ground, together with the table and a fist full of my hair. I realized I could not escape, so I must struggle as much as I could. I grabbed a stool and threw it at the secretary who was running towards the corner of the room. The army representative came back and shoved the table against my legs to block me. As the other two people pushed me down on the floor, he kicked me in the mouth. My mouth filled with blood and my teeth became loose. They beat me as hard as they could. I couldn't move, and I didn't intend to. I just lay there and let them beat me. After a long time, they stopped.

"Are you done yet?" I asked.

The army representative said, "How dare you start a fight."

I replied: "You hit me first. I don't even know your name. Why should I hit you?"

"OK, let me tell you," he said. "My name is XXX. I am the leading representative of the Military Control Commission."

"Let me also tell you," I said. "First of all, I didn't commit any crime. Secondly, I still have the rights of a citizen. If you hit me again, I will fight back. Even if you tie me up, I will still bite you with my teeth." When I said that, I realized my teeth were now as loose as piano keys.

The went away and came back the next day to say: "You didn't tell the truth. You were responsible for the death of a man, not the one on the bulldozer. That had nothing to do with you. We know it. It happened at nine o'clock that night."

The statement was ridiculous. I immediately replied, "My foot was wounded that day, and I left the place at four o'clock. There were many people who can testify for that."

"You are lying," the army representative said. He turned to the other people and told them to handcuff me.

The three men pushed me to the ground, pulled my arms behind my back, and put handcuffs on me. I couldn't move my wrists. Then, they pulled my arms together. I felt the muscles in my shoulders tightening and then tearing apart. I couldn't even sit down with the handcuffs on. Sweat fell from my forehead. I shivered so much that I could hear my teeth clicking. I yelled, "Is there no law anymore? I still have the rights of a citizen."

The army representative did not bother to answer. He kept looking at his watch. Twenty minutes later, they took the handcuffs off. But I felt as if my arms were not mine anymore.

Two days later, they announced that I was formally arrested. I was put in a jail cell near the street. At midnight I was brought to trial. The army representative told me: "From now on, the nature of your case has changed. You are a criminal suspect. And this is the court. You won't get away by refusing to admit your crime. We can convict you even without your statement."

I was furious and replied, "I can only be declared not guilty. Otherwise, you are violating the law."

"Well, we will give you some experience first," he said.

From then on, they began to starve me, a situation that lasted for two and a half years. Every morning I was given a small bowl of porridge, but it could hardly fill my stomach. Instead, it made me feel more hungry. It is much easier to get hungry when you have nothing to do than when you are busy. I began to lose weight fast. My fingernails became so soft that they could be pulled back and forth, like the soft shell of a crab. Even the hairs of my beard could cut through the fingernails. When I had to climb the stairs, I had to stop and gasp for breath every seven or eight steps. The worst thing was that, when my feet touched the ground, I felt as if all my vital organs were dropping inside my body.

Since the jail cell was right next to the street, I could hear all the noises outside and I could see my home from the window. Damn it. I wish I had been put in another room. Every morning, the aroma of hot soybean milk and fried donuts wafted into my room. Someone once asked me what it was like being in jail. I said it was like lying in a small-sized coffin. The cover of the coffin was right on my nose, and I couldn't move an inch. I didn't commit any crime. I began to feel like I would go crazy.

To come back to the story, after starving me for the first two weeks, I was brought to trial again. The army representative asked me, "How does it feel?"

I said: "Why don't you think of something else. I've already gotten used to it."

This got me into more trouble. "All right," he said. "Bring in the ropes."

This time I was tortured more ferociously. Before they tied me up, they wrapped my arms in four pieces of canvas, so that the cuts wouldn't show later. They tied my hands behind my back and pushed them all the way up almost to my ears. I could almost hear the sound of my muscles tearing apart, and the blood vessels breaking open. It was worse than having my head chopped off. I didn't recover for four months. My arms were congested so badly they had no flexibility, neither did my hands. I couldn't make a fist. I lost the strength to hold things. It was impossible to use chopsticks, and even a spoon frequently fell out of my hand.

After all these tortures, I still didn't know what crime I had committed. I was determined to hold on and find out what I was charged with. If I had to die, I needed to know the real reason first.

One day in March 1970, I was suddenly brought back to the trolley bus company and taken into the auditorium, where it was pitch dark. The windows were heavily draped. I couldn't tell whether there were people in the seats or not. The army representative and other people from the court sat behind a table on the stage. Two rectangular stage lights were directed into my eyes. It looked like judgment day.

They said, "You still have a chance to confess. It's not yet too late."

"I have nothing to confess," I replied.

"OK, turn around," they ordered.

I turned and saw a row of people. They were all my buddies from the rebel groups. The one on the left was my bodyguard. He was escorted by a policeman.

The judge ordered them to testify. After they had done so, I understood what my "crime" was.

They said that at nine o'clock on the night of the armed fighting, under my direct orders, my bodyguard had hit a man from a textile factory with an iron bar. The man's head was cut open, and he died on the spot. I had ordered them to get rid of the body and make up a story to cover up the event.

How, I thought, could they fabricate a tale like that and use it on such a formal occasion. I was furious. They testified one by one, and I retorted to them one by one.

The army representative said, "You have no right to speak." He ordered his people to handcuff me. After that, when I tried to open my mouth, the audience shouted slogans to denounce me. Only then did I know that the auditorium was full of people. Later I was told that people who attended the meeting were all Communist Party members in the company. Non party members were not allowed to participate.

I realized I was in great danger. All those who testified against me were my former buddies. And they all told the same story. If convicted, the crime was punishable by death. It looked as if they were determined to get rid of me, once and for all. I was convicted at the meeting along with my bodyguard. However, I could not understand why he had confessed to something he did not do. Why did he turn against me? Why did he opt for self-destruction?

Although I was convicted, I was not sentenced at the meeting. For that, they still needed my own statement.

The next morning, the army representative read me the meeting minutes from the previous day and asked me to sign it. They wanted to use this as my statement. I asked, "Why is there not a word of my own on the minutes?"

"Because it is not necessary," he said. "Sign it."

I took the pen and wrote on the paper: "This case is far from the truth. I won't close my eyes after I die." At the end I wrote a big character: "Wrong."

The army representative told me, "You can't write like this."

I replied, "I can't put my signature on what you have there. I am responsible only for my own words."

That afternoon I was brought to the court again. They asked me, "Do you think you can reverse the verdict?"

I said, "Yes."

"Let me tell you something," the army representative said. "It is a simple matter to give you a sentence. Right now, the Public Security Bureau, the Procuratorate, and the Court work in the same office. We can make a decision over a cup of tea. Moreover, I will denounce you and let everybody in the city know about your crime. Only then will we execute you."

I said, "I must write a will."

"That is impossible," he replied.

"You are even worse than the First Emperor Qin,"[12] I said. "You don't represent the Communist Party. I have read that all feudal emperors allowed criminals on death row to write a will. If I don't have a will, who can reverse the verdict for me after I die."

He said, "This case is ironclad. No one can reverse it." After that he tore the meeting minutes and my words to shreds.

I was so angry at this that I started to scold him: "Damn you. You have no right to tear that. It is the original evidence. You are no Communist!" Since I was going to die anyway, I had nothing to lose and scolded him more.

After that they tied me up with a big iron shackle, which weighed nearly forty pounds. Many elder inmates said they had never seen such big shackles, which were obviously too heavy for most people. I sat in my jail cell, looking at the ceiling, with no appetite at all. I was angry and furious, and felt terribly wronged. But there was nothing I could do.

An elder cellmate said to me, "Young man, you should not fight them head-on. All they want from you is a statement. If you didn't do it, just be quiet. There is no use arguing. It only makes you suffer more."

Another cellmate, who used to be a pre-trial judge in the Public Security Bureau, asked me, "Did you really not do it?"

I said: "At that time, I was never alone. My enemies tried to capture me, so I had bodyguards with me all the time. On that day, my foot was wounded at four o'clock, and I left immediately. Several people went with me. They accused me of killing the man, but that didn't happen until nine o'clock. How could I be involved? But my old buddies testified against me. They insisted that I lied about my foot injury. They tried to push the time back so that I could be linked to the man's death. But there were other people who left with me in the same vehicle, and I was treated in the company clinic. I wrote down their names, but this was thrown away. When I asked about it, they didn't bother to answer me."

My cellmate said, "You take a piece of paper and write down the whole process in detail, including all witnesses for every period of time. At the end, you should write: 'This is my testimony, forever.' After that, don't hand it to the army representative. Instead, give it to the prison guard on duty. When a guard receives materials from a prisoner, he must file them. Remember, if you really didn't do it, you must not fabricate things. Otherwise, you would have harmed not only yourself, but other people as well. The Communist Party has a policy. No matter what happens at the time, the case will be re-examined years later. You must believe this."

There was no mistaking he was a professional with a lot of experience. My life was spared because of him. Later I learned that what I wrote was indeed filed in my dossier, which may be why they didn't sentence me to death. On the court verdict, it said: "Facing irrefutable evidence, he was extremely cunning and refused to admit his crime." This could refer to the materials I wrote.

I was sentenced to life imprisonment. After that, I was moved to a jail room at the back of the prison. Although I continued to deny the charges, I gave in to my fate. Since I was imprisoned for no good reason, I lost faith in everything. I no longer believed in the law, or in myself. From then on, there seemed to be a bloody corpse sticking to my body. I couldn't get rid of it even if a layer of my skin was peeled. The prison was not a place to reason. There was no use to argue. Since I would never get out, and I had to stay in jail for the rest of my life, I had to find a new way of living. I started to play basketball, my favorite sport, with other inmates. I spent my time doing things for the prison. They did not starve me anymore. I ate and drank as I pleased. Since I was only one step away from death, I called it "living to die." I had already reached the very bottom of the world, and there was nothing more to lose. However, there was one thing I could not forget. Every now and then, I wrote a statement to remind them of my innocence. All appeals I sent out were rejected. To the prison officials, it was the court that was responsible for the verdict. Their only task was to guard the inmates. When a prisoner denied the charges, the prison officials would at most give him some "educational lessons." I had insisted on my innocence all along. As time went by, the prison officials didn't bother to pay attention to me anymore. Even "educational lessons" were dropped. All they had to do was make sure that I didn't escape.

Ten years after I was jailed, when the Cultural Revolution had already ended, I began to feel hopeful again, and regained a desire to live. However, after two successive setbacks, I lost faith again.

In 1980, my sentence was reduced from life imprisonment to twenty years. It was the result of a new policy of the Central Committee to reconsider the jail time for all prisoners with long prison terms. The "Change of Sentence" said that I was given a shorter prison term because I had "admitted to my crimes." What an irony! I had never admitted anything. Nothing they did was based on facts, not when I was convicted, not when they changed the sentence. It seemed that they could justify whatever they did. I believed there was no hope of reversing the verdict. But I wrote another appeal anyway. If I hadn't, they might have really thought I admitted to the crime.

Soon after that, in March 1980, my appeal was again rejected with the following reason: "We have received your appeal and re-examined the case. Based on the main facts of your crime, it was properly handled. Therefore we must reject your appeal."

My heart went cold again. I had twelve more years to spend in jail, which meant that I wouldn't be released until 1992. By that time, I would be nearly sixty years old.

Shortly after that, however, I was suddenly declared not guilty and released. It was really odd. Let me tell you what happened.

One day in March, two people from the court visited me in jail and told me they had to re-examine my foot injury. They asked whether there were any remnants of it.

I said, "Most men have athlete's foot, and the skin peels off all the time. After eleven years, how can there be any remnants?"

They insisted on looking anyway. I took off my shoe for them to look at my foot. There was not a trace of the injury. I realized they wouldn't be checking my foot without reason. There might be some hope of reversing the verdict. I said immediately, "Since you are interested in my foot injury, can I give you some evidence? I have saved the sock I wore on this foot that day. There is still a hole in the spot where the injury occurred."

They were surprised and said, "You still keep your socks from ten years ago?"

I told them that I had left the socks at home. Later, my family brought them to me in jail. One day after a ball game in the prison yard, a fellow inmate played a trick on me by throwing away my shoe and the sock, which left me with only one sock. It happened to be the one I wore on the injured foot that day. Since I couldn't wear only one sock, I put it in my bag, thinking I might use it some day to mend clothes.

They asked me to put the sock on. The hole was right in the spot of the injury. They drew a sketch of the position and took away the single sock. It was very clear now. If they could prove that I was indeed wounded, I would have an alibi. I became a little excited and said, "Can I ask a question?"

"Go ahead," they said.

"I feel very odd. What happened to the witness I mentioned before? He was the driver of the bulldozer whom I saved on that day. He was tall. I don't remember what he looked like because he had blood all over his face. I took him back to the trolley company and sent him to the clinic to be treated. If I hadn't saved him, he would have died for sure. He must remember me. Why did this witness never show up?"

"We met with him yesterday," they said. "He said he didn't remember you."

"That's impossible," I insisted.

They said, "Why don't you put yourself in his position. He was a captive and was horrified by the beating. He didn't know what you were going to do to him. How could he remember you? He only said one thing that could help you. He remembered being pushed onto a vehicle and being brought to a clinic of a work unit for treatment."

"What about the student who went back with me to the factory?" I asked.

They smiled. "Not one, but two students. The one you mentioned is now in Xinjiang. We went there already, and he has testified for you."

Again I asked, "There are many people in my company who can testify for me. Are they all dead?"

"After you go back to your company," they said, "you may find out yourself what everybody said at that time. Cultural Revolution cases like yours ..."

I got angry and said, "Stop it."

This surprised them. "Why?" they asked.

I said, "Don't say it is a Cultural Revolution case. I can't stand it. What is a Cultural Revolution case? What about the Movement Against Three Evils and Five Evils? Anti Capitalists? Elimination of Counterrevolutionaries? Catch Counterrevolutionaries? The Four Clean-ups? What were the two factions of the Cultural Revolution anyway? People fought and killed each other. What for? Love? Hate? Or pure murder? Although I didn't kill the man at No. 609, he died after all. Why? You go to ask the real killer. I bet he couldn't tell you the reason either. Even if you were to ask Chairman Mao, he wouldn't be able to answer your question, no matter how great he is."

They didn't know how to respond to that. Before they left, they simply said, "Take care of yourself. We will make it clear."

From that visit, I knew the verdict would be reversed. At that time, many people who were wrongly accused and imprisoned during the Cultural Revolution died or were paralyzed as a result of heart attacks when they were suddenly declared not guilty. They couldn't stand the sudden rise and fall of their destiny. There were many such cases in the prison where I stayed. Later, the authorities gained more experience. Before they released a person, they gave him some hint first, so that he would be mentally prepared.

It happened as I expected. A few days later, I was brought to the front office. People from the court and my company were already there. The judge said: "Everyone stand up." He even turned to me and said, "Don't put your hands on the desk. Stand upright!" Then he read a ruling, which was:

"XXX was involved in a murder case. On October 13, 1972, he was sentenced to life imprisonment by the Military Control Commission of the Public Security Bureau of T City. After a re-examination of the case, no evidence was found to link XXX to the death. It is hereby ruled that the original sentence be rescinded. XXX is now declared not guilty, and is to be immediately released."

After the judge finished reading, he smiled at me. The inmates who were watching outside shouted: "All right!"

The judge said to me: "Your salary will be paid to you from the day you were arrested. Due to the financial difficulties of our country, your wage scale will not be upgraded for the time being. That will be resolved later. Remember, when you go back to your work unit, you are not to start trouble with your company leaders. You can blame the Gang of Four for everything. Your company helped a great deal in re-examining your case. If there is anything you can't straighten out, come talk to us at the court. You can go now."

After that, I was asked to gather my belongings from the jail cell and go back to the trolley bus company. A car was sent from the company to meet me. I returned to the jail cell and gave all my stuff to the other inmates. Like that, I left the place that had imprisoned me for eleven years for no good reason. I tried to stay calm. I was a man and was guilty of nothing. I was forcefully brought there. I would leave on my own two feet.

When I returned to the company, my old buddies were all surprised at the changes in me. Ten years before, I was an energetic young man. Now I looked like a dying corpse. They all confessed to me what they did. It was really awkward. I told them, "Everything is past. At that time, I didn't have a chance to escape. If I had, none of you would be living now. Time has settled all the bad feelings."

Later, I found out what had happened, and I didn't really blame them anymore.

On the day I was imprisoned, all my buddies were rounded up as well. They were forced to testify against me. They were brought to a place where they could hear the screaming of the tortured. They were horrified. The army representative also brought their family members, their wives, children, and parents, to cry in front of them and beg them to make a clean break with me. They were ordered to say what they were told. In the end, they fabricated the story and were released.

A woman at the company clinic was exceptional. She had treated the wound on my foot and she insisted on testifying for me. The company leaders assigned her to a new job outside the clinic, then another one, until she was finally forced to leave the company. She went to Beijing to work at the Ministry of Forestry. When the court decided to re-examine my case, they found her in Beijing. She cried and showed them a copy of the testimony she wrote ten years before. She told them, "At that time, my mother said to me, the young man has no chance to live. But he can't die because of us. You must tell the truth. I wrote this testimony. It has been ten years now. Why didn't they accept it?" Several times I wanted to go to see her and thank her for her honesty. In those years, there were not many people who could have done as she did. Later I heard she emigrated to Macao.

My bodyguard was also down on his luck. When the army representative questioned him, he was offered a deal. If he testified against me, they said he would be released. But when I was convicted, so was he. He was sentenced to fifteen years in jail. On the day of the conviction, we were brought to jail separately. He screamed and shouted, "Damn it! You promised not to convict me, but you did. The thing never happened. It is a lie!"

The policeman who escorted him said, "Shut up! Why didn't you say it earlier!"

I don't blame him. He was as wronged as I was. We both spent eleven years in jail and were released on the same say.

I was told that after he was convicted, his father obtained a hospital report about the man who was killed. The man had not been cremated, but was buried in the ground. The father demanded that the body be unearthed and re-examined to find out whether his head was really cut open by an iron bar. But no one listened. After the Gang of Four was overthrown, the textile factory re-examined the case and concluded that the man had been shot to death by an opposition faction. The killer was from the textile factory, and the two men from the trolley bus company (i.e. me and my bodyguard) had nothing to do with it. But for a long time, these facts were ignored. No one knew why.

Much later, I learned more about the matter. Long before I was arrested, the textile factory had already identified the killer. But suddenly there was a big turn of events, and somehow I became involved. I have thought about it over and over again, and I suspect there was a conspiracy against me. Beyond this smaller conspiracy, there was a bigger one. However, I don't want to believe in a conspiracy theory because, if there really was a conspiracy, I was merely a sacrificial object.

Until I die, I do not want to admit that I was just a sacrificial object, for if I do, life could only be more meaningless.

In that era, everybody was a sacrificial object.

—AUTHOR

FOOTNOTES

1. One *jin* equals half a kilo.

2. In 1957, the CPC started another Party-wide rectification campaign against bureaucracy, sectarianism, and subjectivism.

3. A document passed by the Eleventh Plenary Session of the Eighth Central Committee of the CPC on August 8, 1966, officially known as "The Decision Concerning the Great Proletarian Cultural Revolution."

4. A "cow shed" was a room used to lock up people. It was so named because the word "cow" was listed in the beginning of a four-word phrase: cows, demons, snakes, and monsters. This derogatory phrase

was used to refer to class enemies in general during the Cultural Revolution.

5. Cultural Revolution Groups were set up at different levels, including the CPC Central Committee. Those at the local level were responsible for carrying out the policies of the Cultural Revolution.

6. Party leaders who sided with Jiang Qing and Lin Biao during the Cultural Revolution.

7. Here it refers to the second Central Cultural Revolution Group, which was established in 1966 with Chen Boda as its director. Most of its members sided with Jiang Qing, and were responsible for the extremist policies of the Cultural Revolution.

8. Zhou Enlai was the popular Premier of the State Council who is believed to have saved a large number of Party cadres from persecution.

9. Starting in 1967, the PLA was sent to various work units to "give firm support to the revolutionary left." The move was in part intended to stabilize the situation, but it had many negative consequences.

10. During the Warring States Period (475-221 B.C.), China was divided into seven separate states. When the state of Wei attacked the state of Zhao and surrounded its capital, the state of Zhao asked for help from the state of Qi. Instead of sending troops to fight the invading army of Wei, Qi's troops surrounded Wei's capital. Therefore the state of Wei had to withdraw its troops and the state of Zhao was rescued.

11. The Three Essays refer to three articles by Mao Zedong: *Serve the People, An Old Foolish Man Moves the Mountain,* and *In Memory of Norman Bethune.*

12. Emperor Qin was the first person to unify China and declare himself an emperor. He was known to be a ruthless ruler.

A Man
Without a Story

沒有情節的人

MALE, *age 28 in*

1966

SCIENTIFIC
RESEARCHER *at a*
science academy in
S City

M Y life has been largely uneventful, without many ups and downs. As a writer, you probably prefer stories with complicated plots, but my story has almost no plot at all. However, I believe it may still be appealing to you. That's why I decided to contact you. The fact that my life has been uneventful was the result of my careful design. It is like some novels or movies that are intentionally made without suspenseful plots. But for a person to come through the turbulent Cultural Revolution without a heartbreaking experience was by no means easy. It took clear-headed and careful planning to achieve that. Let me tell you how I did it.

I was born to a poor peasant family, and was therefore well treated after Liberation. I went to high school and college on a government stipend. Naturally I became a member of the Communist Youth League. I felt I was living a perfect life, one full of happiness and joy. Intellectuals like myself were political favorites bound for fast promotion. Therefore we were not prepared for the upcoming political changes. I lived a relaxed and careless life, with little or no self discipline.

Bad luck first struck me in 1957 when a new policy of the Communist Party called on the people to "speak out freely and air views fully." With abandon, I followed the instruction of the Party and said things that other people would not dare to say. As a result, I was immediately removed from my position as director of the school newspaper, became the target for criticism and struggle, and was forced to undergo self-criticism. I was accused of having forgotten my class roots, of becoming a degenerate, and of airing "Rightist" views. Fortunately my head teacher was a good man. He insisted that I could be redeemed through education, which prevented the authorities from officially designating me a "Rightist," although at school I was treated as one, and the Communist Youth League gave me a "serious warning." For me, it was like thunder out of the blue sky. As if hit by a big club, I collapsed in one blow.

As a result of what happened in 1957, many people of my generation found that their characters had more or less been twisted. Those who were originally talkative and optimistic now became taciturn and cunning. It was a big change. I regarded myself as one of the few who had maintained a sober mind, knowing that I was no longer a political favorite. Even so, I wanted to do something meaningful, and so I started to look for a way in which I could achieve this goal. If it were just for myself, I would have easily given up my ideal by drifting with the tide. However, I was not a selfish man, and I wanted to make contributions to my country.

After 1957, I was sent to the countryside for a short time to be re-educated through physical labor. Being the son of a peasant, farm work was nothing new, and so it was no big deal for me to toil in the field. However, I was not allowed to read professional books. Once I was caught reading an English-language book and was accused of being a "white expert," who wanted to learn a foreign language so as to take the capitalist road. Several times I was criticized for that. But how could I waste time by sleeping late and shooting the breeze, as most other people did. I wondered what I should do in that situation. It turned out that the more I was criticized, the more clear-headed I became. A sudden inspiration told me to buy a set of the English edition of "Selected Works of Mao Zedong." When the Brigade Party Secretary saw me reading this, he asked, "How can you be reading this capitalist stuff again?" I replied, "Look, this is not capitalism. This is the English edition of Chairman Mao's works." This answer left the Party secretary speechless. After all, he could not forbid me to read Chairman Mao's works. Because of this small victory, I decided to buy the English editions of all Marx's and Lenin's works, as well as *Beijing Review*[1] and *China Reconstructs*,[2] so as to practice my English. This victory also taught me how to make the best of a dire situation. One can survive in the crack of a stone, if one can find the opening.

After a period of time in the countryside, I returned to college to continue my study. I was a major in Botany. One of my teachers had studied herbicides in the United States. His knowledge had freed farmers from manual weeding. I was greatly motivated by this. Growing up in the countryside, I knew all too well the hardships of the primitive farming methods used by many generations of my ancestors. I was determined to devote myself to research on and the production of herbicides, so as to free Chinese farmers from the hardships of manual labor. But China's ecological situation—its soil, weather, and the types of weeds—is vastly different from those of foreign countries. To produce suitable herbicides demands a large amount of scientific research. It might take me my whole life-time to succeed. But I was not going to change my heart.

After graduation I was assigned to the Academy of Agricultural Science. By then I had gone through the "Movement of Four Clean-ups" and the early stages of the Cultural Revolution. I realized that there was not a single place in China where I could focus on scientific study. People every-where were obsessed with political struggles. There were too many petty politicians bent on persecuting and fighting each other. One day you might be a victor, and the next day you might be the victim. It seemed that people were intoxicated with political fighting. If I wanted to achieve my lifetime goal, I had to find a perfect way to do it, as I had done a few years before in the countryside through practicing English by reading Chairman Mao's works.

I made a thorough analysis of myself. I had a good class background, which would prevent me from becoming the main target of persecution. On the other hand, I had made mistakes, which meant that I could no longer be a political favorite. I was right in-between the two extremes, a situation I decided to turn to my advantage. I couldn't have a career if I was the main target of persecution. Neither could I accomplish anything if I was a political favorite. Moreover, I was blessed with two personal advantages. First, I specialized in Botany, which meant that I could lose myself in the countryside without getting involved in the political struggles of the city; second, I was born in the countryside, so rural life was no hardship for me. Having made up my mind to return to the countryside, I wrote a proposal to my work unit, stating that I was willing to go to the front-line of agricultural production, stake root in the countryside, so as to combine scientific research with the practice of production. In the meantime, I said, I could be re-educated by the poor and middle peasants, and remold my ideology. All these were popular jargon terms at the time. Since I appeared to be sincere, my proposal was quickly approved by the academy.

Thus, for more than a dozen years that followed, I stayed in the countryside and visited nearly all the villages in the vicinity of S City. The 250 plus kinds of weeds there seemed to be growing in my heart. I developed herbicides at the Botanical Research Station and tried them out in the field. Once successful, we could start mass production.

The Cultural Revolution at that time was still going on. Occasionally I would be asked to go back to the academy to participate in meetings and factional fighting. Whenever I got such a notice from the academy, I asked the commune or county leaders to request a leave on my behalf. I had a good relationship with the villagers, who had greatly benefited from the herbicides with which I experimented. They were therefore quite willing to ask the academy for permission to let me stay. I intentionally kept a tight schedule, tilling experimental fields and conducting on-site instruction sessions. Whenever the academy called on me to go back to participate in political struggles, the village cadres shouted into the phone, "We poor and middle peasants need him right now. We can't let him go." Thus I was excused.

I worked diligently and cautiously. Every day I kept a record of the day's work. In ten years I filled ten big volumes with notes, the purpose of which was to be prepared in case I was ever questioned. There was one time when the academy conducted a political inspection campaign and sent a group of investigators to check on my work performance. The county leaders told them that I was doing extremely well by showing a complete willingness to be re-educated by the poor and middle peasants, fearing no hardship, fighting selfish behaviors, and studying Chairman Mao's works every day. The rural cadres knew they had to make such exaggerated statements in order to get the investigators off my back. In addition, they showed the investigators several volumes of my work notes. Thus the investigators could find no fault with me and soon left. In this way, I successfully stayed away from the political movement and focused on scientific research. For me, the countryside was a big political umbrella. Without its protection, I wouldn't have been able to accomplish anything. At the same time, I had to work twice as hard to keep the umbrella, so that it would always be there for me. But I had no complaints about working hard. After all, that was exactly what I wanted to do. Don't you agree this was a perfect situation?

Time is limited. I could hardly afford any setbacks in my life and career, and had to know how to protect myself. During most of the Cultural Revolution, I was able to maintain a sober mind. But I knew I would sooner or later get myself into trouble if I never showed up at political study sessions. Therefore I chose to attend some important meetings, such as the ones that took place whenever a new Central Committee document or Chairman Mao's "Newest Instructions" were to be studied. I had to make absolutely correct judgment on which meetings to attend, which to avoid. Every time I returned to the city, I would visit some colleagues who were friendly with me, to be briefed on the current situation. It was important to understand the big political picture. Otherwise one could get into trouble even when one stayed away from it. The most important thing was to keep a distance in political debates. When I had to write a big-character poster to show my stand, I would not mention anybody's name. I pretended to be a simpleton on personnel matters. If I was asked to expose somebody's problems, I would say, "I'm not close to that person, and I don't know any problems to tell you." During the factional fighting, I was asked by one faction to join their side. But I told them, "I'm not a clear-headed person. If I join you, I may not be of any help to you, and I might ruin things for your team." Thus I was excused.

I tried to act like a nobody. When I attended meetings, I always sat in the far corner of the room, never talking to people. I learned not to look into other people's eyes, for if I did, I would have caught some attention. I wanted to be ignored and forgotten. As a result, all my colleagues regarded me as a timid simpleton with no political importance, which was the perfect result of my careful design. I achieved what Zheng Banqiao, the famous Qing dynasty painter, advocated: Be content to be a simpleton! Of course, I was not really a simpleton, but I had to pretend to be one.

There were many people who appeared shrewd and energetic, and who tried to show off during political movements. But in the history of China's political struggles, such people could only triumph for a short time. After they climbed to the top, they became the target of the next struggle. As soon as there was a change in the political climate, they were destined to be toppled, and the most powerful tool their enemies could use was political accusation. If a person was politically persecuted, it would take several years to recover. Life is short. Such persecution could completely ruin a person's life and career if it happened a few times.

Despite my soberness and caution, I was almost caught up in trouble in 1975. One day the head of the Municipal Agricultural Office suddenly declared that the proletarian method of farming was to turn the soil deeply. This was the method advocated by activists of studying Chairman Mao's works. He said, however, that some people had countered this method with a Western bourgeois method, telling farmers not to weed and till. He called that lazy farming and ordered people to find out who was behind this. As I said earlier, sometimes trouble got to you even when you tried to stay away from it. It turned out that I was the one they were looking for. I was so scared I couldn't sleep for a few nights, waiting for the worst to happen. Fortunately the county leaders explained that the herbicides had been produced by the working class. They had helped rid the fields of weeds, which was why the peasants didn't have to weed manually. As a result, they said, the output in the fields had become much higher and the poor and middle peasants had welcomed this new method. The municipal leaders sent people to investigate, and they found out that the herbicides were truly effective. Thus the case was dropped. This was the only time in ten years that I nearly got myself into big trouble. But it was a close call.

Today many people tell me that I have been the luckiest scientist, one who avoided persecution and whose career was not interrupted during the Cultural Revolution. That is the opinion of the outsiders. I have a different view of myself. In 1979, when science was finally given enough attention in China, I got a chance to go abroad, and I was appalled to find out how far we had lagged behind the Western countries. Over 80 percent of our population are peasants, but only a small number of people are engaged in agricultural scientific research. Primitive farming methods are still dominant in many areas, where peasants still rely on nature and experience to do farming. In Western countries, farmers account for only 3 to 5 percent of the total population. The rest of the people can be engaged in scientific research, arts, and education.

From my own professional point of view, China has about 1.6 billion *mu*³ of cultivated land area, which could increase to 2.1 billion if double cropping in some areas were used. Every year each farmer has to spend three work days hoeing up weeds for each *mu* of cultivated land, which adds up to 6 billion work days spent on manual weeding by Chinese farmers each year. If each work day is worth a minimum of five yuan, the total cost amounts to 18 billion yuan, which is an astronomical sum. As an agricultural scientist, I feel guilty about this huge waste of wealth.

However, few scientists went through the Cultural Revolution without being persecuted. Except for a small number of those engaged in national defense projects, almost all of them were the targets of condemnation. After the Cultural Revolution, some of them gave up their careers; others found it impossible to make up for the lost time due to the lack of access to new information. I have to admit that I was among the lucky ones. But that was by no means a favor from the god of destiny. Instead, it was the result of my carefully designed way of life due to the political lessons I learned in the 1950s. Although I did not fall victim to the Cultural Revolution, and could even be counted as a "success story," the mere fact that a scientist like myself, who wanted to devote his talent to his country, was forced to twist his character in order to survive was a tragedy itself. I had to pretend to be a silly and inept simpleton, and make other people look down upon and be disinterested in me. Every day I tried to lose myself among the masses of people, even wishing I could hide in my own shadow.

If you write a novel without a plot, all it lacks is suspense and a climax. But to actually live a life without a plot is boring and depressing. Sometimes I couldn't even feel my own existence, as if I had been digested by some powerful being. It is true that I have had a successful career, but I had to pay a dear price for it. Have you ever experienced losing yourself? If you have, you will understand my heartfelt bitterness. Unfortunately my only choice was to lose myself in the crowd if I wanted to do something meaningful. Otherwise I would have been dragged into the political movement and become a sacrificial victim of politics. Of course it would have been more tragic if I had not made any contributions to the society and the country. Why did I have to put myself in such a miserable position in order to be understood, and to contribute to the country? Today I have a strange feeling about the "country." Sometimes I feel it is a specific and holy existence. At other times I see it as an empty and brutal force. Once I had a rather absurd feeling that the country was cut into small pieces and held in the hands of many people. Do you also feel that there is a distance between you and the country? Why?

In feudal times, the dictator of the state was the state itself.
—*AUTHOR*

FOOTNOTES

1. *Beijing Review* is a weekly news magazine published in five different languages, including English.

2. *China Reconstructs* is a monthly magazine published in over a dozen languages, including English. It was re-named *China Today* in 1990.

3. One *mu* equals 0.1647 acres.

Two Women of No. 63

VICTIM ONE

FEMALE, *age 48 in* 1968

HOUSEWIFE *in* K City

VICTIM TWO

FEMALE, *age 54 in* 1968

MIDDLE SCHOOL TEACHER *in* K City

D URING the Campaign to Clean-up Class Ranks in 1968, a Nazi style illegal prison was set up at a notorious factory in a big city of North China. It was called No. 63. There, many intellectuals and cadres underwent inhumane persecutions. Ten years after that, when the Gang of Four was overthrown, it was publicly denounced. An exhibition was held to expose the unspeakable cruelties that occurred in the prison and its clandestine organization. Today all the remnants of the prison have disappeared. When I interviewed some of its survivors, I found it hard to believe that these things happened there only a dozen years ago. How could China, a nation with 5,000 years of civilization, suddenly become so crazy and savage? As the survivors recounted their experiences, they were obviously still suffering from the terror of their experiences. The wounds on their souls were still bleeding.

Before I recount in detail the stories of two women, I want to briefly relate what other survivors have said about No. 63, so that readers can have an overall knowledge of the notorious facility.

A: "It was originally the instrument and meter plant of our factory, and was later turned into a warehouse. It was a big 200-square-meter room, like a theater. In spring of 1968, the Special Investigation Team (SIT) began to use it as a "cow shed" to lock up people. They brought in plasterers and carpenters to partition the large room into many smaller rooms of six or seven square meters each. The windows were all nailed shut, and glass windows were painted over to prevent view. Rooms on the outside were surrounded with iron bars. Those on the inside were left only with a tiny hole in the door, about the size of a coin, which was used as an observation hole."

B: "Why was it called No. 63? Because its phone extension was 63."

C: "No. 63 had strict rules. People were not allowed to address each other by name. The inmates could only be called 'this one' or 'that one.' They had to lower their heads while walking, and could not look sideways. I was imprisoned there for more than a year, but never knew that many of my colleagues were imprisoned there as well. Even today no one knows exactly who was locked in the room at the south end. Among the prisoners were an engineer and his wife. More than a year after the engineer died, the wife was still asking people to send matches to him because she thought he was still alive."

A: "The guards at No. 63 worked three shifts, seven or eight people to a shift, about thirty in all. During its existence, over one hundred people were imprisoned there. There were two major groups of prisoners. One was called the Petofi Club.[1] It was composed of engineers and technical experts. The other group was called the Third Party, and was made up of Party members and cadres. This group was called the Third Party because the accused were no longer considered members of the Communist Party, nor were they members of

Kuomintang,[2] the Nationalist Party. For the most part, they were arrested on fabricated charges made up by some members of the Revolutionary Committee, who wanted to get rid of their enemies within the Party. People in both of these groups were the most brutally tortured."

C: "I have seen many movies about the fascist concentration camps in Europe. I must say that No. 63 was even worse than those. Some of the torture methods here wouldn't be found in concentration camps. For example, one of the means of torture was to force a prisoner to lie on his stomach while a guard scrubbed his feet with an iron brush. If the person couldn't stand the pain and itch, he would actively move his arms and legs in a manner that looked like a duck swimming on the land. This torture was therefore named 'A Duck Swims on the Land.' In another torture, a prisoner was forced to sit on a burning cigarette. This was named 'Smoking Anus.'

"Among the prisoners was a senior engineer, a boiler expert. He was the only one who was crippled but managed to survive. He has been hospitalized ever since he was released. We had arranged for you to interview him, but the doctor would not allow it. All his fingers were nailed through, and most of his ribs were broken."

D: "Since I have a good class background, I was tortured for only a short time before I was asked to deliver food to the prisoners, clean up the feces and urine, and work the night shift. Every morning I put a bucket in the corridor for all the prisoners to use as a toilet. As soon as a prisoner started to urinate, however, a guard shouted 'time up.' Only two minutes were allowed for a bowel movement. No. 63 was full of bedbugs. Once a prisoner couldn't sleep because of this. I offered to help him catch bugs and we caught more than one hundred in a few minutes. However, one of the rules at No. 63 was not to kill bedbugs. They were natural tools for punishing prisoners."

C: "There was a young man who was terribly wronged. He was a worker. The reason he was brought to No. 63 was that he had an argument with the chairman of the Revolutionary Committee over the allotment of an apartment. The man had a bad temper. The guards threw him under the bed after a good beating. But he still would not budge, so they tied him to a chair with iron wires until the wires cut deep into his skin. Today people can still see the cuts on his legs. But that was not all. The guards struck his penis with wooden sticks until it bled. He has never been a normal man since. It is a shame that a worker could be treated so mercilessly, let alone the intellectuals."

A: "They tortured the prisoners whenever they wanted to. For twenty-four hours a day, beatings never stopped. Sometimes the screaming of the tortured was so loud that the guards were afraid it might be heard outside. So they played loud music on an old-style gramophone to cover the noise. The music was always the same song by Tie Mei from the opera *The Red Lantern*.[3] Whenever Tie Mei sang, those of us inside knew someone was being tortured. Today the model plays from the Cultural Revolution seem to be popular again. When I hear them, I still seem to hear the prisoners screaming."

C: "They asked electricians to change the power voltage from 220 V to 24 V because they feared some prisoners might commit suicide by touching the electrical wires. The light bulbs were covered up with iron wires. There was nothing in any room that could be used for suicide. However, if people really want to die, they will find a way. There was a man who made a living by fishing in the East Sea before Liberation.[4] He was accused of being a pirate and was brutally tortured. One day he picked up a big nail from the ground and used the brick that supported his bed to nail it into his own head."

D: "A seventy-year-old engineer was thrown into the freezing cold outside his jail room for a whole day and night. He fell into a coma. Later the guards put on white outfits and entered his room claiming to be doctors sent to treat him. They raised him in the air, spun him around fast, and told him that was what it felt like to take an airplane. "Isn't it nice to take an airplane?" they asked. After that, they put him on the floor for a 'massage,' trampling across his back with their feet.

"On another occasion the guards forced other prisoners to beat the engineer. They called this 'black against black.' I saw one of his arms hanging down, like it was broken. Later he became mentally disordered. His room had the awful smell of feces and urine. When the guards asked me to give him a bath, I saw scabs all over his body and found that his arm had been dislocated. No one bothered to send for a doctor. He died with the dislocated arm."

A: "The news about No. 63 was completely hidden from the outside. Those who were released did not dare to say a word for fear of being brought back there for more torture. Outsiders tried to stay away from it. There was a man who one day happened to stop to tie his shoelaces near No. 63, and was subsequently suspected of spying. The guards took him in and gave him a good beating. In our factory of two thousand workers, No. 63 was a mystery, a hell.

"There was a time when No. 63 got overcrowded. The guards needed additional space to lock up more people. So the authorities decided to set up a branch in a smaller warehouse. They brought in plasterers to partition the new facility into small rooms, the size of a full-size bed. Six rooms were partitioned on one side of the warehouse, and eight on the other. Later they saw the plasterers whisper to each other as they were working. The authorities became afraid that things might get out of control. Therefore this facility was never used for a prison after its completion."

Eventually, the news that people were tortured to death at No. 63 reached Beijing. On June 24, 1970, Chen Boda and the chairman of the Municipal Revolutionary Committee came to the factory to inspect the progress of "grasping revolution and promoting production."[5] As soon as the government officials left, the prisoners at No. 63 were released, one after another. Later the whole building was torn down on the excuse of needing reconstruction.

For two and a half years, numerous innocent people were tortured at No. 63. Even after the facility was demolished, the ghost of it continued to haunt. For a long time afterwards, those who were responsible for the crimes there went unpunished. They continued to be factory leaders. Some were even promoted. The building was actually torn down to get rid of the evidence of their crimes. It was not until after the Cultural Revolution that the victims were rehabilitated, and the chief instigators were arrested and convicted. However, the court of the law could only punish the guilty. It could never heal the wounds of the victims.

I drew this conclusion from my interviews with the two women of this chapter. One of them was the wife of a victim, the other was a survivor of No. 63. As they told their stories of twenty years ago, their hearts were still raging with anger.

BETWEEN LIFE AND DEATH

DON'T WORRY. I can handle it. After going through those horrible things, it should be easy to merely speak about it. Since I knew you were coming, I started to clear up my head and prepare for the interview yesterday. I thought about it for a whole night, but I'm losing track now, so I might be a little incoherent... No, my heart is pounding fast again.

My grandfather was Zheng Xiaoxu. He was the teacher of Pu Yi,[6] the last emperor, as you saw in the movie. Grandpa was with the emperor most of the time. He seldom tended to family matters. In a family like ours, children were not told of important things. When I was asked about my grandparents during the Cultural Revolution, I didn't know anything about them to tell.

My husband, Lao Liu, was a mechanical engineer. He had been doing technical work ever since he graduated from the Mechanical Department of Northern University (renamed Tianjin University after Liberation). He didn't have a good class background either. His father, Liu Guanxiong, was the navy commander during the Qing Dynasty, an old bureaucrat. For these reasons, we were destined to be the target of persecution.

During the Campaign of the Four Clean-ups, Lao Liu was arrested, but only for a short time. Then the Cultural Revolution started. We were caught completely unprepared. One day, the Red Guards from Lao Liu's factory came to our home, many carrying pickaxes. They dug into the floor as well as the steps outside the house. They even searched through the ceiling and cut open the sofa, looking for weapons. We had an old bed, in which there were two holes. No one ever thought about how the holes might have gotten there. The Red Guards, however, insisted they were bullet holes and asked me to hand over the gun and bullets. I was horrified. I didn't know what had happened to Lao Liu. When he came back that evening, our home was a mess. He tried to comfort me by saying: "Don't worry. Many homes have been searched." I calmed down a little bit. I had been a housewife my whole life. Lao Liu and I grew up together. Our two families had been friends for generations. We got married when I was twenty-two, and I had followed him ever since. I felt safe when he was with me.

The next day the Red Guards came for another ransacking. We lived in the "New Village," as did most of the other engineers. They gathered all of us outside and paraded us through the streets. They put dustpans and woks on our necks and forced us to say: "We are monsters and demons." They also brought the Party secretary to join us. They made a big red umbrella with our names on it and forced the Party secretary to carry it. The implication was that we were the monsters and demons protected by him under his red umbrella. All this happened so suddenly that we were completely overwhelmed. We walked in the street in great humiliation.

Our home was ransacked five times. They took everything in the drawers, including things that we had kept for many years, such as Lao Liu's books, technical materials, and diary. Lao Liu loved photography, and we had a lot of photos at home. After their ransacking, our home was scattered with torn pictures. Kids from the homes of families that were not ransacked gathered outside to watch. After that, we were kicked out of the "New Village." A cart was sent to take our things. We were only allowed to bring daily necessities, such as kitchen utensils, a quilt, a table, and chairs, but not our mirror, which they said was a "demon detector." We were brought to a simple building surrounded by water. But the local residents refused to let us "dirty monsters and demons" stay. They got us off the cart, only to publicly denounce us. After they were done, we were put back on the cart and taken to a deserted building, called the "trash building." There, we lived in a small ten-square-meter room.

Every day we were interrogated by people from the factory. They went to Lao Liu's elder brother's home in T City and found an old uniform worn by his father, when he was a navy commander, and some photos of Qing Dynasty officers. These were used as evidence that Lao Liu "attempted to restore the reactionary rule." How absurd it was. Even if Lao Liu had attempted to restore the old rule, how could he do so in a Qing Dynasty uniform in the 1960s? They also forced me to write to Pu Yi to ask for old photos, which they could use as evidence of our attempt to restore the feudal dynasty. Fortunately Pu Yi replied that he didn't have any. Otherwise it could have been worse.

We were totally numb and couldn't see any way out. Not long afterwards, however, they told us that our problems had been cleared. They even returned Lao Liu's watch. We were a little relaxed, but only for a few days. Then they came back again, accusing Lao Liu of organizing the Petofi Club.

I didn't know who Petofi was. I told them it sounded like a foreign name, and that we had never seen him in our home. I was later told that it was a counterrevolutionary organization, one attempting a military coup. I felt my heart almost jump out of my body.

Lao Liu and I came to the factory before Liberation. At that time, it was almost a deserted place. Technical experts like Lao Liu worked with high salaries. There was not much to spend the money on, so we often gathered together to have parties. Lao Liu was a very hospitable man. He liked photography, ice skating, and tennis. I enjoyed singing Peking Opera. We didn't have children, and our house was spacious. Almost all engineers who lived in the "New Village" would gather in our home. This went on until the start of the Campaign of the Four Clean-ups. After that, no one was in any mood to party. Among the residents at the "New Village" was a man who many years ago was a member of a youth organization of the Kuomintang. When the Cultural Revolution started, he became quite scared. To save himself from trouble, he wrote a big-character poster, accusing us of organizing the Petofi Club. All of the people he named ended up being persecuted.

Lao Liu was scared. He was a timid man to begin with. He kept crying until his eyeballs nearly popped out. I had always looked to him for confidence, but now I had to comfort him. I said: "We are like animals. After we are beaten, we will stand up again. All we did was to have parties together. We did nothing wrong. What is there to be afraid of?"

In my heart, though, I was more afraid than he was. I could tell things were different from the time our home was ransacked. The first time they attacked randomly with a big stick, but without a specific target. Only those with bad luck got into trouble. This time they had chosen their targets.

Those on their list could not escape. How I wished someone would come in and shoot us dead right then and there.

July 3rd was a very hot day. That evening Lao Liu and I were sitting outside to get cool. As soon as we returned home, a group of people came in. They ordered us to sit across the lane and not talk to each other. I was terrified by the noise of their hitting and breaking things in our home. Then they asked Lao Liu to go with them.

Suddenly Lao Liu grabbed my hand and cried. I felt his tears on my hand. Yet he tried not to make me feel worse, saying, "Don't worry. We don't have a big problem. I'll come back when everything is cleared. You should have confidence in the policy of the Party."

I had a folding fan in my hand, on which I had handwritten Chairman Mao's poem "Ode to Plum." Lao Liu said, "Why don't you give it to me."

It was very odd for him to ask me for the fan. Later I understood that he then knew he would not come back. When I gave him the fan, he shook my hand vigorously. I did not know that we were to part forever.

After he was taken away, I was left puzzled. Those people asked: "What are you going to do?"

"I don't know," I said.

"Why don't you come with us. You can help him with washing and cleaning. You can also stay close to him," they said.

I decided that if I went with them, I could stay with Lao Liu and know of his well being. I believed that they invited me to go with them out of good will and had no idea that this was a trap. They wanted to force me to confess and use that against Lao Liu. I sat in the back of their vehicle and entered the factory. I was brought to a huge building. This was No. 63. They pushed me into a small room and locked the door. I saw a pile of straw and broken quilts on the floor. Then I suddenly realized that I was in a prison. That night they came to interrogate me. They asked me to hand over evidence of our counterrevolutionary activities. Since I had no evidence to give them, they beat me up. For two and a half years, they gave me brutal beatings. My hair was pulled out in clumps. I hid the hair under the quilt and hoped that some day I might get out and sue them. After the Gang of Four was overthrown, I was asked to take the stage to denounce them. A high ranking leader encouraged me to say whatever I wanted to. I spoke for more than an hour, my heart pounding fast.

In the beginning, I was asked to admit that we made transmitters, had underground meetings, and read reactionary pledges. They placed three bottles of urine and one bucket of feces in front of me. When I didn't admit what they wanted, they poured the urine and feces into my mouth. They fabricated all kinds of things, such as tales that we displayed the Kuomintang flag during our underground meetings. They tried to force me to write this down. When I refused, they tortured and scolded me even more. Never before had I heard such dirty words as they used.

I was only allowed to sleep after midnight, and was woken up at five. There was an interrogation and beating every day. The torture was deadly. Once, three men pushed me to the ground and kicked me all over my body. Blood came out of my nose. They used a piece of paper, on which I had copied Chairman Mao's "Newest Instruction," to block the blood. My mouth was so swollen that I couldn't eat for many days. Every time I was tortured, I believed I would die.

They had many ways to torture people. Sometimes I was made to carry a pile of iron chains and run around a chair. I was not allowed to stop until I passed out. There were two young men who were particularly ferocious. They held me up in the air, one of them holding my head, the other holding my feet, and twisted me. It was so painful I felt all my bones must have broken. I couldn't help screaming. They played loud music to cover the noise.

Of course I couldn't admit to the charges. If I did, they would use that against Lao Liu, who would definitely die. I would rather die myself than have Lao Liu tortured to death.

Another torture was starvation. Several times I was not given any food for a couple days. I was so hungry that I chewed like an animal on the straw under the quilt. I swallowed the straw. Later, I often hid some leftovers, such as half a bun, under my quilt in preparation for the next starvation. The food often went bad, and I had diarrhea as a result.

After a period of time, I learned not to fight them head-on, but to talk nonsense.

They asked, "Whom did you play cards with at the club."

I answered, "With Chiang Kai-shek and Madame Chiang."[7]

They asked, "What did you save the old uniform for?"

I answered, "I put it on every day to commemorate the Kuomintang."

After I began to talk such nonsense, I was tortured more severely. One day they told me, "Today is your execution day." They covered me with a cotton coat and put me on a jeep. Then they drove around for more than an hour. Actually, they were only driving around in the back of the factory. When they finally stopped, I was pushed out of the jeep and taken into a room. There were several rows of people there, some in army uniform.

They asked me, "Where is your transmitter?'

I said, "I threw it into the river."

They asked, "Where did you get the design of the transmitter?"

I said, "I bought it at the Xinhua Bookstore."

When they heard this nonsense, three men hit me with sticks, another with the back of a knife. There was a man there who had not beaten me before. I thought he was sympathetic to me. But this time he beat me too, and more ferociously than the others. After that, they hung me up for more beatings.

The next day, one of them came into my room and said, "If you really don't have the transmitter, the question will be cleared sooner or later. Your legs look so swollen, and I know some medicine. Let me help you. But don't let anybody know about it."

I wondered how he could suddenly become so nice, and I didn't know how to thank him. However, his treating my legs was only an excuse. He wanted to rape me. I screamed for help, but to no avail. I fought with all my strength... After that, I really wanted to die. Life could only be more miserable if I lived.

A woman worker who worked night shifts said that I should not think about death. I thought of Lao Liu again. If I died, how could he live when he got out? I wish I had known then that he had committed suicide three months after he got to the jail. He couldn't stand the torture and broke his own head with bricks that were used to support his bed. I remember seeing him through the crack in my door shortly after I was locked up. I saw him being pushed by two people. I thought he was still alive. We were both in No. 63, but he had no idea that I was also there, and I didn't know that he had died long ago. Had I known he was dead, I would not have lived to stand the tortures.

One day in the spring of 1971, they suddenly told me, "Your husband alienated himself from the people by committing suicide on September 28, 1968..." They said other things, but I heard only one sentence: "You must make a clean break with him." I felt totally numb. I didn't cry. Later they came back and asked me to put in writing that I would sever all relationships with him. I burst out crying and called for Lao Liu.

My mind was in chaos, and I couldn't control myself. One moment, I felt the news was not true, and that Lao Liu was still alive. I thought that he had confessed and been released. Some day he would come on a bicycle to meet me. I wouldn't mind if we had to wander around the rest of our lives like beggars. The next moment, I felt the news was true and went out of control. I cried and cried, calling Lao Liu's name, as if he were in front of me. The guards said that I must be haunted by a ghost.

As a result, they told me, "Our factory is a production unit. We can't let you stay here forever, at such a high cost..." Then they kicked me out. I was determined not to return to the small room at the trash building. Every little thing there would drive me crazy. So they put me up in another place, and had two women workers take turns looking after me. They were afraid I might commit suicide. I learned afterwards that there was an investigation into No. 63. They feared that I would add one more name to the list of the dead.

When Lao Liu died, the crematorium refused to take his body. The guards at No. 63 burned his body with firewood. The remains were locked in a simple wooden box. One day, they came to me with a white bag and said, "He deserved it." I opened the bag and put the box on the floor. It was Lao Liu. I fell on the floor, yelling, "Help..."

From then on, I made a big cloth wrapper and put it on the bed. I put Lao Liu's clothes and hat on it. He was Lao Liu! Every day I stayed home to accompany him. He was there to accompany me too. When I ate, I put a pair of chopsticks in front of him. He just stayed there, never moving, never saying a word. I didn't need him to speak. As long as he was there, it was fine...

Later my stepdaughter came home. Other folks asked me to get rid of the wrapper, for fear that it might scare my daughter. I moved it to another place.

My stepdaughter settled in the countryside in Inner Mongolia at the start of the Cultural Revolution. Her fate was not much better than mine. Her birth father was a childhood friend of Lao Liu's. Lao Liu and I had no children. We adopted her when she was forty days old. Her birth father's name was Zhu Wenhu. He was an electronic engineer at Lao Liu's factory. Because he often came to our home, he was imprisoned in No. 63 as the number two man of the Petofi Club. He had a bad temper and was therefore tortured more ferociously than most of the others. Several times, he was forced to sit on burning cigarettes so that he couldn't have a bowel movement. Three of his ribs were broken, and he died in the hospital. After his death, the hospital was forced to provide false testimony that he died of heart failure. There was an X-ray photo of his chest showing a broken rib. They changed the name on the photo for fear that someone would look into the matter later.

My stepdaughter lost both of her fathers, her birth father and her stepfather, to No. 63. I lost Lao Liu. Until today, I still don't know why I have lived. Tell me, why am I still living in this world?

Death is an empty blank with many question marks.

—AUTHOR

ETERNAL MEMORY

I AM "THE WOMAN WHO SENT MONEY TO THE DEAD," whom you heard of. All my misfortune is highlighted in that phrase. I may look very calm to you now, but this phrase is an abyss for me. As soon as it comes into my mind, I fall to its deepest bottom.

My husband died at No. 63 on December 27, 1969. I never went to No. 63. I learned about it later. Several engineers died there. But if you knew Lao Qian, my husband, you would know he was no troublemaker. He was in charge of material supply at the factory for twenty years. He never took even a small thing from there. Why then should they take his life by hanging and beating him to death?

Lao Qian and I grew up together. He was a bad-tempered, but honest and hard-working person. We lived a simple life, but maintained our integrity. He was a minor cadre for many years, but never a leader of any sort. I was an ordinary teacher. We have five children. Most of our income was spent on their education. They all went to college. When the Red Guards ransacked people's homes during the Cultural Revolution, we were among the poorest families in the factory. Not a single valuable thing could be found in our home. Half of our suitcases were empty. We only had 100 yuan in our bank account. The only thing they could find that might be out of ordinary was a dining knife, which they displayed at an exhibit as a dagger and evidence of Lao Qian's guilt.

Lao Qian was accused of participating in the Petofi Club at Engineer Liu's home. If you believed what the accusers said, you might believe that there was indeed an underground organization at Engineer Liu's home. But how was that possible? I went there often myself.

Shortly after Liberation, this place was like a swamp. The two visionary leaders of the factory, Fan Xudong and Hou Debang, tried to recruit as many qualified people as possible. They sought all the top graduates from Yenching, Fudan, and Nankai Universities. They also hired many technical experts to whom they gave high salaries. For a time, the factory was crowded with talented people. Premier Zhou Enlai called it a "basket of talent." All these people took residence in the "New Village," which was made up of several rows of new houses. At that time, there was no recreational place to go after work. Yet intellectuals need some kind of spiritual satisfaction. Engineer Liu and his wife loved to entertain people. They were very hospitable, and their home was spacious. Therefore, the co-workers often gathered at their home to sing songs and play cards. There was no gambling. We remembered each other's birthdays with potluck parties at Liu's home. We had good relations with one another.

Lao Qian and I did not live in the "New Village," but in a place called the "Triangular Area." Lao Qian loved Peking

Opera and he was a good *huqin*[8] player. I liked to sing Peking Opera, so did Engineer Liu and his wife. We often sang together. It was that simple.

Most of the intellectuals did not have good class backgrounds, and they were watched from early on. I remember once seeing a representative of the neighborhood committee peeking into Liu's home from the top of a tree when we had a party there. At the time, I thought he just wanted to have some fun himself.

My youngest son loved the radio, and there was always antennas on top of our house. One day, the neighborhood committee and the police came on the excuse of checking out the electrical wires. Later, when the case of the Petofi Club was made public, they became intent on finding an enemy transceiver. They wanted to find it, and then go to Beijing to tell the news to Chairman Mao himself. It was not until then that I realized we had been watched all along. I was horrified just thinking about it. My son-in-law brought some electrical parts and ear phones back from the Korean War. They had been left behind by American GIs. Fortunately, my youngest son took all of them with him when he went to study in Xinjiang. Otherwise they would have been used as undeniable evidence that the transceiver was in our home, and we would all have died.

At the start of the Campaign to Clean-up the Class Ranks, Lao Qian was questioned about this matter. But he was not locked up in a cow shed, and was allowed to come home every day. One day he didn't come home. I waited till midnight, and then became really worried. I went out into the dark to look for him, but to no avail. At one o'clock, a group of people from the factory broke open the door and ransacked our home. I asked: "Why is Lao Qian not back?" They replied, "He won't be back for a while." From that night on, I never saw Lao Qian again. When he left home in the morning, everything was normal. There was no need for any heartbreaking farewell. But that was the end of everything. How could it happen so easily?

From then on, there was almost no news of him. The only thing I was told was that he was very thin and pale, and that he was made to sweep the courtyard with a big broom.

This, in fact, was totally false. He was locked in No. 63 and tortured. If he had been sweeping the courtyard, that would have been much better. I was a high school teacher and had a work unit, so they didn't lock me up. Engineer Liu's wife didn't have a job, so she was locked up and underwent unspeakable tortures. She was locked in the same place as her husband, but she didn't know that her husband had died until two years later.

At the time, I felt more optimistic about Lao Qian, and with good reason. They stopped paying salaries to other people who were arrested, but Lao Qian's salary was paid as usual. At first, they even allowed me to send stuff to him. I often sent him cigarettes, toothpaste, soap, cookies, and clothes. Every month I went to the factory to get his salary, and I would take out 40 yuan and send it to him. But they never allowed me to go to see him in No. 63. Everything I sent to him was directed through the SIT. I wondered why he was the only one whose salary was not stopped. The only logical reason seemed to be that his case was not as serious as the others. Some day, I thought, he would come home safely. This was my hope and fantasy.

More than a year had passed. One day after Spring Festival in 1970, when I went to school, a teacher asked me, "Do you have any news of Lao Qian?"

"No," I said.

He lowered his voice and rather mysteriously said, "I heard that Lao Qian died."

"That's impossible," I replied. "Why would they keep paying his salary if he died? Why wouldn't they tell me? I received his salary a few days ago. And I sent him money too."

How stupid I was! I didn't believe it when I was told of his death. Actually he had died several months before. But I had good reasons not to believe he had died. After the conversation at the school, people from No. 63 came to my home asking for more money and clothes. They said the money I sent was not enough. I even gave them a new cotton-padded jacket to bring to Lao Qian. As usual, I went to get his salary every month and sent part of it to Lao Qian through the SIT. Each time they took the money without hesitation. I would have had some doubts if they had showed any sign of hesitation. How could they be so cold-hearted and cheat a helpless woman like that? Can you imagine what they were thinking of when they took the money from me?

Another four months passed, and No. 63 started to release people. But those who came out tried to stay to themselves and not to speak to others. Once I saw Engineer Liu's wife on the street. She walked along the foot of the wall and seemed to be afraid of seeing people. She looked absentminded. I dared not speak to her for fear that it might give her more trouble. I could only wait. Now that they released Engineer Liu's wife, I thought, Lao Qian would come out soon.

At the end of June, representatives from the factory and my school came to my home. They looked calm, but nervous. After sitting for a while, they told me that Lao Qian had died.

"When?" I asked, still not believing it had happened.

"December 17, 1969," they said.

I tried to stay calm, and asked, "How did he die?"

They would not answer that, but told me, "Your husband died. But his problem is not cleared yet. At this time, he can't be rehabilitated. We will treat it as a death on the job. Since everyone in your family has a job, and there are no children anymore to support, you won't receive any compensation. His salary will be stopped from today. That's all."

I said, "That's very strange. We grew up together. Our two families have been friends for several generations. He started working immediately after graduation from college. That's all his experience. What question could you have about him that can't be cleared. Also, how did he die? What made you decide to treat it as a death on the job?" But they would say no more.

Until today, I still don't understand why I didn't scream and yell at the news. That's what I should have done. Poor Lao Qian, you died six months ago, but I didn't know it. Why didn't you come into my dreams and let me know? Can you be playing tricks on me, and trying to land me a sudden and deadly blow, like they did?

After that, an army propaganda team[9] moved into the factory. An old friend of my son-in-law's happened to be a member of it. He broke into No. 63 and found out what really happened. Lao Qian was tied up by his wrists and ankles. They raised him in the air by tying the ropes to the four corners of the room. After giving him a good beating, the guards went out to have a drink. They got drunk and completely forgot about Lao Qian. When they came back again, all his limbs were twisted and contracted. They took him down, only to find he was already dead. This is what they called "death on the job."

Even in feudal society, setting up a clandestine tribunal was forbidden. A county magistrate would be removed from office if a suspect was beaten to death in court. How could they hang Lao Qian up and beat him to death? How could they not tell me about it for over half a year? How could they come to my home to ask for money and clothes after Lao Qian was dead? I brought the case to the city officials, and to Beijing, but no matter where I went, I got the same answer: "The question is too complicated to be resolved."

After the Gang of Four was overthrown, and the wrongful cases of No. 63 were rehabilitated, I finally understood that the questions were made "complicated" at the top. Today the chief instigators and murderers have been arrested, but how can we ever know what tortures Lao Qian went through, and who else was there to beat him to death? The Cultural Revolution is over, leaving many families broken and many people dead. All the wrong doings have been attributed to the Gang of Four. People are smiling at each other again, as if nothing happened. Where can you now find those people who tortured others? You can only hope that they still have some conscience. But I have not yet heard of anyone who suddenly found his conscience and confessed to the victims.

We found Lao Qian's ashes in an urn after searching in several places. At the time, it was handled with no care. Even the people who handled it forgot where they put it. Now we have the ashes in a good urn, and have placed it in a funeral home. Every year, during the Qingming Festival[10] and December 17, the day he died, our whole family goes there to pay respect. On January 16 of the lunar calendar, which is his birthday, I go there alone. We never burn mourning paper. We just go to see him. He didn't get happiness in the human world, where else can he get it?

You see, I am very calm now.

But once at a banquet, an abalone and chicken soup was served. I immediately took two bowls and said, "This was Lao Qian's favorite when he was alive. He asked me to have one more bowl on his behalf." People immediately became quiet. No one said a word to comfort me. They knew there was no use. They could only say, "All right, all right..."

Another time, I was walking by West Lake in Hangzhou. I suddenly thought of him and missed him dearly. I don't know why I should think of him in such a beautiful place. From then on, I have tried to avoid going to beautiful places...

There is never an end to the result of evil.

—*Author*

FOOTNOTES

1. Petofi was a Hungarian poet who is well-known in China. The term "Petofi Club" was first coined by Mao Zedong in 1966. It referred to underground organizations aiming at sabotaging the Communist Party.

2. The Kuomintang, or the Nationalist Party, was founded by Dr. Sun Yat-sen and later headed by Chiang Kai-shek. It was engaged in civil war with the Communist Party for many years before it was defeated in 1949 and retreated to Taiwan. After 1949, the Kuomintang was regarded as the arch enemy of the people in China.

3. *The Red Lantern* was one of the eight model plays during the Cultural Revolution. Tie Mei was the heroine of the opera.

4. In 1949, the Communist Party defeated the Nationalist Party and established the People's Republic of China. Therefore the pre-1949 years were referred to as before Liberation, and the post-1949 years as after Liberation.

5. "Grasping revolution and promoting production" was one of the popular political phrases used during the Cultural Revolution.

6. Pu Yi, the last emperor of China, was featured in *The Last Emperor,* a movie by the Italian film maker Bernardo Bertolucci.

7. Chiang Kai-shek was the leader of the Nationalist Party and was regarded, after 1949, as the arch enemy of the people in China.

8. *Huqin* is a two-stringed musical instrument that accompanies the Peking Opera.

9. The PLA were stationed in various work units to help stabilize the situation.

10. The Qingming Festival, on April 5th, is a traditional Chinese festival to pay respect to the dead.

The Cultural Revolution Lasted 2,000 Years

文革兩千年

MALE, *age 41 in* 1966

***EDITOR** at a publishing house in T City*

You may want to write about a person's ten years in the Cultural Revolution, but I need to tell you about my experience of fifty years. Don't worry, I will keep to the subject. You got to understand, my friend, that my Cultural Revolution started fifty years ago.

If you knew all the ups and downs I experienced during the past five decades, you would also come to the conclusion that the Cultural Revolution started long before 1966. In fact, one might say that the Cultural Revolution has been going on in our country for 2,000 years!

Let me give you my reasons for saying so, along with my experience.

For several decades, I could not fully understand what was happening to me. I took part in the revolution fifty years ago, only to be treated as a counterrevolutionary much of the time. Never did I get out of the circle labeled the "enemy." I never understood why until 1968, when I was tortured and locked up in a single room near the H River as a "special agent" by the Storm and Thunder rebel group. The building used to be the warehouse of our publishing house. All the books had been sent to the paper mill to be recycled. They were now considered part of the Four Olds. The empty little room was saturated with the aroma of old paper, old floorboards, and old bricks. The window was sealed and pasted over with newspaper. At night, I could clearly hear the gentle flow of water in the H River and the occasional sound of people rowing boats there. I couldn't help thinking of my far away hometown by the side of the Hutuo River. I thought of the thatched cottages that turned all green in spring time. I grew up by that river, and often bathed in it. When I first joined in the revolution during the Anti-Japanese War, we crossed the river every day to fight the enemy. For many years, my life was occupied by only two things: revolution and the enemy. I was part of the revolution, but the enemy eventually turned out to be myself. As I recalled the years of my life, I suddenly felt the pain from the torture disappearing from my body. Instead, it turned inward and condensed in my heart... I don't know how it happened, but I suddenly understood everything. It was as if the clouds finally melted, and the mist dispersed. Some people say that such a sudden awakening results in an ultimate freedom. But I must say it is just the opposite. Awakening can only add to the pain.

There are two clans in our village, one with the surname of Wang, the other with the surname of Li, like myself. The two clans have been fighting from the earliest times. Never has there been reconciliation between them. In my memory, there were three massive battles, all of which were bloody. One of my uncles was crippled during the fighting, and has since been called Li, the Lame Man. When I was a small child, my grandmother told me that during the early Qing Dynasty, one of the Wang's passed the imperial examination at the provincial level, which made him a *Ju Ren*, the highest official imaginable among the villagers. It was a big deal, as if a dragon had been born to the village. The new status of *Ju Ren* made the man a big bully. When he walked in the village, he always had his arms crossed in front of his chest, with a sorghum stalk in his hand. Whenever he ran into someone from the Li family, he beat up that person with the stalk.

The key position in the village was the village head. Whoever occupied that position can overpower anyone from the other clan. And the Wang's have always lorded it over the Li's. It was so during the rule of the Japanese invaders, and it remained unchanged when the victorious Eighth Route Army[1] took over. From the strife in this small village, you can trace the evolution of history and find the roots of the Cultural Revolution. But I didn't understand this at that time.

Our village was in an old liberated area and a famous anti-Japanese revolutionary base in central Hebei Province. After the July 7th Incident,[2] people's morale in fighting the Japanese was very high. At the time, I was a fourteen-year-old student, and my feeling for the Communist Party was deep and pure. I literally believed in every word the Party said. When Lu Zhengcao's[3] army arrived, I was too excited to sleep at night. If an Eighth Route Army soldier happened to look at me, I would feel happy for days. I loved reading and writing, and I was a good speech-maker. Therefore, I was made head of the Children's Corps. Every night we went from household to household to help the adults read the *Textbook for the People*. We also propagated anti-Japanese ideas and the policies of the Communist Party. Even adults were touched by my enthusiasm.

At that time, the village launched a campaign against smoking and alcohol. Wall posters were seen everywhere criticizing those who smoked and drank, especially the cadres. These were early forms of what we call today big-character posters, or one of the "Four Greats"[4] during the Cultural Revolution. The village head had a liking for smoking, drinking, and gambling. I wrote a little essay about this, only a few sentences. It was meant to be a good-willed criticism. It went like this:

"Some people speak against smoking, but they smoke pack after pack themselves; Some people speak against drinking, but they drink bottle after bottle themselves. How can they do this?"

It was a mild and childish piece. Don't forget I was only a fourteen-year-old kid. Before I put it up on the wall, however, I lost it on the way to school. The paper was picked up by the security picket in the village, who was also a member of the Wang family. He turned it over to the village head, and it became evidence that I was a "special agent." The village head said that since he represented the Communist Party, whoever opposed him was against the Party, and whoever went against the Party was a special agent for the Kuomintang. The security picket proposed that I be buried alive. The incident was reported to the district. At that time, there was a cook in the district who happened to be a member of our Li family. He pleaded with the district chief, saying I was only a kid and was just making a nuisance. The district interfered, and my life was spared. But the village still made a case of it and secretly labeled me a "suspected special agent," which has followed me as the first page of my dossier ever since. Even the Hutuo River couldn't wash away that "historical problem." It started me on a treacherous journey of misery for half a century.

You may not understand how a fourteen-year-old could be labeled an enemy because of just a few words. But the reason was simple: They could not put up with the fact that I, a member of the Li family, was head of the Children's Corps. As a result, I was dismissed from the position. Politics became quite ugly against such a backdrop. I had an uncle who attended a teacher's college for one year before the July 7th Incident. Because of his education, he was active in village affairs. When the Communists took over, he was afraid to get in touch with the Party for fear of making trouble. As a result, the village cadres in the Wang family declared him a "Kuomintang agent," a label that put the whole Li clan in a submissive position. Because of my uncle, every member of the Li family became a suspect.

In order to get out of this treacherous situation, my elder brother married the daughter of a security official in the county and moved to another village. I didn't stay much longer either. After finishing primary school, I went to a junior high school in Anping County. I thought I had left all my troubles behind, but I didn't know that I had brought with me a political black spot that was not going to be erased.

After graduating from high school in Anping County, I became a teacher at a village school. At that time, I was only sixteen and had no idea that my dossier was following me like the shadow of a ghost. All the villagers appreciated the good job I did, and I felt good about myself. So I decided to apply for Communist Party membership. I was determined to follow the Party and participate in the revolution for the rest of my life. I asked the village head: "Is there a Party branch (*zhi bu*) in our village?" He didn't answer my question directly, but joked with a pun: "There is not a weaver (*zhi bu*) in our village." In the beginning, I thought he was just treating me as a kid, and was not serious about my inquiry. Later I found myself being transferred from village to village, without any reason. It was as if I had tuberculosis. Everyone tried to stay away from me.

In 1942 the Japanese invaders launched a vicious mop-up operation against the revolutionary base. The county government arranged secret shelters for all my colleagues, except me. I had to go back to my home village to hide. One day someone found a reactionary slogan on the snow-covered ground in the village. Without even asking me, the village cadres from the Wang family recorded this in my dossier, one more evidence that I was a suspected special agent. Although I didn't know this at that time, I clearly felt that I was being pushed out the door of revolution. However, I still regarded myself a revolutionary and was determined to devote myself to revolution. I couldn't resign myself to doing nothing in the village, which was now occupied by the enemy, so I decided to join the Eighth Route Army. Fortunately all the village cadres from the Wang family were in hiding at the height of the Japanese operation. A member of the Li family, the cook who saved me from being buried alive, had been elected village head. He wrote my recommendation letter, which I sewed inside my shoes. After innumerable hardships, I finally found the Eighth Route Army. Before I did, however, I came close to being caught by the enemy ten times. Somehow I managed to escape or was protected by local villagers. One time, I was captured by the Japanese soldiers. But because one of my eyes is strabismus, the villagers told the soldiers: "This cross-eyed man is an idiot." Thus the enemy was fooled and I was saved. When I finally found the Eighth Route Army, it was as if I had found my own mother. The feeling was really good.

I started as a secretary for the Political Department of the Eighth Division of the Central Hebei Military Region. There, I enjoyed a short period of joy and happiness. I was surrounded by trust, care, and love. When I developed a high fever, the comrades took turns looking after me day and night. Every hand, rough or smooth, touched my forehead, and my eyes brimmed with tears. For the first time, I enjoyed revolutionary love, which is truly better than maternal love! Since I liked to write, I wrote all sorts of articles—short stories, poems, plays, news reports—for the *Central Hebei Herald* and *Front-line News*. I can't claim that they were exceptionally good, but they reflected my true feelings. During that time, I became acquainted with such famous writers as Sun Li, Yuan Qianli, and Wang Lin, all of whom helped me to become a good writer. The Political Department even sent me to the front-line as a war correspondent. For a time, my reports were printed in the *Front-line News* every day. Because my byline often appeared in that paper, I gained a lot of fame. I again decided to apply for Party membership. Leaders of the Political Department were happy about this.

However, it turned out to be a stupid decision. I had been treated well because my dossier had not yet been transferred to the army. But after I applied to join the Party, the Political Department sent people to my village to investigate my background, and they found my dossier. As a result, the clouds of suspicion came back to haunt me. Not only was my application left in limbo, I was not sent to the front-line anymore, although war correspondents were needed to cover the battles in Bozhen Township and Qinxian County. One day, the director of the Political Department came to my room, and, in a rather casual manner, said: "We are now engaged in fierce battles against the enemy. Some special agents have entered our political headquarters to spy for the enemy." I was quite surprised and said: "How can that be possible?" When I said this, he fixed his eyes on me to observe my reaction. Fortunately I did not know that I was a suspect myself. Otherwise my reaction would have been awkward, even though I was not a special agent. And, in such a case, they would certainly believe that I was a special agent and arrest me. Later I found out that Central Hebei and Shandong Province were the two experimental regions of Kang Sheng's[5] Anti-Special Agent Campaign. During that campaign, anyone suspected of being a special agent would be arrested immediately. It was also fortunate that the director of the Political Department had gone through the Long March.[6] He had experienced most of the political campaigns before, such as Yan'an Rectification, the Rescue Movement, and the AB Clique, and knew that many people had been wrongfully accused. When he saw my reaction, he walked out of my room without saying another word. However, I was quietly put under surveillance. From then on, whatever I said or did went into my dossier. It was not until 1949, when I was interrogated by the military court, that I realized how dangerous a position I was in at the time.

Intuitively, however, I could feel that trust had disappeared from the eyes of the comrades. I couldn't ask anyone about it, or plead my case. If I did, I would be suspected even more. Gradually I became quite sensitive. They suspected me, and I suspected them at the same time. I couldn't tell if their attitude towards me was real or not. That was the beginning of the insomnia that I have suffered ever since. The short and beautiful period of joy and happiness I had enjoyed had now passed.

One year later, I suffered lung disease, and was hospitalized in the Peace Hospital of the Central Hebei Military Region. In the beginning, everything was normal—not in a physical sense, but in terms of the political environment. Soon afterwards, however, it was clear that people were trying to stay away from me. I couldn't find anyone willing to play chess with me. When the Chinese New Year came, I was allowed to go home and visit my family. Another soldier, who used to be my student, went with me. On our way home, he didn't say a single word to me. When we were finally about to part, he very hesitantly said to me: "I figure that you are a nice person. There is something I want to tell you. But you should not tell anyone about it." I promised not to. He said, "Do you remember Teacher Zhang who taught with you at the same time? He was a special agent and has committed suicide."

I was completely taken by surprise. "How could he be a special agent?" I asked. "His father died in a Japanese bombing. He was loyal to the revolution and was an honest man. I remember there was a village cadre who had affairs with many women and embezzled public grain. Zhang was the only one who dared to criticize the cadre in a wall poster."

"That was why he was made a suspect of special agent," said the student. "He was first kicked out of the school, and then became a worker at a drug plant. Later, the Army launched a campaign to dig out special agents. They studied his dossier and found out he was a suspected special agent. He was given a good beating. Afterwards he hanged himself. It is said that your name was also in his dossier, and that you had conducted activities as a special agent with him."

I asked, "What activities?"

He said he didn't know.

I was terrorized, and tried to remember what the two of us had done. I could only think of one thing. When Teacher Zhang wrote the wall poster, he ran out of ink. He came to borrow ink from me. The next day, the security picket of the village also came to borrow ink from me. I was a little surprised about it at the time. Now I understood that he was looking for evidence. How scary it was!

The student then asked, "There was someone from the Military Region who talked with you about a month ago, right?"

I said, "Yes. He was a special representative, a nice person. He asked about my family background, and was very concerned about my health too. What's wrong?"

The student said, "He was not a special representative, but a detective from the Security Department of the Military Region. At present, there is an internal movement against special agents. When the old cases were re-examined, your name was found in Teacher Zhang's dossier. Originally, they had planned to arrest you in the hospital that day. But after talking with you, they found that you didn't look like a special agent. At that time, I was working in the Security Section of the hospital. When I heard about it, I was really worried about you. They could have arrested you right then and there."

Although it was winter, it was not very cold. Yet I trembled so much that I could hear my teeth clicking. But after the severe fear left me, I became fearless. I wanted to dig out all the accusations that had stuck to my back for so many years. I wanted to stand naked in front of the Party and have every one of my cells examined to show them I was a real revolutionary. Then, after this surge of emotion, I realized I was completely lost. There was no way I could prove my innocence. It was as if I had been grasped by a big iron fist, and was helplessly manipulated.

Not long after that, the War of Liberation[7] started. Our troops moved to Baiyangdian, where *Front-line News* was headquartered. Since the newspaper was short handed and I was an old author, the director wanted to have me on staff. I was quite excited about this. I was asked to go to the Organizational Department and go through the formalities, which again resulted in trouble. Not only was I not allowed to work at *Front-line News*, but I was sent to the Party Rectification Class at the Military and Political Cadres School. Despite its name, not everyone in the class was a Party member. However, everyone was there because of some sort of historical problem. I was still naive about this, though. I thought that I would only need to answer a few questions, and my problems would be cleared, as in the classical Peking Opera play, *Joint Trial by Three Courts*. But what actually took place at the school was far from expected. People in the class were asked to struggle against each other. When one person was criticized, everybody but that person was told about the alleged wrong-doings. Since people vied to show their loyalty to the Party, they struggled against each other ferociously. One night, I was on sentry duty along with a young soldier. I said to him, "Can you tell me what I did wrong? I am really wronged. I have always been loyal to the revolution. Why am I treated as an enemy all the time?"

The young man was from the countryside and looked honest. He figured that I was an honest man too, and so he asked me, "Did you write a reactionary slogan on the snow ground of your home village during the Japanese mop-up operation? When you worked at the Political Department of the Eighth Division, did you tell a security officer that you wanted the Kuomintang plane to throw a bomb? Also, when you wrote to your wife, did you tell her that Fu Zuoyi's[8] troops had planned a surprise attack on Hejian? People wonder how you could know the enemy's plans before hand." Besides this, he told me many more things about the accusations against me.

I shuddered at what he said, and felt powerless to prove my innocence. Most of the accusations were based on distorted facts, so distorted that my original purpose was completely misinterpreted. Take the bombing by Kuomintang planes for example. Once I was on a business trip with a security officer at the Eighth Division, and he said to me, "Xiao Li, you are a good writer. How do you obtain all the materials that we can't find?" As he was speaking, there was a Kuomintang plane flying above us. So I used the plane as an example and said, "Look at the plane above us. You don't need to write about this because it is not worth reporting. However, if the plane bombs the village ahead, you can write about that." I was talking about the value of news reporting. But when it was recorded in my dossier, I was accused of hoping for the bombing by an enemy plane. As for the surprise attack by Fu Zuoyi's troops, it was passed on to the soldiers by Division Headquarters, in order to get everyone prepared. But they insisted that I had obtained the information from the enemy. Even worse, they had censored my letters to my wife. If I were truly an enemy, they would never have been able to collect so much detailed information against me. During the Cultural Revolution, a rebel asked me, "Do you know how many materials you have in your dossier? They would fill more than a cart." I could not understand why they spent so much time and energy investigating a loyal revolutionary like myself. I decided to do something extraordinary. The next day, the instructor of the Party Rectification Team came to talk to me again. I couldn't stand his pressure, so I rushed out of the door and attempted to jump into the river. I was stopped. The instructor got furious. He immediately organized a school-wide meeting to denounce me. A day later, I was escorted to the military court as an "active special agent." They forced me to provide evidence that I was a special agent. I said, I could only prove that I was a revolutionary. If they insisted that I was a special agent, they would need to provide the evidence, which they didn't bother to do. Instead, they put me in shackles. It was the first time I was ever handcuffed. Forty-seven days later, the country was liberated. When I heard this news, I was quite excited. But looking at the shackles on my hands and the iron bars on the wall, I felt a flavor of bitterness. Whenever I am reminded that I greeted the national liberation in shackles, I can't suppress my dejected feeling. It puts my heart in a dark shadow.

My experience has proven that when people speak favorably of you, it isn't worth anything, because no one puts this in your dossier. If you are accused of, or simply suspected of, having done something wrong, however, it is most likely written in your dossier. Once something gets into your dossier, it is never taken out and follows you throughout your life. Can you guarantee you are a good guy in your dossier? You know you are honest and loyal to your country and your work. You think that you have nothing to hide, and that you are guileless. But in your dossier, you may appear to be a completely different person, one with smirches all over. When it comes to others making a judgment about you, you will be viewed and treated according to what your dossier says.

The military court sent people to all the villages, schools, and troops I had been in. No one could provide definite evidence to show that I was a special agent. Fortunately, in my home village, the old cadres had been replaced. Although the new cadres were still from the Wang family, they had no direct conflicts with me. When they talked to the investigators, they didn't add new accusations. In the end, the military court released me with an ambiguous verdict, saying that I would be "judged according to future behavior. If you behave well, your problems can be cleared. Otherwise you must still carry the mental burden." I entered the New China with the burden of an unclear personal history.

In the first few years after Liberation, I was in several work units. Because of my uncleared historical records, I was never put in important positions, which didn't matter much to me. All I was asking for was the right to work hard, and not make mistakes.

In 1955, while working in a publishing house in B City, I was put in charge of an editorial department, with the vague title of "Person in Charge." Yet I was enthusiastic about the assignment. Then, suddenly, the Campaign to Root out Counterrevolutionaries[9] started. My old problems once again surfaced. I was severely criticized and underwent endless interrogations. For me, it was yet another ferocious struggle. Although I suffered a great deal during this campaign, the positive side of it was that my old problems were finally cleared. My work unit sent four or five people to all parts of the country, such as Yunnan, Guizhou, and Sichuan, even Inner Mongolia and Xinjiang, to investigate my case. They interviewed nearly all my former colleagues, and re-examined the matters I was once involved in. I must thank the Party Committee of Anping County. They said: "During the Movement to Suppress Counterrevolutionaries,[10] we investigated the whole county and had a complete list of special agents. He was not on the list." It was only one sentence, but it cleared up all the clouds that had been hanging over me for years. I was finally vindicated and received a new verdict, which said: "After investigation, the case of XXX as a suspected special agent must be dropped."

I was first made an enemy of the people in 1939 when I joined in the Children's Corps. It was not until 1956 that the accusation was finally dropped. No one asked about my long and sorrowful seventeen years of bitterness. Only I knew how I got over it. On the day I was declared innocent, I stood on stage and couldn't stop trembling. When I went home, I didn't celebrate it with drinking. Nor did I shed any tears. It was as if I had been given a second life. I couldn't recognize myself.

Now please allow me to say something superstitious: I believe in fate.

What is fate? Fate is something that you can't control, but that controls you mercilessly all the time.

To me, good fortune is like a bird. It never stays above my head for too long. This is the characteristic of my fate.

The Party general secretary of our work unit wanted to promote one of his protégés. Only I was an obstacle because of my professional ability and my position. He therefore tried to push me out. It happened that one of my former leaders was planning to set up a new publishing house in T City. I asked to be transferred to the new place. Since I was willingly vacating the position for the Party secretary, my application was quickly approved. For the first time, I went to a new work place with a clear personal history in my dossier. However, in less than one month after working at T City, the Party Rectification Movement started. It was 1957.

One day, I received a letter from my former work unit in B City, written in the name of the Party branch of the editorial department I used to work in. In all sincerity, they invited me to go back and help them rectify my case. Since it was hard to refuse the request of a Party branch, I went back and spoke for two hours at the meeting. I talked about how I was wronged during the Campaign to Root out Counterrevolutionaries, and I made a few criticisms on the Party general secretary, who also attended the meeting but didn't say a word. I could see that his countenance was clouded. But I didn't know that the two-hour talk would put me back on the same disastrous road I had previously traveled for another twenty years.

After talking at the meeting, I went back to T City. Soon after, the Anti-Rightist Movement started with a vengeance. I was again asked to return to my old work unit, this time in the name of the General Party Branch. As soon as I arrived, I was declared a "Rightist," and the Party branch of the editorial department was declared an "Anti-Party branch." Among the fifty or so editors in the publishing house, twenty-five were labeled "Rightists." They were all accused of "opening fire on the Party" for their criticisms on the Party general secretary.

Later I found out that the Party general secretary and the Party branch secretary belonged to antagonizing factions. During the Rectification Movement, the Party branch secretary wanted to get rid of the Party general secretary. Because of my sufferings during the Campaign to Root out Counter-revolutionaries, the Party branch secretary believed I was still holding a grudge against the Party general secretary and decided to use me as a pawn in his fight against his enemy. When the Anti-Rightist Movement started, however, I became an instant victim when the Party general secretary regained the upper hand. Isn't there a resemblance between this and the struggles between the Wang and Li families in my home village? To use today's terms, it is called a historical, or cultural odd cycle. Although I was not sure when the cycle started, I could clearly feel its existence. And I have fallen into the cycle time after time. This was the second time.

Looking back, it was by no means a matter of rejoicing when I came to T City in a relaxed mood. In fact, I was once again embraced by the dark shadow of fate. Only I didn't feel it at first. When my dossier was transferred to T City, something even worse had been added to it. Before that, I was only "suspected" of being a special agent. This time I was unmistakably a "Rightist." Before I even had a chance to enjoy my cleared status, I turned from one type of enemy into another. The only difference was the name.

Now let me return to the Cultural Revolution.

I had only myself to blame for my bad luck during the Cultural Revolution. I was an old "Rightist," a dead tiger. No matter who was struggled against, I was put in a minor role. I was not the major target. When the Cultural Revolution started, the Party secretary intended to get rid of the director. Since I had been working closely with the director from the beginning, I was used as evidence that the director had "put a Rightist in an important position." The purpose of denouncing me was to kick out the director. Later, when the Campaign Against Capitalist Reactionary Line started, the director gained the upper hand and the Party secretary became the target of struggle. As a result, I was no longer struggled against, nor was I given any important thing to do. I was left alone to myself. Still later, there was a campaign to Clean-up Class Ranks. The Party secretary staged a comeback, and the director once again was struggled against. Since I did not take part in the director's faction, I was again left alone. At that time, there were two types of "monsters and demons." The more serious ones were locked up in "cow sheds." The less serious ones were allowed to go home every day. I belonged to the second type and was rather fortunate considering the situation.

In our publishing house there was a female editor, who was professionally very good. Her ex-husband was a Kuomintang army officer. Due to political reasons, she was labeled a "special agent," although she didn't do anything she was accused of. During the campaign to Clean-up Class Ranks, she became the major target of struggle, the purpose of which was to justify the charges against the director. Under the director's big red umbrella, it was alleged, all bad elements were protected.

I should have stayed away from someone labeled a "special agent." But one day when I got off work, she was sweeping the courtyard as I walked by. When she saw that I was alone, she gave me a piece of paper. I took it home and read it. She wanted me to send a message to her son-in-law, asking him to tell her younger brother to hand over the draft of a big-character poster she had written at the beginning of the Cultural Revolution to the Special Investigation Team of the publishing house. I figured that she didn't want to involve her family. Therefore I became sympathetic and did as she requested. To my surprise, she later confessed that she did this because she couldn't stand the torture. I became an "active counterrevolutionary" immediately, because I had delivered a message for a special agent, and so I was locked up in a "cow shed." Every day, I was tortured with unspeakable cruelty. They used sticks to squeeze my fingers. They hung me up and beat me until my ears started bleeding. Even today I still can't get my arms back into their normal position. I was forced to say that I saw a transmitter and cipher code at her home. The woman editor later tore up her bed sheet and hanged herself. Even though she died, I was still forced to say that she had a transmitter. I could not understand why they insisted on making a fabrication sound like a real thing. Once they asked me to admit that I was a special agent who got away with it during the Campaign to Root out Counterrevolutionaries, and that the woman editor and I belonged to the same clique of special agents, the head of which was the director. I suddenly understood that the purpose of torturing me was to get evidence against the director. It was like the earlier days when the Party secretary was the target of struggle. At that time, a non-Party member was asked to strip the Party secretary of his Party membership!

Ten years after I was cleared of the "special agent" label, I was once again made a "special agent." For the third time, I fell into the historical odd cycle and became a victim of factional fighting. Only occasionally did I manage to get out of it, but almost before I even realized this, I was again back in it, each time deeper than before. Of course I was only involved in a small and specific cycle. Didn't Lin Biao[11] and the Gang of Four play with such an odd cycle themselves, only to a much broader extent? What has fallen deeply into the giant and irresistible odd cycle is our disaster-ridden nation.

I must truly thank the Third Plenary Session of the Eleventh Party Central Committee,[12] which has put the wrong back to right. It also put an end to that disastrous and absurd era. What lessons can I provide for our people from my own experience? I feel that in the past several decades, several centuries, and several millenniums, our people have spent too much time and energy hurting each other. It is necessary, of course, to fight over matters of principle. But when personal motives are involved, not only is the fighting void of principles, but it deeply harms the country and the people. In the end, all that is left is the tired out self. You have probably read more history books than I. Can you tell me how we can rid our nation of this odd cycle?

The bigger odd cycle is the cultural odd cycle.

—AUTHOR

FOOTNOTES

1. After the Communist Party and the Kuomintang agreed to join forces in fighting the Japanese, a branch of the former Communist army was renamed the "Eighth Route Army."

2. The July 7th Incident was also known as the Marco Polo Bridge Incident. On July 7, 1937, Japanese troops launched an attack on

Chinese troops stationed in Lugou Bridge (Marco Polo Bridge) near Beijing. The incident marked the beginning of the War of Resistance Against Japan.

3. Lu Zhengcao was one of the Communist generals.

4. The "Four Greats" refers to the four methods used in mass struggle sessions: speaking out freely, airing views fully, holding great debates, and writing big-character posters.

5. Kang Sheng was the advisor to the Central Cultural Revolution Group. He was in charge of intelligence and security for the CPC for many years, and was responsible for the persecution of a large number of Party cadres.

6. In 1934-1935, Communist troops were forced to leave their base areas in Jiangxi. After many hardships and setbacks, and a journey of 25,000 *li*, mostly on foot, they finally arrived at Northern Shaanxi where they set up new revolutionary bases.

7. War of Liberation (1945-1949). After Japan surrendered in 1945, the Communist and the Nationalist forces were engaged in a civil war, which resulted in the total defeat of the Nationalist army and the establishment of the People's Republic of China.

8. Fu Zuoyi was the commander of Kuomintang troops stationed in Beijing during the civil war. Facing an imminent attack by the Communist army, he surrendered so that the city of Beijing could avoid bloodshed.

9. In July 1955, the CPC Central Committee issued the "Directive on the Campaign to Root out Counterrevolutionaries." It was intended to dig out hidden counterrevolutionaries. The campaign lasted two years.

10. In October 1950, the CPC Central Committee issued the "Directive on Suppressing Counterrevolutionary Activities." The movement aimed at wiping out antagonist forces and local bandits, and lasted until the end of 1953.

11. Lin Biao was designated Mao's successor in 1968, and died in a plane crash with his wife and son when they tried to escape after failing to assassinate Mao.

12. The Third Plenary Session of the Eleventh Party Central Committee (December 1978) was a watershed conference of the CPC Central Committee. It shifted the Party's policy from class struggle to economic modernization. The meeting marked the beginning of the policies of economic reform and opening to the outside world.

Hair Cut by
a Ghost

FEMALE, *age 33 in*

1966

UNEMPLOYED *in T*
City

I AM telling you my personal story. When you write about it, though, I don't want you to focus on me, but on another person.

Before I start, you must promise not to laugh. I have told the story to several other people, and they all laughed. As soon as they started laughing, I stopped, for I can't stand someone laughing at other people's misery. So can you promise not to laugh? You do? Then I will start.

I

On a late autumn night of 1964, I had a horrible night-mare. I dreamed that many devils and demons were licking the skin on my head with their tongues. Yes, tongues of various colors, blue, red, green, purple. Some of them were multi-colored, but all were shining brightly. Still deep in sleep, I wondered how they could lick the skin on my head. What happened to my hair? All of a sudden I woke up with a scream, so loud that it woke my husband. When he turned on the bed light, he stared at me as if he was seeing a ghost. Pointing at my head, he was speechless. I raised my hand to my head, and it felt like a water melon, round, hard, and slippery. I was totally bald. Where was my hair, I wondered. Then my husband and I saw a pile of my hair on the pillow. We were stunned. Suddenly I remembered a bizarre and horrifying story that I had heard as a child, a story of a ghost cutting people's hair. But I had never imagined that it could happen to me.

I covered my head with both hands and cried.

If you had seen my hair before, you would've definitely marveled at its beauty. I dare say that not many women, Chinese or foreign, had as beautiful a head of hair as I did. My husband said that he first fell in love with me because of my hair. In the hair salons near my house, I never had to pay to have my hair cut. The proprietors all asked me to be a model for their new hairstyles. Unlike many other women, who had to rely on heavy make-up to compensate for their lack of natural beauty, my hair was beautiful enough for me to stand out wherever I went. Now that my hair was suddenly gone, I looked worse than any of the women with the worst hair. My bald head looked like an egg. How could I go out and face other folks again? For a woman who cared as much as I about her looks, the loss of hair virtually amounted to a death sentence.

My husband was even more worried than I was. He visited many doctors, looking for a cure, and came back with all kinds of pills and herbs. I even tried secret recipes from ancient times, like the one you wrote about in your novel *The Miraculous Pigtail*.[1] However, none of them worked. My head was still as bald as a porcelain pot. My husband refused to give up and continued to look for doctors who could help me to grow hair. Eventually, I became tired of this, and one day I yelled at him furiously, "Do you not like me anymore because I'm bald? Do you want to desert me? Do you love me or my hair? If you only love my hair, why don't you take it and leave. Listen carefully, I won't try any more treatments."

After that, he had no choice but to give up. However, one month later, I received a large parcel from the Shanghai Stage Costume Factory. It was very odd because I never even went to the theater to see performances. How could I have anything to do with stage costumes? My husband was standing beside me, not saying a word, as I opened the parcel. It was a woman's wig! I tried it on and it fitted perfectly. On the sides of the wig were two exquisite plastic hooks to hook onto my ears. I could hardly call it a wig because the hair looked so dark, shiny, soft, and natural. It was almost as beautiful as my original hair. I asked my husband, "Did you order this?" He just smiled and didn't say a word, which was always his way. He was an engineer at a radio factory, and always preferred action to talking. Every time he did something for me, I'd say, "You are so nice." For him, that was all he needed to hear from me.

It turned out that a wig actually had lots of benefits. In many ways it was even better than real hair. For example, real hair has to be cut and made up once in a while. This is not necessary with a wig. Moreover, since you can't see the back of your head in the mirror, it's hard to make up real hair by yourself. With a wig, you can take it off, put it on a table, and work on it before putting it on your head. It is especially convenient when you give yourself a perm.

Whenever I did up my hair, I would lock myself in the room, close the drapes and take off the wig. I never looked in the mirror without it. If I did, I might find that I looked like the evil spirit depicted in the classic novel *Strange Stories from Liaozhai*.[2] With the wig, however, I felt sure that no one could imagine that I was actually a bald woman whose hair had been cut by a "ghost." Even my husband looked at me in admiration because of the beautiful "hair." He never came into the room when I was working on the wig, and he knew exactly what I was afraid of seeing and saying.

II

My husband was a senior engineer. Consequently, we became a target of attack when the Red Guards started to ransack houses. After all, that was what the Cultural Revolution was partly about. It called on the uneducated and ignorant to attack the intellectuals. The Red Guards who raided our home were mostly young kids, each with an ax in hand. They smashed whatever they saw and didn't leave a single item untouched. What I feared most, though, was that they would cut my hair. And they did, because my hair was too outstanding. Among the Red Guards were some young women who were jealous of my beautiful hair. It is no secret that women are jealous of other women's beauty, while men are jealous of other men's success.

I was pushed to the ground by a dozen hands and I saw my hair fall as two scissors mercilessly cut through the wig. The Red Guards pushed me as hard as they could, as if they were afraid that I might put up a fight. But how could I dare to fight? If I did, my wig might fall off and my bald head would be revealed. After they finished messing with my hair, they seemed satisfied. They cursed me some more and then left.

I cried my heart out. How could I live with such disheveled hair? My husband didn't bother to comfort me, but busied himself cleaning up the mess. I was so angry that I yelled at him, "Is that garbage more important than me?" Without saying a word, he continued to comb through the room, until he had cleared away all the trash in front of the wardrobe. Then he stood on a chair, reached to the top of the wardrobe, and produced a parcel wrapped in old newspapers. When I opened it, I saw it was a brand new wig. And before I had a chance to open my mouth, he said, "I had ordered an extra one a long time ago, just in case."

At that moment, I felt he was truly marvelous. I had heard from his colleagues that he always knew what would happen next and so made the necessary moves accordingly, like a great chess player. Of course, he didn't know how to play chess. He devoted all his talent to the development of radios.

But I have to blame myself for all the mishaps.

At that time, we were not completely out of danger yet. I should have wrapped up the wig and hidden it. Instead, I removed the damaged wig and put on the new one. But the mirror was broken, so I couldn't see how it looked. Suddenly there was a loud bang on the door. It was kicked open, and the same Red Guards returned. At that time I couldn't understand why they had come back. Later I found out that they wanted to take the leather hand bag on the clothes hanger. My husband had bought the bag for his use on business trips. The Red Guards wanted to take it away. When they saw me, however, they screamed. The looks on their faces were exactly the same as my husband's when he first saw my bald head.

"Who are you?" they asked.

I didn't know how to answer and simply said, "It's me."

"What happened to your hair? Tell the truth. If you play tricks on us, we will beat you to death," threatened one Red Guard. After that, they all shouted: "Beat her up."

I was terrified, not knowing how to handle the situation. My husband jumped in front of me. He was shaking so hard that his knees bent forward, as if he was about to kneel down and beg them not to hurt me. Unable to come up with an excuse, he told the truth. He said that my real hair had been "cut by a ghost" and that I was wearing a wig. "She is not intending to cheat and play tricks with you young revolutionary fighters," he said. To prove it, he turned and took the wig off my head. Looking at my bald head, the Red Guards burst out laughing. A woman Red Guard said, "How can a bourgeoisie demon like you care about her looks!" She turned to the other Red Guards and said, "Let's burn her wig."

They grabbed the wig from my husband's hand and lit it with a match. Almost instantly the wig was aflame and turned into a pool of dark dust. After that, they left, with the leather bag.

This time I didn't cry, but my husband did. He seldom cried, but when he did, there was no way I could stop him with words of comfort. He turned to me and said, "Please forgive me. I have done harm to you. I was afraid they might beat you to death."

Moments of joy and happiness may not be remembered for long, but those of sadness can hardly be forgotten.

III

From then on, I had no choice but to wear the damaged wig. It was short, messy and miserably uneven, like the heads of some men whose hair has disappeared in patches. In those days, thousands of people were forced to have their hair cut. But their hair would eventually grow back. But mine wouldn't. For a long time after the situation quieted down a little, I felt too ashamed to go out. My husband had to do all the shopping. I waited until winter time, when I could finally go out with a scarf on my head. However, I had to worry about the days ahead. What would I do when the weather got warm again?

Soon after that, the Red Guards split into different factions, fighting each other. People like us were not bothered anymore. One evening, my husband asked me, "Can you give me the wig and let me repair it for you?" Not knowing what he meant to do, I declined. The next day he made the same request, and I refused again, because I didn't believe he could make it look any better. A few days later, I got quite sleepy one evening and went to bed rather early. Subconsciously I felt the wig being removed, but when I realized it was my husband removing it, I pretended to be asleep and didn't open my eyes. He took off the wig and went into the next room, closing the door behind him. I couldn't hear any sound after that. I got up from the bed and walked to the door, trying not to make a sound. Through the keyhole I saw my husband working on my wig under the light bulb. On the table was a bunch of hair, the same hair that had been cut off by the Red Guards! I didn't know it, but he had kept all of the hair. He always knew what to do next! At the moment, he was using a pair of tweezers to pick up each hair and glue it to the wig. It was as if he were restoring a cultural relic. I can never forget what I saw through that keyhole. As I stood there, tears rolled down my face. I didn't want to disturb him, so I returned to bed, covering my head with the quilt and cried. I don't know how I fell asleep. When I woke up, he was standing there smiling. His red eyes told me that he didn't sleep for the whole night. Suddenly I realized the wig had been returned to my head. I have no idea how he had put it back on. I sat up on the bed, and the beautiful and shiny hair was hanging down to my shoulders and back.

VI

My husband left me long ago. He was removed from his position as an engineer and sent to a plant to be reformed through physical labor. There he died in an accident. It seems as if he had even anticipated that. After his death, I found an undated letter in his desk drawer. It was addressed to me, like a will. It was full of complaints about me. He even cursed me and listed all the unhappy incidents in our marriage. I wondered how he could have held all of these things against me for so long and hidden them so deeply in his heart. For a time, I hated him for this hypocrisy. I thought that all the love he had shown me was nothing but a performance. He had actually hated me in his heart. What a hypocrite! Because of that, I didn't feel it was too big a loss when he died, and was able to cope with the matter rather easily. Later, a friend of mine reminded me, "Is it possible that he wrote the letter because he feared you couldn't bear the loss of him? Maybe he has done that out of his true love for you."

I thought about it and realized that she was right. How could I ever understand the way he loved me, even after his death?

Don't think I'm not sensitive enough to understand true love. Today you can find all sorts of wigs at beauty salons. But I am still wearing the one he repaired for me. There is one thing about this wig: it will never turn gray. And of course that is what he wanted too. He wanted me to be forever young.

Love can be tested in adversity.

—AUTHOR

FOOTNOTES

1. *The Miraculous Pigtail* is a novel by Feng Jicai that has been made into a movie. It has also been translated into English.

2. *Strange Stories from Liaozhai* is a classic Chinese novel by Pu Songling of the Ming Dynasty. It contains many stories of ghosts and demons.

Dead Face

死
脸

MALE, *age 5 in*
1966
KINDERGARTEN
Child on M Street
in R City

I AM often drowned in a deep sea of agony, so deep that I can hardly lift up my chin. It is all because of this "dead face" of mine—an expressionless and lifeless face. I cannot change my face because I cannot change my personality. Whenever I look at my cold, stiff, and motionless face in the mirror, a strong abhorrence overwhelms me. I hate the Cultural Revolution.

The other day I told you I wanted to talk about my experience during the Cultural Revolution. You dismissed me with a laugh: "You were no more than ten years old during the Cultural Revolution. What extraordinary experience could you have?" Frankly speaking, I was quite angry with you. If it were a few years ago, I would have started a big argument with you. Of course, I'm not going to quarrel today. I only want to share with you something that has been buried deep in my heart for almost thirty years.

When the Cultural Revolution began, I was only five years old. But some images of it are still strikingly clear in my mind. I remember watching one person being paraded by a group of people on the street, a big white board hanging from his neck in front of his chest. I didn't know what was written there since I hadn't yet learned to read. A big tall hat was jammed onto his head. He was pushed and pulled by people who were hitting gongs. When they took him to his own house, he was made to stand on a table in front of the door. People angrily waved their fists and shouted slogans. I have long forgotten what I did at the time. I can't even remember how I felt. I could have been either scared or just curious. But I do remember that my family only allowed me to watch from inside our door. Because my grandfather was a capitalist, his house had been raided. I was picked up from kindergarten and was sent to my maternal grandfather's house. My mother's father was a senior clerk in the old society and had some stock in a company. He was labeled a "capitalist's running dog." Since danger might fall on him at any moment, the family was quite nervous. But I didn't feel the tight atmosphere at all. I sat at the door step, watching many red flags fluttering in the wind. They looked quite beautiful to me. Only years later did I know that these were the symbols of the Red Guard movement.

After a while, I was sent back to my grandfather's house. Every room in the house was sealed with paper ribbons except one, which was left for my parents to live in. My grandfather went to stay with a friend of my father's, a man of great integrity who agreed to hide my grandfather despite the possible danger of being caught. My grandfather owned a flour plant and a welding factory in the 1940s, and was quite wealthy, which made his neighbors jealous. I was later told that when the neighbors raided our house, they charged wildly, striking and smashing everything in sight. Soon the house looked as if it had just been hit by a powerful bomb.

At that time the adults were busy minding their own

business. My father was a teacher. Since he did not have a good class background, he was also living nervously. But no one expected that a small child like me could be hit by the Cultural Revolution as well.

In our neighborhood, there were many more poor people than rich ones. We were among the few rich families that were ransacked. Therefore, I was named a "bastard" by other kids my age. Children from families with good class backgrounds attacked me at will. When I walked on the street I would sometimes be hit by a score of rocks coming from nowhere. When I stayed at home I would sometimes be startled by violent banging on the door, followed by a moment of uproarious laughter. The scolding of "bastard" never left my ears. On the front door of our house, children from other families wrote slogans in chalk: "Down with the capitalist bastard XXX." XXX is my name. At the time I felt as if I was an enemy of the whole world. I hid myself in the house and I was scared to go out alone. One day my father asked me to buy some cigarettes for him from the store. I sat there, not moving an inch, until my father got furious. On the way home I ran into some neighborhood children. They pushed me against a wall and started a struggle session right there. Two kids pulled my arms up from behind, while others pressed my head down. All the children shouted slogans and spat at me. They didn't stop until a passing adult yelled at them. When I got home, I wanted to tell my father about the incident, but he started to blame me for coming back too late, and so I swallowed every single word. I swore to myself that I would never tell him about any of my miseries, no matter what happened to me.

I started school when I was seven, only to find that I was the only "bastard" in my class.

I hated school and was especially afraid of going on the road to and from school. Humiliation was waiting for me at any moment. Once again, I became the target of attacks and pranks by my classmates, who treated me like a toy that could be tossed around. While in class, I always wished that the teacher would stand by my side a little longer, because as soon as the teacher walked away, the other students began to attack me. Those who sat beside or behind me struck me hard with sharp pencils. Once a student who shared the desk with me pretended to be listening attentively to the teacher, but instead was actually pinching me hard on the thigh from under the desk. If I had reported this to the teacher, my class-mate would have accused me of framing him and engaging in "class revenge." At that time, political slogans like that were very powerful weapons. I could only endure it and hold back my tears. But deep inside, I developed a rebellious tempera-ment. I knew that tears were a sign of weakness.

I was preoccupied with hatred. I hated the neighbor-hood kids, my classmates, and their parents. Sometimes, when I couldn't tolerate it anymore, I fought. But it was always me who took the loss. The teachers were naturally partial to those students with good class backgrounds. When my father learned about my fighting, he would give me another beating because he was afraid of my making trouble. But I was a rebel at heart. If the kids dared to bully me, I would risk my life to fight. Often I was beaten until I had bruises on my face and wounds on my body. Coming home with dark eyes, I would talk to nobody when they asked me what had happened. At that time there was a very famous song: "The Cultural Revolution Is Good." You must know the song very well. When we sang this song in chorus, I would change the lyrics to "the Cultural Revolution is no good." If I was discovered doing this, I would have been charged with a crime punishable by death. Luckily everyone sang the song at the top of their lungs, and nobody realized that I had changed the lyrics. You can imag-ine how much I hated the Cultural Revolution.

I tried to stay away from other people, especially chil-dren of my own age. I believed that adults did not harbor as much hostility against me, but kids my own age considered me their enemy. I lived a nervous and tiring life. Only when I lay in bed at night did I feel a little safer. The night time belonged to me, a time when I could fantasize being a super child with so much power that I could throw all the kids who had beaten me onto the ground till they begged for their lives on their knees. But when daylight came, a strong and deep sense of terror overwhelmed me once again. I felt lonely, cold, and helpless. The only person who showed me any sympathy was the mother of a classmate of mine, who was from a worker's family. One day she said to her son, "Why don't you go and play with XXX (my name). He is a smart kid and a good student. He will have a bright future." It was the first time in my life I heard such a complement. For a while, whenever I thought of these words, I had a warm feeling. How I longed to talk to her. Yet I was also afraid to do so, because I had forgotten how to express my feelings to other people.

During the second semester in the fourth grade, I started to excel in my studies and to score the highest marks on every exam. The teacher hinted to me that I might have a chance to join the Little Red Guards. I was quite excited, and felt as if I was now on top of the world. But something unexpected happened. On the school's playground, someone wrote a counterrevolutionary slogan: "Down with Chairman Mao." It was written on the red brick wall with white chalk. It became a serious incident. The police was sent to investigate the case. It was believed that one of the students had written the slogan. All of a sudden, I felt my classmates' attitude towards me changed. Nobody talked to me. They only looked at me out of the corners of their eyes, and they gossiped behind my back. In class, the teachers ignored me when I raised my hand to ask questions. It appeared that I was naturally the one who had written the slogan, for I was a "bastard" of the counterrevolutionary class.

But the investigation showed that the slogan was written by a boy from the fifth grade. He was from a family that had been poor for generations and had harbored deep hatred for the exploiting class. He wrote the slogan and then reported it, because he wanted to be a "hero." The incident was over, but I could never forget my classmates' attitude, their subtle behavior, and the gossip behind my back.

Gradually I became sensitive, vulnerable, and suspicious. Whenever my classmates talked about something, I felt they were talking about me and I reacted strongly. What I did not know was that I had developed a personality that would later cause many problems for me.

After I was enrolled in middle school, I left the original environment behind. My new schoolmates knew nothing about my background. You might think that my psychological problems would have disappeared. But just the contrary. My personality problem now started to surface. Only then did I realize that I had so many weaknesses.

I couldn't get along with others, I didn't like to socialize, and I was very defensive. One of my classmates had the habit of teasing and casually touching people. Whenever he walked by me, I would subconsciously raise my arms in order to ward off his unexpected move. All my classmates laughed at me. They couldn't understand why I was so sensitive and on edge all the time. Yes, I was always on edge. Somehow I felt that people wanted to harm me. When I talked to someone and the person lost attention for a second, I thought he was doing that intentionally. He either had prejudice against me, or meant to humiliate me. Then I would be enraged. My relationship with my classmates was tense and antagonistic, and it eventually became confrontational. I felt that they intentionally ganged up to make fun of me. Although there was no longer any political element in these conflicts, they touched my old wound. In the end, my relations with my classmates got so bad that whenever we talked, we ended up quarreling; whenever we quarreled, we ended up in a physical fight. My classmates gave me a nickname "dead face." They only called me that behind my back for fear that I would hear. But when I finally heard this humiliating nickname, I did not lose my temper, but instead sank into a deep agony. When I looked at my face in the mirror, I almost smashed it to pieces. Was I born with such a lifeless and motionless face?

I tried to change myself. But it couldn't be more difficult than to try to change one's personality. What gave me the biggest headache was that I did not know how to get along with my peers. It seemed that I was born afraid of them.

I specialized in computer science in college. After graduation, I worked for a company in charge of project development. Once a middle school classmate came to visit me at work. He was surprised at how much I had changed. He said, "I have never imagined that you could be so talkative. I remember you didn't talk at all in school."

I started to change after I turned twenty-seven, when my sensitive and suspicious personality began to fade away.

There were many reasons. I grew older, became more mature, had more social experience, and was trusted at the work place. But the most important reason was that there was no more political discrimination. Today Chinese society is free of political prejudice. People no longer feel the terror and ruthlessness of political pressure and discrimination.

Political discrimination is a product of the feudal autocratic society. I remember once reading an article in a magazine, which said, "In ancient times people shouted 'long live' on their knees; during the Cultural Revolution, people shouted 'long live' on their feet." This is a vivid and profound description. During the May Fourth Movement,[1] the main theme was to get rid of feudalism and to promote a new culture. However, during the Cultural Revolution, all those feudalistic cultural traditions were revived: the monarchical loyalty, literary inquisition, obscurantist policy, personality cult, blood lineage, and so on. These are all parts of the feudalistic tradition. However, the authorities alone couldn't possibly have replanted these ideas in people's minds. They did it with the cooperation of the people themselves. It seems that China has been possessed by a feudalist soil. Although I can hardly believe that the Cultural Revolution will repeat itself, my personal experience tells me that this is because no one has emerged as its director yet. But China is full of actors and actresses who are ready to put on another show like the Cultural Revolution. Almost every single Chinese was part of the show on the grand stage of the Cultural Revolution. They couldn't all be victims. Otherwise, there would not have been so many tragedies.

The other day after lunch, we were chatting in the office. When we talked about the current problems of society, such as the profit-before-everything mentality, a colleague of mine said, "It is really outrageous. We really need another Cultural Revolution to get things in order." I immediately lost my temper. I shouted and yelled at him, and couldn't control my anger. We almost got into a physical fight.

All my colleagues were surprised at my reaction. I had always seemed to be a quiet, amiable, and cordial person. They couldn't understand why I had suddenly become so agitated, like a crazy bull.

That incident made me realize that I still possessed a vulnerable and sensitive character. I had just buried it deep in my heart. My colleague's words revived my old hatred. On the other hand, the incident might have been a good thing for me. It reminded me that I need to be more careful and exercise more self-control. Only then can I really leave that tragic era completely behind.

At least half of human nature is nurtured after birth.

—AUTHOR

FOOTNOTE

1. On May 4, 1919, students at Peking University took to the street to protest the signing of a peace treaty in Paris that allowed Japan to take over China's Shandong Province from Germany, who had been defeated in World War I. The protest turned into a city-wide student movement, which called for democracy and science.

Seeking Pleasure Out of Misery

"I THROW MYSELF ONTO THE GROUND"

*L*AST time it was you who sought me out. This time I came to you for an interview. I have read your *Ten Years of One Hundred People*. It's no good. Full of crying about wrongfulness and wailing of resentment. To me, it is like suffering from my own misery after suffering through others. I have always been against this way of living. So I'd like to express my opinion.

During the Cultural Revolution, people commented that while others became thinner and skinnier after each struggle session, I became fatter and stronger. I was energetic and my face was glowing with vigor. I remember that Old K, the man in charge of the "cow shed" where I was locked, asked me what kind of counterrevolutionary spirit enabled me to always be in such good spirits. I told him that I had high blood pressure, which forced the blood upward, giving me a red face. It was also called a "death glow." After hearing this answer, he stopped worrying.

Living in China, you cannot take everything too seriously. That is rule number one. Rule number two is that you need to know how to get around. You cannot always fight head-on, for you will definitely hurt yourself if you fight something hard with hardness. Instead, you should take a hard hit with softness, or not take it at all, but let it go—like practicing Tai Chi. Chairman Mao had a famous sixteen-word principle of guerrilla warfare: "When the enemy advances, I retreat; when the enemy withdraws, I chase; when the enemy digs in, I harass; when the enemy exhausts, I attack." I was simply applying Chairman Mao's thoughts to everyday life. If you come hard, I give you soft. If you attack in my face, I return it in your back. If you fight nonstop, I find loopholes and make trouble. As long as I feel contented in my heart, it doesn't matter whether I win or lose.

Last time I told you some of my dirty tricks. I heard you have written a story based on them. I haven't had a chance to read it yet. Today I will just talk about whatever comes to my mind, regardless of whether you've heard it before or not.

I was locked in the "cow shed" at the beginning of the movement, and I was made head of the "cow shed." The reason for this was that my problem was the least serious. My only "crime" was that I was a Kuomintang clerk for six months before Liberation. Every morning I called all the "cows" together for a meeting, but I would only do so in Old K's presence. With Old K in the room, I would bang on the table and shout, "Today, this whole roomful of us bastards..." Of course, Old K was one of the "whole roomful."

One day, Old K seemed to realize this. Wasn't he included in the whole roomful and cursed as well? He bulged his eyes and asked me to explain. I immediately pretended to be innocent and replied, "Didn't you hear me say 'this roomful of us?' Of course the 'us' refers to us demons and monsters. How can you belong to this group?" Old K was at a loss for words. From then on he had to listen to me curse him every day. Don't you think it was fun? If you do not seek fun, you can only feel depressed, shed tears, or take your own life. There was a "petty capitalist" who was locked up with us. He couldn't stand the humiliation, and jumped from the second floor window and died. I thought to myself, what a fool he was. How could he let himself down while others tried to make his life hard?

Don't think everyone in the "cow shed" was a good person, though. In those days, everyone felt insecure and wanted to show a "good attitude" by making other people counterrevolutionaries, so their lives would be a tad easier. Once, an old fart called Old Z sold me out. Old Z's father was a landlord. He was at most the "offspring of a landlord." But since his house was privately owned, he was branded a landlord when the Cultural Revolution started. In order to show his good attitude, he denounced me, accusing me of coining counterrevolutionary jokes in the "cow shed."

This is the joke I told. One day, a man named Q was eating a small piece of beef, which he had brought from home. I made fun of him, saying, "Do you know what you are doing eating beef?" He was not bright enough to understand my question and replied, "I don't know." I quipped, "You are in a cow shed, and so you are a cow. For a cow to eat beef, it is no different from eating yourself." The joke made everyone laugh. At that time, a ruthless and bloody struggle was going on everywhere. How could we "monsters and demons" dare to engage in laughter?

So Old Z reported this to Old K, who called me over to see him. Banging the table and kicking a chair, he accused me of making fun of the revolution. I said, "To eat oneself means self-destruction. I was only cursing him."

Old K was quite clumsy and stupid. Not only was he physically awkward, his brain was dumb, and his mouth was slow. After several rounds of my word games, he was at a loss. But his fury didn't go away. The next day our work unit started a new round of struggle sessions. We were denounced on big-character posters. Old K charged into the "cow shed" and screamed at us. He was, in fact, screaming at me: "You demons and monsters listen carefully. The revolutionary masses have started a new round of struggles against you. How dare you still not admit your crimes. Now everyone of you must act quickly and write a poster, asking yourself if you have behaved. Don't wait for the revolutionary masses to pick you out. This time it will be a big struggle that will last three days and three nights."

I didn't bother to look at Old K. I could imagine his pompous air. Without much thought, I already had a plan. I was determined to make fun of him. So I spread out a piece of white paper—at that time, the revolutionary masses used red paper, but demons and monsters like us could only use white—and began to write: "XXX, I Ask You." XXX was my name. The following was what I wrote:

> The Great Proletarian Cultural Revolution has reached a new climax. The revolutionary masses are wielding their mighty weapons to beat up you drowning dogs. XXX, I ask you. Did you behave? You said you did. No. I don't believe you. You'd better prick up your dog's ear and listen: I warn you. You are at the brink of death. If you do not behave, and if you dare to make trouble, I will throw you onto the ground, let ten thousand feet step on your body, and never allow you to turn over for thousands of generations.

As soon as my poster was put up, Old K couldn't hide his fury. He sent for me. He was so outraged that he hit the table with his fist and yelled, "Where did you get your dog's guts. The revolutionary masses are asking you. Who are you asking? Who do you refer to with all the 'yous' on your poster? Are you pointing finger at the revolutionary masses?"

I immediately pretended to be terrified. With my hands trembling, I looked shocked, frightened, but innocent. I argued, "If I dare to point finger at the revolutionary masses, I'd deserve to die a thousand times. Director K, please don't be angry. I am so afraid when you are angry. Just now you instructed us to ask ourselves. All the 'yous' in the poster, of course, refer to myself.

'You' means 'I' or 'me.' I was only pointing finger at myself."

Old K was muddled. He yelled, "You son-of-a-bitch. If 'You' means 'me,' why don't you use 'me' instead? How can 'You' be 'me'? He was soon confused with the two words. Unable to continue, he banged on the table and shouted, "Get out. Correct at once."

I said, "I accept your criticism and will correct it at once. If I change all the 'yous' into 'mes,' will it be okay?"

"Of course that will be okay. Get out." Old K impatiently shooed me out.

I said to myself, "You stupid bastard, you have fallen into my trap again." I read my poster again and found there were twelve "Yous" in it. I went back to my room, wrote twelve 'mes' on a piece of white paper. Then I took some glue and changed all the "Yous" on the poster into "mes." Afterwards, I went to invite Old K to read it, as if I had done something honorable. This time, the poster read like this:

> *The Great Proletarian Cultural Revolution has reached a new climax. The revolutionary masses are wielding their mighty weapons to beat up you drowning dogs. XXX, I ask me. Did I behave? I said I did. No. I don't believe me. I'd better prick up my dog's ear and listen: I warn me. I was at the brink of death. If I do not behave, and if I dare to make trouble, I will throw me onto the ground, let ten thousand feet step on my body, and never allow me to turn over for thousands of generations.*

Old K's face was suddenly flushed red. Before he could scream, I said with a flattering smile, "You asked me to change all the 'Yous' into 'mes.' I have done that without missing a single one."

Old K was again at a loss for words. The incident made me happy for a whole week. Not only did I have a good appetite, I slept soundly.

I have to say that, although the Cultural Revolution had its way, everyone had his own way of living.

The vigor of life lies in its wisdom.

—*Author*

"Aunt Pig"

MY LIFE AS AN EDUCATED YOUTH was in fact quite interesting. Despite all the hardships, there was a lot of fun. Today, when we reflect on those years, we can always taste a special flavor. I would call it the flavor of salty candy, if you approve of this metaphor.

Those of us who once settled in the countryside as educated youths in H County, W Province, still laugh about the "salty candies" whenever we get together. At that time, we were all young. The youngest was only fifteen or sixteen, and the oldest was no more than twenty. We were full of energy, and we were all trouble-makers. Our most exciting adventure was an incident we called "Aunt Pig." We have kept it a secret ever since. Today is the first time I have made it public.

In those days, the work we did was hard and exhausting, and the food was bad, so we all felt greedy. There were seven or eight of us in a group. If one of us happened to receive a package of brown sugar from home, we would all flock around, tear the package open immediately, and stuff the contents into our mouths. Then a flock of flies would come and stick onto our mouths. No matter what we did, they just would't go away. In that place, even the flies were "short of mouth" and greedy.

Very often we compensated for the lack of good food by talking about it. One day, we talked so much about it that we could no longer stay put. So we decided to steal a pig from the neighboring B village. We worked out a brilliant plan: We would take a few pieces of steamed bread and soak them in liquor, which should be enough to knock out any pig. After that, we would carry the drunk pig back, slaughter it, and satisfy our watery mouths. Such a plan, we thought, would not only work well, but would also give us a lot of fun. As we developed our plan, we felt as if we were putting together a funny joke. Once we decided on the scheme, we all set out to prepare for the action. Someone got hold of a few pieces of corn bread. Another stole a bottle of liquor from the village grocery store. A young man nicknamed Number Three and I went to the brigade headquarters and took an old stretcher. When I saw the stretcher, I came up with another idea, which would remedy a flaw in our original plan. What if we were caught while carrying the pig out? With a stretcher, though, we could say that we were carrying a patient to the county hospital. The stretcher gave us more inspiration, and I was hailed as a hero. The other guys promised that I would be rewarded with an extra piece of pork butt because of it. That promise made me quite happy, and I offered my white bed sheet to cover the pig like a patient. With all the details completed, we consummated our plan. We were so excited, some of the younger fellows couldn't help jumping up and down.

We could hardly wait to start our scheme. That night we sneaked into B village. We heard several dogs barking, but as soon as we gave them some of the liquor-soaked bread, they stopped. The hungry dogs soon became drunk dogs. Without much trouble we came to a pigsty. There was a big fat female pig that we decided to get. We threw a piece of bread in its direction. The pig was lying on the ground, but when it saw the bread, it immediately sprang up to gulp it down in one bite— faster than a cat. We threw it one more piece, then another, till every single one was gone. We then all squatted outside the pigsty and waited for the pig to pass out. But all we heard was the chewing noise and the sound of the pig breathing. We were afraid that the liquor was not strong enough, and regretted that we didn't bring more bread. After about an hour, there was no more sound. We popped our heads over the pigsty and saw that the pig was drunk on all fours. We hurried inside, moved it onto the stretcher, covered it with the bed sheet, and ran as fast as we could out of the village. The pig was really heavy. By the time we realized that we were out of danger, we were soaked with sweat, and our arms were so tired they became rubbery, as if they had no bones.

We decided not to carry the pig back to our village for fear of being caught by other people. Instead, we would take it to a deserted wooded area near H village and slaughter it right there. However, something unexpected happened on the way.

While we were carrying the pig towards H village, we ran into a group of educated youths from Y city. There were five or six of them, men and women. We were totally unprepared, and just wanted to pass by them without much fuss. Unfortunately for us, there was a skinny and tall young man among them, who was very talkative. He asked what we were carrying. For one second, we couldn't think of what to say. Fortunately, I came up with a response. I said that an old woman in our village had suddenly fallen ill and that we were carrying her to the hospital. Hearing this, they all offered to help. We kindly refused their offer. But they introduced themselves as proactive members of the group to study Chairman Mao's works from A village. They were returning home after three days of meetings in the county seat. They insisted that we give them this opportunity to learn from Lei Feng,[1] and set a good example. Citing Chairman Mao's quotations, one of them said, "It is a pleasure to help others." Another asked me what class background the old woman had. I told him that she had been a poor peasant for three generations, which seemed to inspire their class feelings.

They insisted that they help us carry her to the county hospital and began to fight with us for the stretcher. Alas, there was no way we could resist their enthusiasm. In addition, after carrying the stretcher for over twenty *li*, we were exhausted. Moreover, we felt nervous over the fact that they might find out what we were carrying. Finally we gave in and surrendered the stretcher to them. A young woman among their group started to look under the cover, but I immediately stopped her, saying, "It's too windy here. The aunt has a bad flu. She cannot be exposed to the wind." The girl stopped, and helped to cover the pig again with even more care than we had taken. "No wonder I heard this aunt breathing so heavily," she quipped. The guy nicknamed Number Three almost burst into laughter at this. I feared that we could no longer hang on to our plan, and so I said, "If you want to take her to the hospital, then we will go back home."

They couldn't be happier to hear that, and they suggested that we go home and take a rest. Then they picked up the stretcher and walked towards the county seat. And we turned around and headed home.

After only a few steps, we heard a young man shouting to us, "Which village are you and the aunt from?"

I replied without much thought, "The B Village." B village, of course, was the home of the pig.

Then a young woman asked, "What is the aunt's name?"

I replied quickly, "Aunt Zhu." "*Zhu*" is a popular Chinese

sur name and has the same sound as pig.

Then we heard them shouting, "Don't worry. We'll take good care of Aunt Zhu. So long."

"So long," we waved at them to wish them success. After that, we couldn't hold our laughter much longer, and we ran as fast as we could to a place where they were totally out of sight. Unable to contain ourselves, we fell on the ground, laughing, rolling, somersaulting. We felt happier than we would have if we had eaten the pig.

The following is what we later heard happened.

According to people in the county, it was already eight in the morning when the educated youths arrived at the hospital. They called for emergency, and the doctor came out. The doctor went up and patted the body. Before he could call out "Aunt," the "aunt" gave out a big roar, jumped up, and started running hysterically. Because it was still covered with the sheet, nobody could tell it was a pig. Everyone was shocked to see that an old woman could be so swift and wild.

Alas, how could you tell a Cultural Revolution experience without this?

The true flavor of the salty candy is the salty bitterness inside the sweetness.

—*Author*

"Returning the Clock"

I'VE READ SOME OF YOUR STORIES about the Cultural Revolution. They were all sad ones. I felt uncomfortable reading them. So I want to tell you something that I was very proud of, a success story.

At the end of 1969, I was sent to settle in O village, R County, R Province. There I lived for five years. When I finally could see some light at the end of the tunnel and had a chance to return to the city, I had to get the approval of the brigade's Party secretary and his stamp. That secretary was, in one word, a bastard. He was really a snakehead, cruel and greedy. Even the old time local tyrant, Liu Wencai,[2] was no comparison to him. Three of the female educated youths in our village were raped by him. Well, I shouldn't get into that. Let's just talk about me. I knew it wouldn't be easy to escape from his hand and was prepared to be blackmailed by him. He was known to be greedy, and I decided to bribe him. But even bribery wasn't an easy matter. I had to make sure that I gave him the right stuff. His nephew was a squad leader in the civilian army, who was also his trusted follower. So I sounded out his nephew and was told that the Party secretary needed a grandfather clock. At that time, the brigade leaders often held meetings at his house. A clock would make it very convenient for them. I asked his nephew what kind of clock he wanted. That jerk darted a look at me and said, "Of course, one that has a wooden box outside and a swinging pendulum inside." I was outraged. Such a clock would cost me eighty yuan, or at least two months of my father's salary. The bastard was too greedy, I thought to myself.

However, I am not a person who can suffer a loss. That night I tried to work out a plan, and I came up with a brilliant idea. I wrote a letter to my uncle who was working in Beijing, explaining my situation and asking him for a favor. I said that this would be the first and last favor I would ever ask of him. I begged him to send me a clock at whatever cost, and I promised to return it within three months.

My uncle worked as a dispatcher at the Beijing Railroad Bureau. Since he didn't smoke or drink, he was able to save some money. My parents often turned to him when they had difficulties. Soon after I sent the letter, I received a clock from him. Attached was a letter consoling me, but there was no mention of my promise to return the clock. He had probably dismissed it as an empty promise.

With the clock in my possession, I was able to put on a show.

The clock was really a handsome one. Wooden box with bright paint. The inside was made of copper, with Chairman Mao's quotations engraved in red. Three hands ticked elegantly and vividly. At the bottom was a glass door, through which one could see the pendulum swinging gracefully from left to right. My uncle was really nice to send me this clock. I was moved by his kindness.

Yet I had to wait for the best moment to give the clock to the secretary. I waited patiently for five days until I heard that he was cited and praised at the commune. On his way back, his mouth was stretched by his smile from chin to chin. I saw my moment. Holding tightly onto the clock, I walked into his house. It was an effective move. Seeing the handsome clock, the secretary smiled so widely that his eyes reduced to a thread. He said, "You have done very well here. I won't let other people go. But you will have my approval to leave."

I handed over my reference letter right away and said in a flattering tone, "Next time when I need to be re-educated, I will come to your village again." The secretary reached underneath a pillow for his stamp, breathed hard on its surface to moisten the ink, and banged the stamp on the letter with a big noise. Viola. Green light. I could go. Everything was done.

With this letter in hand, I went to the commune, the county, the province, and then to my far away hometown. After more than a month of traveling back and forth, and miles of red tape, I finally managed to get everything ready. I came back to the village, packed, and bid others farewell. Now it was time to get my clock back. Here is what I did, which I had planned from the very beginning.

One day, when I heard that the commune leaders were coming to inspect the village, I waited for them to gather at the secretary's house. Then I pushed his door open and stepped inside. The room was full of people. It was pretty hot and stuffy, and was full of the choking smell of tobacco. When the secretary saw me, he said, "So you are leaving. But don't forget us. If you do, we will go and look for you." His warm words were not meant for me, but for the commune leaders. I signaled that I had something to talk to him about and grabbed his sleeve. When we were in the doorway, I put my mouth up to his ear. He turned his cheek and asked, "What?"

I said, "I am very embarrassed to tell you, but the clock that I lent you was borrowed from my uncle. Now that I'm going back, I have to return it to him. Otherwise it will be hard for me to step into his house. Can I have the clock back, please?" I pretended to lower my voice as if I didn't intend to let others hear me. But my controlled voice was just loud enough for everyone in the room to hear it clearly.

The secretary's face suddenly turned pale. He was trembling. Since his face was so close to mine, I could see his expression clearly. But he was "checkmated" by me. He had no choice but to say, "Okay, okay. Take it, take it." Of course I knew that he could have beaten me to death if the commune leaders hadn't been present.

Without even bothering him, I slipped out of my shoes, stepped onto the bed, and took the clock. I left by announcing, "I'm leaving." He did not see me off, but I could imagine how he felt at the moment.

When I returned the clock to my uncle in Beijing, the whole family was confused. But after I told them the story, everyone burst out laughing.

I am proud of myself for this. During the Cultural Revolution, it was the only thing I did on my own.

You should applaud for me.

Happiness always lies on the side of resistors.

—AUTHOR

FOOTNOTES

1. Lei Feng was a PLA soldier, a heroic figure who was known to be willing to help other people. Since the 1960s, the CPC has repeatedly called on the people to "learn from Lei Feng."

2. Liu Wencai was a notorious landlord in Sichuan Province who was known to have viciously exploited local peasants before Liberation.

EPILOGUE

THIS YEAR BRINGS US FACE TO FACE WITH TWO ANNIVERSARIES: one, the thirtieth anniversary of the beginning of the Cultural Revolution; the other, the twentieth anniversary of its collapse. The sensations these two anniversaries evoke in us could hardly be more different. The first reeks of death—a weighty, oppressive, bitter, and mournful scent. The second is like a rebirth, though it hardly allows us to relax. The first anniversary inspires us towards rationality, vigilance, introspection, and scrutiny. The second tends more towards the emotional, but it is a mixture of a hundred different emotions. Hemmed in by two such anniversaries, the Chinese people are now traversing a spiritual terrain one hundred times more arduous than the treacherous mountain paths of Sichuan.[1]

It is under such conditions that I have at last completed this volume, a spiritual history of people who suffered during the Cultural Revolution (CR). This is a thorny flower that I have placed on the grave of the CR, which itself once buried the hopes and ideals of an entire generation. As I stand silently before this stone-cold grave, the voices, tears, and stories of the people I interviewed grow louder and louder in my ears, until suddenly they become the sorrowful thunder of an entire generation.

In the eight years since I first announced my plans to record the experiences of ordinary Chinese people during the Cultural Revolution, I have received over 4,000 requests, by letter and telephone, from individuals asking me to be their spokesman. A writer who takes on the role of spokesman for the people often must sacrifice the pleasure of venting his own anger, but instead is entitled to enjoy the noble solemnity of duty to a higher cause. In writing this volume, the highest principle I set for myself was to respect and abide by the truth. To this day, I believe that I have successfully completed my mission to create a record of the Cultural Revolution.

The inexorable procession of time has ensured that the Cultural Revolution is already a historical concept. But a catastrophic history is always imbued with two implications: the first is a dead history, the second a living history. For dead history, all that remains is a pile of wreckage that can never regain life; living history bequeaths its damage to later generations. Living history belongs in the realm of current events; dead history is nothing but a process of eternal ending. This ending, however, is not a cover-up, nor a forgetting, nor a pretending-not-to-know. It involves sober self-examination and careful analysis. Only when we are able to turn the end-point of catastrophe into the beginning of a cure do we have the right to say that the Cultural Revolution has truly come to an end.

Appended to this book are excerpts from interviews with twenty young people who have no first-hand experience of the Cultural Revolution—people born after 1976—in which they discuss their impressions of the CR. The contents of these interviews should be enough to put us on guard. Tragedy is always repeated in the midst of ignorance, but it can never be replayed among the vigilant. This is the reason I felt the imperative to complete the present volume.

As this book is going to press, I wish I could leave blank several pages, to make room for the confessions of a true repenter. Even though I have said, "an unrepentant people is beyond hope," I have also said, "the pure life begins with repentance, and the ugly life comes to an end amidst guilt." I have listened to the remorseful words of several people whose good consciences were bothered by their experiences, but I must say that I have yet to come across the kind of out-and-out courageous repenter I had hoped to meet. When will such people, driven by their conscience, come knocking at my door? Not until that day will I be able to believe, beyond any doubt, that wisdom and civilization have returned to their rightful place—be it in a single person, or in our whole society.

Of course, I do not intend to point the finger of blame at the innocent Chinese people. Goethe once said of his German compatriots, "When I think of the German people, I cannot help but feel my spirit sadly wounded. As individuals, each one is worthy of admiration; but as a whole, they are equally worthy of pity." I believe we Chinese are just the opposite: as individuals, each of us has weaknesses and flaws; but as a whole, the Chinese people is truly worthy of admiration!

The Cultural Revolution played on human weaknesses, such as selfishness, covetousness, weak-will, jealousy, and vanity. But it also drew on people's virtues, like loyalty, kindness, simplicity, and courage, and used them to augment its own strength. The real tragedy of the Chinese people is that both poles of human nature were manipulated. However, if such loyal, kind, and good people were given the opportunity to act on their essential goodness, what great accomplishments could they achieve? This potentiality is already evident among the events of recent years. Thus, in now attempting to write an epilogue to the CR, our aim is not to awaken old hatreds, to express our bitterness, or to seize upon the mistakes of history to enter into a trial of strength with the corpse of a deceased politics. Instead, we are courageously facing ourselves, solemnly facing our past, bringing forth from dusky shadows the cloudless sun of tomorrow's brighter day.

To sum up, the only way to close the final chapter of the Cultural Revolution is to remember it truly and thoroughly.

—Written the night of the 30th anniversary of the publication of the May 16th Circular [2]

FOOTNOTES

1. "The mountain paths of Sichuan", or *shu dao*, is a symbol of hardship and difficulty. The Tang Dynasty poet, Li Bai, once wrote: "It is more difficult to walk the mountain paths of Sichuan than walk up to the sky."

2. "May 16th Circular" of 1966 marks the formal start of the Cultural Revolution.

APPENDIX I

Cultural Revolution in the Eyes of the New Generation

INTRODUCTION: Over the past few months, I interviewed several dozen people who did not experience the Cultural Revolution firsthand—that is, people born after 1976. I asked them about their impressions of the Cultural Revolution, the reasons for these impressions, and to tell me their own stories and opinions. The youngest person I talked to was just twelve; the oldest was twenty. What follows are excerpts from these interviews that provide a record of the younger generation's understanding of, and attitude towards, the Cultural Revolution, as well as a glimpse into the values of China's young people in the 1990s.

—*The Author*

MR. FANG (b. 1976, age 20, college sophomore)
I like history, so I've paid some attention to information about the Cultural Revolution.

My generation, we don't have any memories of the CR, so we can only use our powers of reason to think about it, without the slightest emotional involvement. Instead of hate and love, we think in terms of good and bad. My personal opinion is that there were some positive aspects of the CR. If the CR hadn't been so vicious, so out of control, so extremist, the Left would never have lost power. Today's economic reforms were really helped along by the CR. So the CR did make a contribution to Chinese history. Of course, that wasn't the original intention behind it. The effects of the CR were exactly the opposite of its goals.

MS. PI (b. 1978, age 18, junior in high school)
I don't want to know about the Cultural Revolution. I'm sick to death of hearing mom and dad talk about it. Whenever they start, I tell them, "I know you had it rough, but that was years

ago! You need to live in the present, not the past. You want my sympathy? Fine, I sympathize with you, but what good does sympathy do? Are you afraid the CR is going to jump up from behind you and begin all over again? Go out on the street and look around. Where's it gone to? Show me a single Red Guard, a single big-character poster! Private businesses are every-where, you think they're all going to be labeled 'capitalists'and be struggled against?" When my parents hear this, they shake their heads and tell me I don't understand. I say they have a bad case of "CR phobia."

MR. ZHAO (b. 1977, age 19, worker)

China won't have another CR. These days people are really money-conscious—they'd do anything for a buck. No one these days can get people all riled up over some cause. The only way to get people's attention these days is with money. The CR was mainly about people's spirit. I've heard that in those days folks used to get all worked up over some little event, and they'd all start crying. People were so sincere, it must've been great! I mean, would people like that hurt each other on account of personal desires? No way! Another thing is the model operas. They're better than the traditional Peking Opera, and they're pretty moving. Some folks talk about "thoroughly negating the CR." Well, first off, I don't think you can negate the model operas.

MR. ZHANG (b. 1977, age 19, college freshman)

I'm not much interested in politics generally, much less the CR. The CR is a problem for my parent's generation. My impres-sions of the CR come from listening to the old folks telling sto-ries. The CR had a big impact on them, but it doesn't on us. It doesn't have a thing to do with our lives. If you told me right now we were going to start up the CR all over again, I wouldn't oppose the idea at all. I think it might even be fun. First, because I don't think the CR was such a frightening thing; sec-ond, because it would be something different, a new experience I'd like to try. Yeah, it'd be fun.

MS. LIAO (b. 1984, age 12, fifth grade student)
I know about the Cultural Revolution. It's the story of Chairman Mao fighting against a big bad guy!

MR. SUN   (b. 1976, age 20, taxicab driver)
I never saw the CR, but it's gotta be better than what we got these days! These days, people are just nastier than you can imagine. You're a salaried worker, so you ain't got the money to go to nightclubs, am I right? Those places are *demented*! Anything that flies, crawls or swims, anything you got, they'll eat it off a plate! There's only one thing they won't eat—shit! And then there are the girls who work the clubs at night. Of course I know all about them, they're always taking my cab to work! They take out their little mirrors and put on their lipstick right there in my cab. They make more money in one night than you make in six months. They get wads of cash for keeping those rich guys company. You think the CR could have come up with such insanity? Whaddya say? You askin' me how much I make? I make a hundred yuan a day. Whaddya say? Wasn't the CR all about struggling against capitalism? Well, I say struggle away! Anyhow, first get those rich jerks! Just get rid of them. That's enough. Kill their insanity!

MS. WAN (b. 1979, age 17, high school sophomore)
Right now we're studying the CR in our history class. The textbook isn't very specific—no one really understands what happened. I'm not that interested, I just want to pass the final exam. My mom says during the CR, our society was really chaotic, and awful things happened to good people. What I think is that Chairman Mao must have already lost his power, otherwise how could he have been unable to control the Gang of Four? Mom also says that during the CR, workers didn't go to work, and students didn't go to school. So I think it couldn't have been all bad! You didn't have to go to class, but you could just hang around and have fun, and criticize the teachers—what a blast! Some of my classmates say, why not have another Cultural Revolution, then we wouldn't have exams! I've also heard people say that the CR set China's development back a hundred years. I don't know if that is true or not— how do you figure a hundred years? There's no way to measure it.

MS. MA (b. 1979, age 17, high school sophomore)

My feeling about the CR is that it's mysterious and complicated, a little terrifying, but also kind of funny. I've heard that people made Mao pins as big as dinner plates, so you couldn't pin them on your clothes, but had to hang them on a string around your neck. Were people like that nuts, or what? Also, my dad says when he went to Beijing to see Chairman Mao, he rode his bike all the way there. How could he do such a silly thing? You couldn't get me to ride a bike to see anyone! Stuff like that I just can't really comprehend. It's weird. Don't you think it's abnormal? I wish I had a better understanding of the CR, but I don't know where to begin.

MS. FU (b. 1980, age 15, 8th grade)

When the CR started my dad was only around ten. Most of my impressions of the CR are from TV shows. I think the CR is kind of funny, but also maddening! The more patches you had on your clothes, the more revolutionary you were. The people with knowledge were the ones who were struggled against. I don't think anything like the CR will happen again. These days no one person could rally the whole country around a single phrase. These days people use their brains and think twice before doing anything. And if I decide I don't agree, you can bet I'd resist!

MS. CHANG (b. 1983, age 13, 8th grade)

I don't know much about the CR. My father was sent to Inner Mongolia as an educated youth, but he never talks about what happened there. Our textbook doesn't say anything about that stuff, and my classmates almost never talk about the CR. None of us are really clear about what went on, and anyhow it's got nothing to do with us. Only once, my grandma said that during the Cultural Revolution her hair was all shaved off, and she walked around wearing a cap to cover her bald head. When my Dad saw her, he asked her what had happened, but she wouldn't talk about it. He told her to take off the cap, and she just cried. I think the CR is a little scary. But that's it.

MS. HE (b. 1977, age 19, first-year college student)

Back then people had ideals, people were so honest—what charming times! I can't imagine what the CR was like in any detail, but was it like the May 4th Movement? There were parades, speeches, struggles, and there were two factions and a lot of violence, but it was a struggle over beliefs! That kind of life appeals to me. Even if this honesty was betrayed, I would still like it because I am honest like that. These days there's no way to live with such high ideals.

MR. LIU (b. 1980, age 16, ninth grade)

I know the CR was bad. I've heard my old man talk about it. But I don't understand why people didn't fight back. I said to my father, what right did they have to confiscate your stuff, to beat you up? Why didn't you beat up on them? If it was me, I'd sure go at it with them. If the CR happened again, I for one wouldn't be afraid. I'd beat up people and confiscate their property too. I'd mop the floor with anyone who had hurt our family.

MS. LIN (b. 1984, age 12, 5th grade)

I don't know what the CR was. I'm not sure what it was about. I know there was fighting during the CR. Was it for the building of the New China? They fought against the Japs, right?....no no, it was against Chiang Kai-shek's counterrevolutionary party. I've heard of the Gang of Four—that was Chairman Mao's wife, plus Lin Biao, but that's all I know.

MR. TIAN (b. 1979, age 17, high school sophomore)

Everyone says the "cult of personality" during the CR was a bad thing, but, as far as I can see, it was OK. So many people responded to a single command! If people are all of one heart and mind, they can accomplish big things. What we're lacking these days is precisely that kind of moral backbone. Hardly anyone these days talks about "the people" and "the nation" and higher causes like that. I've heard that people threw themselves into their work during the CR, that at quitting time they'd voluntarily refuse to go home. People nowadays are too much into money. But what I don't understand is why people seem to avoid the topic of the CR. We were reviewing for our history exam, and the teacher said, "You won't be tested on this part, don't bother preparing it." This part was the part of the textbook that talked about the CR. The only thing my grandparents will tell me about the CR is "You mustn't talk about these things!"

P. Guo (b. 1977, age 19, clerk)
Think about it: if the CR was wiped off the records of Chinese history, how could you connect the pre-CR society and the reforms of the post-CR period? This just goes to show how important the CR was. We shouldn't too easily negate a whole period in history. I never witnessed the CR, but everyone says that back then there were no drugs and no prostitution, right? So as I see it, history isn't as simple as math, where $1 + 1 = 2$, and $2 - 1 = 1$. There were some good aspects of the CR, some very good aspects.

N. XIE (b. 1978, age 18, vocational school student)
The problem with the CR was that political relations became more important than any other kind of relations. The problem these days is that money relations are more important than any other kind of relations. In the CR you'd never think in terms of getting paid for your work; these days, you'd never think of working without getting paid. In the CR, one man spoke for millions; these days, nobody listens to anything anyone says. I think it'd be best if we could combine the good aspects of the CR and of the current situation, and come up with something halfway in-between.

MR. YUWEN (b. 1979, age 17, high school sophomore)
Most of my impressions of the CR come from listening to my father. He wore several "hats" during the CR, maybe because he was an intellectual. It seems to me that even though he was unfortunate, he wasn't like some kind of tragic hero. He had to just swallow his pride and take all that abuse. When he does talk about the CR, he always sighs a long sigh. There's nothing I can do for him. I believe that under any condition it's wrong to humiliate people, to make them swallow their pride.

MR. ZHANG (b. 1977, age 19, clerk)

Everyone has different opinions about the CR, so I have very confused impressions of it. Some folks say that during the CR, life was real tough, that college graduates made only fifty yuan a month. But others say that prices were really low, that a pound of meat cost less than one yuan. Some folks say that during the CR, there was a lot of violence, that it wasn't safe to walk the streets; others say that officials were really honest, and that public security was actually quite good. Some say that Chairman Mao made mistakes, while others say that Chairman Mao was great, that he really knew how to rally the people and inspire the whole nation to act in unison based on his words. I don't know who is right and who is wrong. It doesn't add up to a coherent story. I once asked someone who'd been through the CR about all this, and he said everyone was right. When he told me that, I was even more confused.

MS. YU (b. 1976, age 20, worker)

In my village I heard some people talk about the CR, but not many. Folks there care about their crops, not about politics. They don't have the time or interest to ask much about it, so long as it doesn't interfere with the essentials of their daily life. Wasn't the CR an anti-Leftist thing? I don't know anything else about it. Anyhow, what use would it be knowing about it?

MS. JIA (b. 1977, age 19, peasant)

The CR was a struggle against bad people, mostly against landlords, eh? But all the old landlords are long since dead and gone. Today some people are small merchants, and some hire other folks to work for them, so they became landlords too! So who will be revolted against if there was another CR? Now that everyone wants to make money, no one thinks about that kind of stuff anymore. Only when people are poor will they become revolutionary!

MS. ZHU (b. 1976, age 20, second-year junior college student)

The old folks seldom talk about the CR with us, probably because we don't share their experiences, and so don't have a common language. My own opinion about the CR is that Chairman Mao's original intentions were good. He sent intellectuals to the countryside, hoping to support the more culturally backward parts of the country. But exactly the opposite happened, and he ended up spoiling the careers of a lot of talented people. In those days, young students were hot-blooded and raced impulsively to the aid of their fatherland. This was good for the country, but in the process they lost their sense of self-worth. The impact of the CR on our generation is indirect, but it's still there. Personal relations are more complicated. We tend not to trust each other, and so on. This is definitely related to the way people slandered and ratted on each other during the CR. I think the negative aspects of the CR outweigh the positive aspects. I'm glad I'm living in these times, instead of back then.

Appendix II

An Interview with the Author Feng Jicai

INTERVIEWER: Dietrich Tschanz (Switzerland)[1]
TIME: June 5, 1995
FORM: International phone call.[2]

INTRODUCTION: In 1986, I became intrigued with your project and translated the preface to *Ten Years of One Hundred People* (hereafter *Ten Years*) which had appeared that same year in the journal *October*. Last year, I began to gather the material needed to write a critical article on this project. In the course of this preliminary work, I encountered a lot of problems, and hoped I might approach you to get some help.

My article will be divided into two parts.[3] In the first part, I will introduce your motivations, main ideas, the writing and publishing processes as well as the methods you use in your work. In the second part, I will give a critical evaluation of your work. Here I hope to address questions like, Does your work belong to the category of literature or history? What are the specific qualities of "documentary literature"? What is the difference between this form and the "literature of the legal system," a sensationalist literary form currently in vogue? There are also many other questions which I hope you might answer.

QUESTION: As far as I know, you started your literary project by placing an announcement in various newspapers. In it you asked for personal accounts of the Cultural Revolution. What were the actual contents of this announcement? What was your intention in drawing up the announcement? In which newspapers did you have it published? It seems that initially you wanted to limit the range of your interviews to Tianjin, but soon after that extended it to include the entire country. Why did you make this change?

ANSWER: This announcement was first published in the *Tianjin Evening News*, but later distributed by the *China News Service*, and, as a result, big and small newspapers throughout the nation competed with each other to reprint it. At that time, the Cultural Revolution (hereafter CR) had been over for only ten years, and people's wounds had not healed yet; since they had no outlet for their distress, the response was of course enthusiastic. The announcement had three main contents: first, I wanted to record for the victims of the CR the journey of their spiritual experience; second, I interviewed only common people, and refused celebrities and high status individuals; third, I promised to conceal their names and the concrete names of all relevant places and people, and to guarantee that I would never reveal any of them to the outside world. I did this mainly because I believe that the experiences of the common people always represent the authentic experiences of a particular period; there will always be people who complain of injustice, and who speak of the sufferings of celebrities and high status individuals and erect a monument to them and write their biography. That is why I devoted myself to the silent and unknown people, and to all moral beings who had to swallow insults and humiliations. Secondly, I stress the revelation of the soul. The experience of the soul is the deepest experience. As an author, I inevitably attach particular importance to what the soul endures. Furthermore, I had to keep secrecy for the interviewees' sake, because even though the CR is over, these people are all still alive, and the old scores are not settled yet, so I had to guarantee their security. It seems that all these considerations of mine were quite realistic, and this is why I got such an enthusiastic response. All told, I received around 4,000 letters from people who wanted to talk to me. I really couldn't store that many letters at my home, and so I got rid of most of them. I did this to keep the promise I made in the announcement to keep strict confidentiality, because some of the topics which these letters touched upon cannot be written about at all.

I began this work in Tianjin. Since I live in Tianjin, it was very convenient to begin work from there. But, very quickly I expanded my project to other parts of the country. From the very beginning, when I started planning this literary project, my field of vision encompassed the whole country. The Cultural Revolution covered the entire 9.6 million square kilometers of China; almost no one could escape this disaster, in the way that the sea makes everything salty. I had to search for the most profound, representative, and unique examples from the scope of the entire nation, for only then would I be able to depict the range and depth of this unprecedented disaster.

Q: How did you conduct the interviews, and where? At your or at the interviewee's home? When you did the interviews, was there a third person around? Did you check the veracity of the material you gained in the interviews? Or was there simply an unwritten contract of trust between you and the interviewee?

A: As for the place where the interviews were conducted, I always asked the interviewee to make his own choice. If, for example, the interviewee's story was too personal, and it was thus inconvenient to conduct the interview at his home, he could come to my home or choose another place. Outside of Tianjin, the interview was often conducted in the hotel where I stayed, because this sort of interview is the kind of conversation which relies on absolute trust and sincerity. Most of the interviewees were very anxious to meet me and treated me as their close friend; this is why their innermost thoughts and feelings, which they could hardly suppress any longer, came out in a torrent. So, both the interviewee and I didn't want the presence of a third person. The third person would have felt like a barrier, or could even have been disruptive. Only if there were the two of us, could we be very natural during the interview, have a wholehearted engagement, talk either with joy or sadness, or become agitated together. I didn't try to gain material from the interviewees simply to write this book. I was driven solely by a holy responsibility, that is, to speak on behalf of the people.

In general, after the interview I didn't do any verification. Verification could have exposed the interviewee. The interviewees did everything to seek me out; they were full of things they wanted to tell me. While talking, they shed tears and revealed to me personal secrets they had held back even from their family members... There was no need to verify their statements. What's more, they knew that I wasn't there to redress the wrongs done to them, that their names would not appear, that nobody would know who they are, and that even the people whom they denounced in their stories had no way of finding out their identity. So why should they lie to me? Before each interview, I explained to the interviewees why I wanted to write this book. I always told them that this book was not for me; it was not only for them, but was foremost for the one generation of Chinese who had suffered through this calamity. I wanted to tell all this to the later generations, so that they never ever would have to repeat our suffering. Whenever I reached this point in the interview, they were always very moved. Only when I succeeded in turning my responsibilty into their own, was I able to get truly valuable things.

Q: What questions did you ask during the interview? Can you tell us something about how you conducted the interviews?

A: I first let them recount whatever was on their mind. That was most important, because if you have them answer questions, they are not only restricted, but also lose the mood needed to tell their story. To conduct an interview involves my entering the world of the interviewee, not the interviewee entering my sphere. So, I addressed my way of asking questions to their feelings. In general, I asked the following questions: first, about their experience and the incident; second, about the true emotions of the interviewee during the incident; and third, about how, in retrospect, the interviewee assesses his experience during those ten years. These were, more or less, the questions I asked.

As for the interview process and form, if a person sought me out and told me that he wanted to talk, I first had a simple conversation with him. I listened to the intensity of the interview request and roughly what he had to say. If I was moved by his or her story at the outset, and if this story was distinctive, then I designated him or her as an interviewee and arranged for another meeting. If someone from outside of Tianjin wrote to me and wanted to talk, I replied with a letter in which I asked what he or she wanted to talk about. If the value of his or her answer wasn't great, I left it at that; if the opposite was the case, however, I devised a way to meet that person. During the interviews, I used two methods: I recorded the interview and simultaneously took handwritten notes. The notes were intended to register the main points, and the recording was meant to capture everything, including the manner of speech and the emotion in the person's voice. This helped me to get closer to who the interviewee really was when I revised the text of the interview. This book of mine is the history of the interviewees, told by the interviewees. The truth is more important than everything else. I didn't want the CR to "become deformed" by my book; otherwise, it would have lost its true value.

After the interviews, I always proceeded quickly to the revision work. This revision work was divided into two parts: First, I listened to the recording and jotted down the most crucial portions on paper. The second step was based on the first one: I consulted the notes I made during the interview, used literary devices, and then wrote. I didn't necessarily proceed immediately to the second step.

Q: How many times did you interview a person?

A: In general, once, the time ranging from half a day to one full day. Sometimes, a second day was needed, either because there was too much ground to cover, or because of compositional considerations, if for instance there were not enough details.

Q: Could you please talk about how the interview went for "Was I Really Guilty?"

A: Aya! That was really a very painful interview. She approached me first and wanted to talk, but then refused to speak when we met. She wept and cried aloud. The interview was conducted in a room of her work unit; she chose the place. Because I was a victim of the CR myself, I understood her frame of mind. I suggested to her that we not talk that day, and maybe we should talk some other time. But then, she couldn't help grabbing me and beginning to speak. The deep pain and torment of her soul still moves me to this day. The day after the interview, I got a phone call from her husband, who told me she was in bed with high blood pressure. As a result of this interview, she got sick for an entire month. This is what is called, "remembering once is like shedding a layer of skin." After that interview, an old woman wanted to talk to me; she cried her heart out, but was unable to speak. I refused to further interview her. For the interviewee, this kind of conversation is the equivalent of an intense reliving of the horror of the CR; it really is too painful. From then on, I flatly refused to interview old and weak people.

Q: In the Japanese edition of *Ten Years of One Hundred People* you said, "What distressed me the most was that in the end I had to part with some stories which, though their mood and expression moved me to tears, remained vague and general once they were written down, because the persons narrating the story could not provide any vivid and specific details. I had to increase the number of interviews so that I could select from among them the stories which were representative, profound, and distinct. At the same time, I had to examine and select these stories from a literary standpoint, because this is a literary project." Could you please tell me the criteria you used to select the stories?

A: The bulk of the interviews were not incorporated into the book. Some of them were not selected because the interviewees were not good at conveying their own experiences and were inarticulate; they had only strong emotions, but couldn't provide concrete details; others were not selected because the stories were similar in content, they only concerned the interviewee's suffering, but had little happening on a deeper level. In this book I wanted to choose the oral reports of at least several dozen people and refer to some two hundred people. I took them to be representative of the generation of the CR. Since there are around one billion Chinese, each person represented at least one hundred million people; so, there absolutely had to be a variety of stories. If there was one identical story, then its exemplarity was diminished by one percent, and its impact and coverage diminished by one percent as well. To avoid repetition, three things, namely incident, character, and theme, had to be totally unique. The most crucial part was the uniqueness and depth of the theme. These were the standards I used to choose the stories.

A big disaster can precipitate all kinds of strange social phenomena. If I only had paid attention to the strangeness, brutality, and sensational quality of the surface of the incident, my book would have only satisfied the curiosity of people, and lost its value as an object of serious reflection and source of inspiration. What I fear most is that later generations will adopt a sensationalist attitude towards the suffering of an earlier one. However, whether a literature can be established hinges upon whether the characters can be established or not. So, I placed heavy emphasis on whether an interviewee had his own thoughts, events, experiences, and details. Without lively and distinctive details a character cannot be lifelike. Otherwise these interviews would resemble a person's diary and wouldn't be worth reading.

Q: So, in other words, you selected these stories more according to the criteria of a writer than of a historian?

A: To this I would answer that my project has multiple features. First, there is a historical aspect to the project; it is a historical record. The compositional principle underlying this book is an objective and faithful conception of history. Second, there is a sociological aspect to the project; as a thoroughly socio-political event, the CR is rich in sociological meaning. I have always believed that a work like *Ten Years* could be more appropriately carried out by a sociologist. So, I paid close attention to the sociological implications of my interviewees' words and made them an integral part of my stories. Third, there is a literary dimension to the project. I am a writer who cannot shirk my vision and stance as a writer. But this is not fiction, it's "documentary literature."

Q: What is your definition of "documentary literature"? How do you view the relationship between documentary literature and fiction. Mr. Li Jianjun in his article "The Hardships and Warnings of the Awakened" called your book a work of fiction. Do you agree with his assessment? To which category does your work actually belong?

A: I think one has to be very clear about the differences between news reporting, documentary literature, and fiction. First, there is the relationship between news reporting and documentary literature. Though both must use real people and real events, must be faithful to the objective facts, and must use the interview format, after the interview, one reports, while the other records. The former is not literature and does not permit any fabrication; the latter belongs to literature and allows for fabrication. When we compare documentary literature and fiction, we see that documentary literature has its origin in real people and real events; it is writing based on the facts, whereas fiction is writing based on the imagination. In fiction, one fabricates at will, and can indulge fully in fabrication without any restraints or limits; but documentary literature can only be a kind of "limited fabrication." Like fiction, it has a story and characters, but it is not fiction; there can be no concept like "documentary fiction." What I mean by "limited fabrication" is the following: assuming that the original form and the spirit of real people and real events are not altered, one is allowed to fabricate—including fictional settings, non-major events, and secondary characters—and add necessary details to enrich, deepen, and strengthen events and characters.

> Fabrication is a purely subjective act. Therefore—
> fiction gives free rein to subjectivity;
> news reporting prohibits subjectivity;
> documentary literature cannot indulge in subjectivity and distort objectivity.

My *Ten Years* differs from ordinary works of documentary literature. Because I see the truth of the original shape of things as being of utmost importance, I had to keep even any "limited fabrication" to a minimum. I didn't fabricate secondary characters, their environment, settings, or non-major events. I put all my effort into the interviews themselves. I let the interviewees talk as much as they wanted, and chose from these interviews the most expressive, vivid, and distinctive plot elements and details. For example, in "It's Hard to Explain," the menu which the starving prisoner sticks to his belly, or in "The Stream of Miserable Consciousness," the attempted suicide by eating flies, are the interviewees' real experiences. I used my writer's vision to select those details, not my imagination to fabricate them. I am convinced that at times the impact of life itself is unparalleled in its power, especially in an era when there was such a big catastrophe. I see the interview process as the equivalent of the composition process in the writing of a literary work. For example, the protagonist in "A Person Without a Story" told me in the interview that during the CR he could live in peace only after he had transformed himself into a "vanished" person. When I asked him how he made himself vanish, he said that he turned himself into a shadow "without anything," without friends, character, temperament, or substance. I felt that these details were not exciting enough and so I persistently asked him question after question. Finally, he provided me with a revealing detail. He said that at the time he did his best to avoid looking into other people's eyes—because only if you look into another's eyes can he remember you. Not even Balzac or Faulkner ever thought of this detail. It is in this manner, that is, by using authentic material, that I create real characters; and it is with the details told to me by the interviewees that I fill out their image. This is very much like the restoration of ancient objects: the materials that are used must originate from the period. In this way, the original environment of the story is preserved, and it also possesses literary quality.

Second, I place heavy emphasis on the development of the main idea behind the story. During the interview, I pay particularly close attention to what makes a story thoroughly unique. For example, in "Away from Madness" the first utterance of the interviewee is "I was a non-participant!" I immediately grasped the uniqueness of this story—here was an example of a non-participant. This was a fairly common group of people during the CR; but they had a particular attitude towards the CR. Though the interviewee was more interested in talking about his experiences as a Red Guard and his meetings with Chairman Mao, I concentrated on his inner transformation from an ardent revolutionary to an indifferent on-looker, and used this to explore the foundations of human nature. I regard the interview process as a process of literarization.

In my view, documentary literature is the literarization of real people and real events. The character *ji* (to record) in *jishi wenxue* (literally: the literature of recorded reality) refers to the interviewing and writing; the character *shi* (reality) refers to real people and real events; and the word *wenxue* (literature) refers to literarization. In writing this book, I made one rigorous demand of myself: that I would derive as much material as possible from the interviewees to reconstruct the story. Hence, I firmly believe in the historical as well as spiritual truth recorded in this book. The stories originate in the grim truth of life, and therefore I have to be absolutely truthful in my work.

Q: Could you please talk a little bit about your working procedure?

A: Sure. Because this book uses the "faithful record of an oral report" form, the whole process consists of the following steps:

1. interviewing,
2. going through the recording, and
3. writing.

I have already talked a bit about the interview form. The main thing is first to identify the unique cases by going through the letters and preliminary conversations, then during the interview, to make this uniqueness the goal of "questioning that goes to the bottom of things." But I don't want to repeat here what I have said already.

As for going through the recording, the content of the recording has to be faithfully put down on paper, regardless of whether it will be used in the writing process or not. Only the repetitious parts are not written down in the same manner.

As for the writing, I would like to talk about this in some more detail:

The first step consists of studying the recording, that is, looking for the main points in the text of the recording. These main points include: 1) the basic views of the narrator; 2) the thread of change in the thought of the narrator in the course of the last ten years; 3) the individual character of the narrator; 4) the details which can express the distinctiveness of the story and person; and 5) the salient features of the narrative logic and of the language.

After determining the main points, I have basically settled on the focus and writing style of the entire story, and clearly formulated what I will and won't write.

The next step is the cutting. In the process of writing, I usually employ only the method of cutting rather than the method of adding things. I remove unnecessary passages to achieve the shape I want in a story, much like a gardener prunes trees. I am confident of this technique of writing because during the interview I have asked the questions I need to and go then "to the bottom of things." The writing of documentary literature begins with the interview. However, after material has been removed, the text is fragmented and must be relinked and reorganized. This linking is done in accordance with the narrator's mental state and not in simple chronological order. This mental state includes the trail of the narrator's thought, his character traits as well as his inner world and feelings. For example, in "The Stream of Miserable Consciousness" I seized upon the characteristic of incoherence and chaos in the narrator to show at the same time his totally contradictory state of mind, and the disorder and absurdity of the era. So, cutting means disrupting the original order of the narrative and reorganizing it; this reorganizing is an art and may be likened to cinematographic montage. The cutting of raw material in documentary literature is a structural method; its purpose is to strive for the art of the text and a text with artistic qualities.

Last comes the language. Because I use the first-person form of an oral narrator, the character of the person, his psychology and feelings have to be expressed through narrative language. This puts high demands on the language, that is, the language of the narration is the same as the language of the character, very much like the language used by fictional characters in conversations becomes the narration in novels. This, then, makes it necessary to stress the rhythm, logic, and speed of the narrative as well as what I have mentioned before, that is, the speaker's particular habitual words, pet phrases, regionalisms, and level of education. Only if the language style of the narrator is transformed into a kind of unique text, can one accurately represent a person and accurately capture his character.

While writing, I listen over and over again to the recordings to get a sense of the narrator. I believe that if one can express one's sense of a person, one can also represent his or her life.

Q: In the postscript to the 1991 Mainland edition of *Ten Years* you mentioned the names of a few assistants. Could you please tell us what they contributed?

A: From the start, there were a lot of volunteers who offered to help me. Among the people I mention in the postscript, some came at their own expense from far away to Tianjin. They sought me out and told me their story; others helped me go through the recording, and still others were the editors of the book. I am very grateful to all of them. It is precisely because they fully understood the original intention and meaning of this book, that they saw their help as a moral duty, and that I consider them as my truly close friends.

Q: What are the artistic and intellectual connections between *Ten Years* and your fictional works?

A: The themes and forms in my fictional work are quite diverse. *Ten Years* is fairly closely connected with my other novels which deal with the theme of the CR. My earlier works like *Ah!, The Carved Pipe, The Tall Woman and the Short Husband,* as well as many of my other stories are part of the scar period literature; they are mostly about the CR, and as a genre they resemble the "literature of ruins" of postwar Germany. Both these genres sought to reveal suffering and at the same time denounce despotism. I have been particularly eager to record the events of the CR and put them into historical record. In 1980, I wrote an article titled "A Tentative Plan for *An Extraordinary Era,*" in which I proposed, following the example of Balzac's *ComÈdie Humaine,* to move the CR into history through a group of novels. But I found out later that no novel could summarize this complex and strange period when the CR swept across all of China. In the face of such a big disaster, all fabrication becomes superfluous, or even false. Isn't the experience of each person who endured the CR a vivid and profound story? So I came up with the idea of producing a huge work of "documentary literature." In the process of writing, I came to realize that the power of reality cannot be equaled, that reality is in fact the true essence of literature. Here I had finally found the ideal form for "recording history." A literary idea can only have one ideal form; this is the open secret of any successful work.

Q: The first story in the Mainland Chinese edition of *Ten Years* is entitled "Collecting Paper to Save a Husband." You seem to have had a specific purpose in positioning the story here, because the narrator (the military officer) plays the same role in the story as you do in your work. What was your intention in ordering individual stories? Was the arrangement of the stories meant to have a specific aesthetic effect?

A: That's right. You seem to have a very thorough and detailed understanding of the book. The narrator of "Collecting Paper to Save a Husband" still lives in Anhui; he used his own money to come to Tianjin and tell me his story. He was the mil-

itary officer responsible for implementing the policy of rehabilitation at the time. Though the incident he experienced had
happened more than ten years ago, he still had not been able
to put his mind at ease. It was exactly his awe-inspiring sense
of justice, humanistic spirit and standpoint that I wanted in my
book. So I put his story in the front of the book to show the
reader how to approach it. Reading this book requires having a
thoroughly just and conscientious viewpoint. I purposely created this reading perspective. When I arranged the individual stories, I put several powerful stories at the beginning so that the
whole book would have an impact. After that, I sequenced the
stories so that I was purposely alternating stories with different
moods (sentimental, excited, ironic, or serious ones) and different rhythms (agitated, calm, or nagging ones). I expect most
readers will read the stories in this book sequentially, following
the established order. By structuring a book in this way, one can
regulate the readers' impressions, maintain their interest so
they don't get bored, and also leave enough space for them to
reflect themselves. In all this, there is of course an aesthetic
component, because this is a literary work.

Q: In 1986, you published a theoretical article on documentary literature in the *Journal for Literature and the Arts*. In
this article you made the assertion that Chinese readers "don't
like to eat what is thoroughly cooked." Do you still believe this?

A: A reader reads a fictional work mainly for the
author's imagination, a documentary work for the truth of life.
In documentary literature, the reader wants to see the true
face of life or simply be given the raw material which he can
process, contemplate, or assess for himself. Herein resides the
reader's motivation for reading. This is the artistic essence of
documentary literature; it will never change. In addition, good
literature always leaves some space for the reader. The pro-
cessing done by the reader is a form of participation, and can
engender a joy for reading.

Q: Were the maxim-like sentences set in boldface type
after each story your original idea?

A: I think this is my style. Because I always stand outside a story when I write it, I also want to enter it and comment on the characters and their stories. I want to communicate
my ideas to the reader, but at the same time I can't do that too

much; I mustn't think for the readers. That is why I always add a sentence at the end of each story. This sentence is outside the story; in the layout, it has a certain distance from the story. I use such a maxim-like sentence because in these stories the most I can do is guide and inspire the reader, and invite him to follow my conclusion when he or she thinks about the story. This sentence is very short, but a short sentence can make people think; this is the attraction of the maxim. Only when such a sentence is attached, is the text of a story complete, including the pleasant impression of the layout.

Q: To date, you have published twenty-four stories from *Ten Years*. Are there objective reasons for why you haven't finished the project yet? Are you going to finish it in the near future?

A: "Hundred" is a round number in China and does not mean exactly one hundred. Of course, in the beginning I wanted to write about a large number of people. The initial writing of the book went very smoothly, but later on problems arose as a result of changes in Chinese society. In particular, the temptations of the market economy made people less willing to reflect on the past. I once asked a group of journalists from the South who came to the North for a visit whether all Southerners had gone into business and lacked the leisure time needed for reflection and self-examination. I asked why I consistently received so few letters from the South? After these journalists returned home, they wrote articles and reported my words, and after that I did indeed receive mail — a single letter. Perhaps this kind of self-examination doesn't help one deal with everyday matters and doesn't benefit the individual. People don't want to worry; they don't want to reveal their old scars. After 1988, I received fewer and fewer letters from people who wanted to be interviewed. I was really surprised that the social changes and the lure of the market economy could have such a huge impact. My interviews were always requested by the interviewees. I never took the initiative and looked for them. This was because the desire of the other party to speak had to be extraordinarily strong for a story to be adequate, powerful, and unique. Despite this, I haven't abandoned this project, and I have been working on it recently. Next year will be the thirtieth anniversary of the beginning of the CR as well as the twentieth anniversary of its ending. In the coming year, I hope to publish the last batch of stories I have been interviewing for and working on, and bring this project to its fruition.

Q: You said that in this book you wanted to write for the Chinese a travelogue of their spiritual experience. Why do you pay so much attention to the soul? What is the meaning of this term?

A: The soul is the core of a person. The external life of a person can be seen, but the interior life cannot. But a strong and profound exterior life leaves traces on one's heart. The physical pain dissolves with the passage of time, but the scars stay in one's heart and cannot be washed away. The dilemma of human existence is, on the one hand, its exterior difficulties, and, on the other hand, the suffering and unease of the soul. Writers are concerned with human beings, but all writers show even more concern with the hidden soul.

Q: Do you really believe that your book can "call the people to examine themselves and promote the liberation of the people"? How do you hope the people will make an effort to prevent the CR from recurring?

A: I have never believed that literature can have too big a social impact. A literary work can influence someone's thought, but it cannot have any direct effect. An author places a lot of expectations on his work, but in reality the expectations are nothing more than an ideal of what he hopes to achieve. Any work in literary history, even if it caused the strongest sensation at one point, couldn't precipitate changes in society. However, its influence on people's minds is potentially deep and far-reaching. Lu Xun died in 1936, but his critical and uncompromising spirit continues to influence one generation of Chinese intellectuals after another. I believe that literature has eternal value; but one should neither overestimate nor underestimate its influence. This is not a question of size, but of proximity and distance; the effect of literature is long and far-reaching.

Q: In an article published in a 1992 issue of *Literary Criticism* someone wrote that "after its publication *Ten Years* received widespread attention and unanimously favorable comments;" you, however, wrote in a postscript to *Ten Years* that it "unfortunately was not suited to its time ... and was treated, for some unfathomable reason, very coldly by the media." Which of these two statements is the more accurate description of the reception of your work in Mainland China?

A: A work is the child of its author. I of course know its lot best. The readers showed their interest in it; it was a best-seller all along. But why not count how many people among the critics reviewed it? Of course, what the author needs most is readers, not criticism or public opinion; but this reflects a certain critical spirit among critics.

Q: What are some of the left-over evils from the CR which still pervade the social life of contemporary China that cause you concern?

A: The political power of the CR is gone. Of the Gang of Four, three have already died, no one is likely to come forth and say "I endorse the CR," unless he or she is a lunatic. On the surface, there are no left-over evils from the CR, but as a spirit it still exists. In addition, the soil on which such a spirit could grow still exists. This includes, for example, lack of legal consciousness, the rule by man, feudalism, contempt for culture, egalitarianism as well as other ultra-leftist ideas and notions. All this is seemingly very disparate and shapeless, but in a certain political climate it could coalesce into an anti-historical force.

Q: Will there be a CR museum? Would you donate your manuscripts and tapes to this museum?

A: Museums are the memory of history. I believe there will be a CR museum. If one day the CR does indeed enter a museum, we will be able to live without worries, and the souls of a generation of victims will be consoled. But by that time, my book, and everything else, will be a mere detail in that museum.

FOOTNOTES

1 . Dietrich Tschanz is a Ph.D candidate in the Department of East Asian Studies at Princeton University, NJ.

2. This text is based on the transcript of the interview with revisions by the author Feng Jicai.

3. This article entitled "Zehn Jahre im Leben von Hundert Gewohnlichen Menschen: Zu Feng Jicais Projekt der Literarischen Dokumentation der Kulturrevolution" (Ten Years of One Hundred People: An Analysis and Critique of Feng Jicai's Project of a Literary Documentation of the Cultural Revolution) will be published in the journal Asiatische Studien/Etudes asiatiques, 50.1 (1996), p. 109-164.

APPENDIX III

A CHRONOLOGY OF EVENTS (1949-1979)

1949

OCTOBER 1

After many years of war between the Communist Party of China (CPC), led by Mao Zedong, and the Nationalist Party (Kuomintang), led by Chiang Kai-shek, the CPC drives the Kuomintang to the island of Taiwan and establishes the People's Republic of China. Mao proclaims that "the Chinese people have stood up."

1950

OCTOBER 8

Mao Zedong orders the Chinese People's Volunteers to march to Korea and fight in the Korean War.

OCTOBER 10

The CPC Central Committee issues the "Directive on Suppressing Counterrevolutionary Activities." The movement aims at wiping out antagonist forces and local bandits and lasts until the end of 1953.

1952

JANUARY 1

Mao Zedong calls on the people to fight against the three evils: corruption, waste, and bureaucracy. Three days later, the CPC Central Committee issued the "Directive on Immediately Mobilizing the Masses Within a Limited Time to Struggle Against the Three Evils." The Movement Against the Three Evils begins.

JANUARY 26

The Movement Against the Five Evils starts, aiming at capitalists who violates the law by bribery, tax evasion, theft of state property, cheating on government contracts, and stealing economic information.

1953

JULY 27

The Truce Agreement ending the Korean War is signed at Panmunjom.

1954

OCTOBER 4

Mao Zedong gives a talk, "On the Debate and Current Class Struggles in Agricultural Mutual Aid and Cooperation," criticizing the Rural Work Department of the CPC headed by Deng Zihui as "Rightist Opportunists." The CPC Central Committee decides that the cooperative transformation of China's agriculture should be completed by 1957.

1955

JANUARY 20

The Propaganda Department of CPC issues a report to repudiate Hu Feng for his views on literature and art, denouncing them as "downright bourgeois idealism and against the Party and the people."

1956

MAY 26

Lu Dingyi, director of the Propaganda Department of CPC, makes a speech entitled, "Let a Hundred Flowers Blossom; Let a Hundred Schools of Thought Contend," which starts a new policy of openness in literature and art.

1957

APRIL 27

The CPC Central Committee issues the "Directives on the Rectification Movement," calling on the people to help the Party rectify by raising suggestions and criticisms on the Party's work.

MAY 15

In an article circulated among Party cadres, Mao Zedong states that ten percent of intellectuals outside the Party are "Rightists." He says that the Rightists should be allowed to "run amuck for a time and reach their climax."

JUNE 8

The CPC Central Committee issues an article drafted by Mao Zedong, "Organizing Forces to Repulse the Rightists' Attacks." The Anti-Rightist Movement starts. In one year, more than half a million intellectuals are labeled "Rightists."

1958

MAY 5

The Second Session of the Eighth National Congress of the CPC positively evaluates the Great Leap Forward, and proposes to change China's backward economic and cultural conditions as quickly as possible. Mao Zedong claims that China could catch up with Great Britain in seven years, and with the United States in fifteen years. Mao also encourages the establishment of people's communes.

1959

FEBRUARY 27 - MARCH 5

At a Politburo meeting, Mao Zedong admits that the Great Leap Forward has gone a little too far. By then, many parts of the country begin to suffer food shortages and famine.

JULY 2 - AUGUST 16

The Politburo holds an enlarged meeting in Lushan Mountains. The outspoken General Peng Dehuai voices his criticism of the Great Leap Forward. As a result, he is accused of heading an anti-Party clique and is ousted as the Defense Minister.

SEPTEMBER 16

The CPC decides to remove the label of "Rightist" from those who have corrected their views.

1960

MARCH 9

The CPC Central Committee issues the "Directives on the Questions of Urban People's Communes," demanding that all local authorities be enthusiastic about establishing urban people's communes.

NOVEMBER

Famine hit many parts of the rural areas. Many people died as a result. In 1960 China's population decreases by ten million people.

1962

JANUARY 11- FEBRUARY 7

The CPC Central Committee holds an enlarged working conference attended by 7,000 people. Mao Zedong makes a self-criticism for the failures of some economic policies.

SEPTEMBER 24-27

Mao Zedong re-emphasizes the importance of class struggle at the Tenth Session of the Eighth CPC Central Committee. He states that class struggle must be stressed every year, every month, and every day.

1963

MAY 2

Mao Zedong calls a meeting of the Politburo on the issue of socialist education campaign in rural areas. He claims that "severe and sharp class struggle has occurred" in China and calls on a mass movement to repulse the capitalist and feudal forces.

1964

MAY

Defense Minister Lin Biao instructs the General Political Department to compile and publish *Quotations of Chairman Mao*. Lin claims that "Mao Zedong Thought is the acme of Marxism-Leninism of our time."

JULY

According to the instruction of Mao, the CPC Central Committee decides to set up a five-member Cultural Revolution Group, headed by Peng Zhen.

1965

NOVEMBER 10

The *Wenhui Daily* in Shanghai publishes Yao Wenyuan's article "Comment on the New Historical Opera *The Dismissal of Hai Rui from Office*." The article attacks Wu Han, vice-mayor of Beijing, for writing the opera. It is generally believed that Yao's article is the prelude to the start of the Cultural Revolution.

1966

MARCH

Mao Zedong criticizes the authors of *Notes from Three-Family Village* and *Evening Talks at Yanshan*, Deng Tuo, Wu Han, and Liao Mosha, for being "anti-Party and anti-socialist."

MAY 16

The Politburo adopts the "Circular of the Central Committee of the CPC," also known as the "May 16th Circular," which decides, among other things, to dissolve the Cultural Revolution Group, and set up a new one directly under the Standing Committee of the Politburo, with Chen Boda as its director. Members of the group includes Kang Sheng, Jiang Qing, and Zhang Chunqiao. The Cultural Revolution formally starts.

JUNE 1

The *People's Daily* publishes an editorial "Sweep Away All Demons and Monsters." Peng Zhen, mayor of Beijing, is ousted, along with Luo Ruiqing, PLA chief of staff, Lu Dingyi, director of the Propaganda Department, and Yang Shangkun, director of the CPC General Office.

AUGUST 1-12

The Eleventh Plenary Session of the Eighth Central Committee of the CPC is held in Beijing. Mao Zedong writes "Bombard the Headquarters—My Big-Character Poster," which starts the criticism of Liu Shaoqi and Deng Xiaoping.

AUGUST 18

Mao Zedong reviews Red Guards in Tiananmen Square.

1967

JANUARY 1

The *People's Daily* and the *Red Flag* magazine publish an editorial, "Carry the Great Proletarian Cultural Revolution to the End," calling on the people to "launch a general attack on the handful of persons within the Party who are in authority and taking the capitalist road, and on the demons and monsters in society."

JANUARY 6

Rebels groups in Shanghai headed by Wang Hongwen seize power from the Shanghai Municipal Party Committee. The incident is also known as the "January Storm," which sets off a nation-wide campaign by rebel groups to seize power from existing authorities.

1968

OCTOBER 5

The *People's Daily* publishes an "editor's note" in response to Mao Zedong's call for "sending the masses of cadres to do manual labor." As a result, "May 7th Cadres Schools" are set up throughout the country. An overwhelming majority of cadres at government offices and teachers of colleges and universities are sent to such schools to do physical labor.

NOVEMBER 24

Liu Shaoqi, President of China, is formally stripped of his Party membership and labeled a "traitor."

DECEMBER

Mao Zedong calls on the urban educated youths to "go to the countryside be re-educated by the poor and lower-middle peasants." During the Cultural Revolution, over 16 million educated youths are sent to settle in the countryside.

1969

APRIL 1-24

The Ninth National Congress of the CPC designates Lin Biao as Mao Zedong's "close comrade-in-arms and successor."

NOVEMBER 12

Liu Shaoqi, former President of China, dies in Kaifeng, Henan Province, after being politically persecuted and physically tortured.

1970

APRIL 24

China successfully launches its first man-made satellite.

NOVEMBER 16

The CPC Central Committee begins to criticize Chen Boda for his "anti-Party activities."

1971

MARCH 22

Lin Biao instructs his son, Lin Liguo, and other supporters to plan a military coup d'etat, code-named "Project 571," a plot to assassinate Mao Zedong and "seize supreme power of the state."

JULY 7-11

Henry Kissinger makes a secret trip to China. After talking with Zhou Enlai, it is announced that Richard Nixon has been invited to visit China before May 1972.

SEPTEMBER 13

Having failed to take Mao's life, Lin Biao flees with his wife, Ye Qun, and son, Lin Liguo. Their plane crashes at Undur Khan, Mongolia, and all people on board die.

OCTOBER 25

The United Nations General Assembly decides to "restore the rights of the PRC in the United Nations." Taiwan is expelled from the world organization.

1972

FEBRUARY 21

Richard Nixon visits China, beginning the process of normalization of US-China relations.

1973

MARCH 10

Under Mao Zedong's instruction, Deng Xiaoping is re-named vice-premier and put in charge of everyday state affairs.

1974

OCTOBER 10

Deng Xiaoping is appointed first vice-premier of the State Council, which greatly antagonizes Jiang Qing and her followers. Mao criticizes Jiang Qing for having "wild ambitions."

1975

NOVEMBER 2

Speaking of the Cultural Revolution, Mao Zedong says that it should be viewed as 70 percent achievement and 30 percent mistakes. He says, "Two mistakes were made during the Cultural Revolution, namely, striking down everything, and the all-out civil war."

1976

JANUARY 8

Zhou Enlai dies of cancer.

JANUARY 21

Mao appoints Hua Guofeng acting premier to succeed Zhou Enlai, which bitterly disappoints Zhang Chunqiao, a member of the Gang of Four.

APRIL 5

People in Beijing mourn the death of Zhou Enlai, which quickly turns into a political protest. The participants clash with the police. As a result, Deng Xiaoping is once again sidelined and denounced as the behind-the-scene boss of the incident.

SEPTEMBER 9

Mao Zedong dies.

OCTOBER 6

Members of the Gang of Four, Jiang Qing, Zhang Chunqiao, Yao Wenyuan, and Wang Hongwen, are arrested. As a result, the Cultural Revolution finally comes to an end.

1977

JULY 16-21

At the Third Plenary Session of the Tenth Central Committee of the CPC, Deng Xiaoping is again reinstated to his position as vice-chairman of the Party Central Committee.

AUGUST 13

The national conference on education decides to resume entrance examinations for the enrollment of university and college students, which has been abolished during the Cultural Revolution.

DECEMBER 10

Hu Yaobang is appointed director of the Propaganda Department of the CPC Central Committee, a position which enables him to painstakingly rehabilitate the wrong cases of the Cultural Revolution. Because of his effort, a large number of people who were unjustly persecuted during the CR are rehabilitated.

1978

DECEMBER 18-22

The Third Plenary Session of the Eleventh Central Committee of the CPC is convened in Beijing. This conference has been viewed as a watershed event in the contemporary history of China. After that, the policies and practices of the Cultural Revolution are formally abandoned. China has since then shifted from "class struggle" to economic construction and modernization. It is also the beginning of the policy of "opening to the outside world and economic reform."

DECEMBER 25

Hu Yaobang is appointed general secretary of the CPC Central Committee to take charge of the day-to-day work of the Party.

1979

JANUARY 1

China and the United States formally establish diplomatic relations.

APPENDIX IV

KEY FIGURES OF THE CULTURAL REVOLUTION

CHEN BODA (1904-1989) Joined the Communist Party of China (CPC) in 1924. Went to Moscow in 1927. Served as secretary to Mao Zedong for many years and wrote many articles on political subjects. Appointed director of the Cultural Revolution Group of the Central Committee of the CPC in 1966. Sided with Lin Biao and the Gang of Four. Was under house arrest in 1970 and expelled from the CPC in 1973. Sentenced to 18 years in prison in 1981.

CHEN YI (1901-1972) Went to France in 1919 and was deported in 1921. Became a Party member in 1923. Took part in the Nanchang Uprising on August 1, 1927. Became foreign minister in 1957. One of China's ten marshals, he was the target of the Red Guards during the Cultural Revolution.

DENG XIAOPING (1904-) Born in Sichuan Province. Was general secretary of the CPC Central Committee when the Cultural Revolution started. Became the main target of persecution during the CR. Purged twice by Mao Zedong. Regained power after the CR and became China's paramount leader since early 1980s. Hailed as "chief architect" of China's economic reform and open policies.

GANG OF FOUR. See Jiang Qing, Wang Hongwen, Yao Wenyuan, Zhang Chunqiao

HUA GUOFENG (1920-) Joined the Red Army in 1936. Became a member of the Politburo in 1973 and minister of Public Security in 1975. Appointed acting premier in 1976 after the death of Zhou Enlai. Became successor of Mao Zedong after Mao died in 1976. After Deng Xiaoping returned to power, he lost his positions as chairman of the CPC Central Committee and premier of the State Council in the early 1980s

JIANG QING (1914-1991) Joined the CPC in 1933. Went to Yan'an in 1937. Married Mao Zedong in 1939. Gained prominent power during the Cultural Revolution. Became vice-director of the Central Cultural Revolution Group in 1966. Persecuted a large number of personal enemies. Was arrested in October 1976 as head of the Gang of Four. Sentenced to death with a two-year reprieve in 1981.

KANG SHENG (1899-1975) Joined Communist Party in 1924. Was in charge of intelligence and security for many years, and persecuted large numbers of Party cadres. During the Cultural Revolution, sided with Jiang Qing and was advisor to the Central Cultural Revolution Group.

LIN BIAO (1907-1971) One of China's ten marshals and main military strategists. Was designated Mao's successor in 1968. Was responsible for the persecutions of many Party cadres during the Cultural Revolution. Plotted against Mao and attempted a coup d'etat in 1971. Died in a plane crash with his wife and son when they tried to escape after failing to assassinate Mao.

LIU SHAOQI (1898-1969) Went to Moscow in 1921, where he joined the Communist Party of China. Active in labor unions for many years before Liberation. Became a Party theoretician and wrote extensively on the conduct of the CPC. Was the president of China when the Cultural Revolution began, which was designed to destroy him because of his differing views with Mao on a number of economic and political issues. Died in humiliation in 1969. Was rehabilitated after the Cultural Revolution.

MAO ZEDONG (1893-1976) One of the founders of the Communist Party of China. For many years, was the paramount leader of the CPC and of the People's Republic of China. In the early 1960s, he felt he was losing power to Liu Shaoqi, and therefore started the Cultural Revolution to destroy his political enemies within the Party. There are many biographies of Mao written by Chinese and foreign authors. A short footnote will certainly not do him justice.

PENG DEHUAI (1902-1968) Peng first joined the Kuomintang and then the Communist Party in 1927. Was Mao's staunchest supporter for many years. Was chief commander of Chinese People's Volunteers in the Korean War. Became one of China's ten marshals in 1955. Quarreled with Mao on the Great Leap Forward, and was criticized and demoted from minister of defense. Raided by the Red Guards during the Cultural Revolution, and died in 1968.

WANG HONGWEN ((1930-1992) Was a worker in Shanghai when the Cultural Revolution began. Was leader of the January Storm in 1967, an event that triggered a nation-wide campaign by rebel groups to seize power from the existing authorities. It also made Wang a prominent figure. Was selected by Jiang Qing and became a member of the Gang of Four. Rose rapidly in the Party hierarchy to become vice-chairman of the Party in 1975. Arrested in 1976 and sentenced to life imprisonment in 1981. Died of cancer in 1992.

YAO WENYUAN (1926-) A journalist who rose to prominence when he wrote an article attacking Wu Han, vice-mayor of Beijing. The article, "Comment on the New Historical Opera *The Dismissal of Hai Rui from Office*," was published in *Wen Hui Daily*, which was generally believed to be the prelude to the Cultural Revolution. A member of the Gang of Four, he was arrested in 1976 and sentenced to life imprisonment in 1981.

YE JIANYING (1898-1986) Participated in the Long March. Supported Mao for many years. Became one of China's ten marshals in 1955. Member of the Politburo since 1966. Was selected vice-chairman of the Party in 1973. Led a bloodless coup in 1976 and arrested the Gang of Four and their followers, one month after the death of Mao.

ZHANG CHUNQIAO (1917-   ) Rose to prominence during the Cultural Revolution when he sided with Jiang Qing. Was believed to be the real brain of the Gang of Four. Became member of the Politburo in 1969 and vice-premier in 1975. Was arrested in 1976 and sentenced to death with a two-year reprieve in 1981.

ZHOU ENLAI (1898-1976) Zhou's prominence in the Communist Party of China was next only to Mao Zedong. Like Mao, a short footnote cannot do him justice. Zhou was the premier of China since the founding of the PRC. He was known to have saved a large number of cadres from persecution during the Cultural Revolution. He died of cancer in 1976.

ZHU DE (1886-1976) One of China's main military leaders, Zhu was known as the commander-in-chief of the armed forces of the CPC. During the Cultural Revolution, he was attacked by big-character posters, and his house was raided by Red Guards. But he was able to remain unharmed after Mao referred to him as the "red commander-in-chief."